AUTOMOTIVE
BRAKE
MANUAL

by Bob Henderson
and Steve Rendle

**The Haynes Automotive Repair Manual
for maintaining, troubleshooting and
repairing brake systems**

ABCDE
FGHIJ
KLMNO
P

Haynes Publishing
Sparkford Nr Yeovil
Somerset BA22 7JJ England

Haynes North America, Inc
861 Lawrence Drive
Newbury Park
California 91320 USA

Editions Haynes S.A.
147/149 rue Saint Honoré
75001 PARIS

Acknowledgements
We are grateful for the help and co-operation of the Chrysler Corporation, Ford Motor Company, Mazda Motor Company, Nissan Motor Company, Toyota Motor Corporation, Volvo North America Corporation and Sykes-Pickavant Limited for assistance with technical information and illustrations. Kent Reppert II also supplied various illustrations.

© Haynes Publishing 1995

A book in the Haynes Owners Workshop Manual Series

Printed in the USA

ISBN 1 85960 202 9

British Library Cataloguing in Publication Data
A catalogue record for this book is available from the British Library

While every attempt is made to ensure that the information in this manual is correct, no liability can be accepted by the authors or publishers for loss, damage or injury caused by any errors in, or omissions from, the information given.

95-224

Contents

CALIPER PISTON
DUST SEAL

CALIPER BODY

HYDRAULIC SEAL

BRAKE
PADS

PISTON

BRAKE DISC

2112-1-1.33 HAYNES

ADJUSTING NUT
AND SCREW

WHEEL CYLINDER

ADJUSTER SCREW
RETRACTING
SPRING

ADJUSTER
WASHER

ADJUSTER
LEVER

ADJUSTING
SOCKET

LEADING SHOE
AND LINING

SHOE HOLD
DOWN
PIN AND
SPRING

SHOE HOLD
DOWN
PIN AND
SPRING

PARKING
BRAKE LEVER

BACKING PLATE

TRAILING SHOE
AND LINING

SHOE RETAINING
PLATE

LOWER
RETRACTING
SPRING

Chapter 1
Introduction

It's a beautiful summer day. You're hurtling down your favourite stretch of asphalt, enjoying the countryside and your favourite CD. You notice, however, an annoying rattle coming from somewhere under the instrument panel. "I'll have to sort that out" you say to yourself, as you make a mental note to fix it as soon as you get home. You turn up the stereo.

Suddenly, a large estate car towing a caravan pulls out onto the road, not more than 100 yards ahead. Instinctively, you check the lane to your right for oncoming traffic and to your dismay, there's lots of it. With nowhere to go, you hit the brakes. Hard. Hard enough for the amber "ABS" light on the instrument panel to glow, but that isn't what you're looking at.

You breath a sigh of relief when you realise the caravan isn't rushing towards you anymore. After a few choice phrases and an exchange of hand gestures, you pass this rolling roadblock and you're back on your way - nothing lost but a little sweat.

A little sweat and a minuscule amount of friction material from the brake pads, but you're not thinking about your brakes. They performed flawlessly, and besides, you pushed the pedal so you get the credit!

When was the last time you did think about your vehicle's brakes? The sad fact is that most drivers pay more attention to annoying rattles or scratches in the paint, ignoring their brakes until they start making bad noises, the vehicle pulls to one side, the brake pedal feels mushy or, worse yet, they fail completely. Brakes are probably the most abused and neglected components on a vehicle.

While complete brake failure is not a common occurrence, some forms of brake system trouble are all too common. Most can be avoided with a little attention every few thousand miles. The braking system is the most important system on your vehicle. Your life, the lives of your passengers, pedestrians and other motorists on the road all depend upon your brakes.

All vehicles will need some form of brake system repair sooner or later. Wear is an inherent feature of all brake systems - your brakes slowly give their lives so you can retain yours. Due to this continual sacrifice, all brake pads and shoes must eventually be retired, to be replaced with the next generation of new lining. Other problems can crop up, too.

But for many, the braking system represents a portion of the vehicle that just shouldn't be tampered with, and because of this, repairs are usually left to someone else. That's where this manual comes in. It has been designed to help just about anyone repair just about any kind of problem in any type of brake system.

Most modern automotive braking systems are actually quite simple to maintain and repair, provided that each step is performed in a careful, deliberate manner. A considerable amount of money can be saved and much knowledge can be gained by taking on these tasks yourself. This will give you a great sense of satisfaction - not only because you saved a bunch of money and your car wasn't tied up for a couple of days in some shop, but because you'll know that the job was done correctly.

This manual unlocks the "mysteries" of the modern automotive braking system. The procedures illustrated throughout the book are general in nature, but with specific differences in component design pointed out where necessary to help you complete each procedure safely and properly. Included are chapters on component and system operating fundamentals, tools and equipment, troubleshooting, maintenance, disc brake pad renewal, drum brake shoe renewal, handbrake systems, brake pedals and brake light switches, hydraulic systems and Anti-lock Brake Systems (ABS). At the end of the manual there's a glossary of terms used throughout the book. In short, everything you need to know to successfully maintain and repair your brakes and ensure your safety and that of others around you, as well!

Conversion factors

Length (distance)

Inches (in)	X 25.4	= Millimetres (mm)	X 0.0394	= Inches (in)
Feet (ft)	X 0.305	= Metres (m)	X 3.281	= Feet (ft)
Miles	X 1.609	= Kilometres (km)	X 0.621	= Miles

Volume (capacity)

Cubic inches (cu in; in³)	X 16.387	= Cubic centimetres (cc; cm³)	X 0.061	= Cubic inches (cu in; in³)
Imperial pints (Imp pt)	X 0.568	= Litres (l)	X 1.76	= Imperial pints (Imp pt)
Imperial quarts (Imp qt)	X 1.137	= Litres (l)	X 0.88	= Imperial quarts (Imp qt)
Imperial quarts (Imp qt)	X 1.201	= US quarts (US qt)	X 0.833	= Imperial quarts (Imp qt)
US quarts (US qt)	X 0.946	= Litres (l)	X 1.057	= US quarts (US qt)
Imperial gallons (Imp gal)	X 4.546	= Litres (l)	X 0.22	= Imperial gallons (Imp gal)
Imperial gallons (Imp gal)	X 1.201	= US gallons (US gal)	X 0.833	= Imperial gallons (Imp gal)
US gallons (US gal)	X 3.785	= Litres (l)	X 0.264	= US gallons (US gal)

Mass (weight)

Ounces (oz)	X 28.35	= Grams (g)	X 0.035	= Ounces (oz)
Pounds (lb)	X 0.454	= Kilograms (kg)	X 2.205	= Pounds (lb)

Force

Ounces-force (ozf; oz)	X 0.278	= Newtons (N)	X 3.6	= Ounces-force (ozf; oz)
Pounds-force (lbf; lb)	X 4.448	= Newtons (N)	X 0.225	= Pounds-force (lbf; lb)
Newtons (N)	X 0.1	= Kilograms-force (kgf; kg)	X 9.81	= Newtons (N)

Pressure

Pounds-force per square inch (psi; lbf/in²; lb/in²)	X 0.070	= Kilograms-force per square centimetre (kgf/cm²; kg/cm²)	X 14.223	= Pounds-force per square inch (psi; lbf/in²; lb/in²)
Pounds-force per square inch (psi; lbf/in²; lb/in²)	X 0.068	= Atmospheres (atm)	X 14.696	= Pounds-force per square inch (psi; lbf/in²; lb/in²)
Pounds-force per square inch (psi; lbf/in²; lb/in²)	X 0.069	= Bars	X 14.5	= Pounds-force per square inch (psi; lbf/in²; lb/in²)
Pounds-force per square inch (psi; lbf/in²; lb/in²)	X 6.895	= Kilopascals (kPa)	X 0.145	= Pounds-force per square inch (psi; lbf/in²; lb/in²)
Kilopascals (kPa)	X 0.01	= Kilograms-force per square centimetre (kgf/cm²; kg/cm²)	X 98.1	= Kilopascals (kPa)
Millibar (mbar)	X 100	= Pascals (Pa)	X 0.01	= Millibar (mbar)
Millibar (mbar)	X 0.0145	= Pounds-force per square inch (psi; lbf/in²; lb/in²)	X 68.947	= Millibar (mbar)
Millibar (mbar)	X 0.75	= Millimetres of mercury (mmHg)	X 1.333	= Millibar (mbar)
Millibar (mbar)	X 0.401	= Inches of water (inH₂O)	X 2.491	= Millibar (mbar)
Millimetres of mercury (mmHg)	X 0.535	= Inches of water (inH₂O)	X 1.868	= Millimetres of mercury (mmHg)
Inches of water (inH₂O)	X 0.036	= Pounds-force per square inch (psi; lbf/in²; lb/in²)	X 27.68	= Inches of water (inH₂O)

Torque (moment of force)

Pounds-force inches (lbf in; lb in)	X 1.152	= Kilograms-force centimetre (kgf cm; kg cm)	X 0.868	= Pounds-force inches (lbf in; lb in)
Pounds-force inches (lbf in; lb in)	X 0.113	= Newton metres (Nm)	X 8.85	= Pounds-force inches (lbf in; lb in)
Pounds-force inches (lbf in; lb in)	X 0.083	= Pounds-force feet (lbf ft; lb ft)	X 12	= Pounds-force inches (lbf in; lb in)
Pounds-force feet (lbf ft; lb ft)	X 0.138	= Kilograms-force metres (kgf m; kg m)	X 7.233	= Pounds-force feet (lbf ft; lb ft)
Pounds-force feet (lbf ft; lb ft)	X 1.356	= Newton metres (Nm)	X 0.738	= Pounds-force feet (lbf ft; lb ft)
Newton metres (Nm)	X 0.102	= Kilograms-force metres (kgf m; kg m)	X 9.804	= Newton metres (Nm)

Power

Horsepower (hp)	X 745.7	= Watts (W)	X 0.0013	= Horsepower (hp)

Velocity (speed)

Miles per hour (miles/hr; mph)	X 1.609	= Kilometres per hour (km/hr; kph)	X 0.621	= Miles per hour (miles/hr; mph)

Fuel consumption*

Miles per gallon, Imperial (mpg)	X 0.354	= Kilometres per litre (km/l)	X 2.825	= Miles per gallon, Imperial (mpg)
Miles per gallon, US (mpg)	X 0.425	= Kilometres per litre (km/l)	X 2.352	= Miles per gallon, US (mpg)

Temperature

Degrees Fahrenheit = (°C x 1.8) + 32   Degrees Celsius (Degrees Centigrade; °C) = (°F - 32) x 0.56

It is common practice to convert from miles per gallon (mpg) to litres/100 kilometres (l/100km), where mpg (Imperial) x l/100 km = 282 and mpg (US) x l/100 km = 235

How to use this repair manual

The manual is divided into Chapters. Each chapter is subdivided into sections, some of which consist of consecutively numbered paragraphs (usually referred to as "Steps," since they're normally part of a procedure). If the material is basically informative in nature, rather than a step-by-step procedure, the paragraphs aren't numbered.

The term **(see illustration)** is used in the text to indicate that a photo or drawing has been included to make the information easier to understand (the old cliché "a picture is worth a thousand words" is especially true when it comes to how-to procedures). Also every attempt is made to position illustrations on the same page as the corresponding text to minimise confusion. Some procedures are largely made up of illustrations and captions, with little or no accompanying text. The two types of illustrations used (photographs and line drawings) are referenced by a number preceding the caption. Illustration numbers denote chapter and numerical sequence within the chapter (eg 3.4 means Chapter 3, illustration number 4 in order).

The terms **"Note,"** **"Caution,"** and **"Warning"** are used throughout the book with a specific purpose in mind - to attract the reader's attention. A **"Note"** simply provides information required to properly complete a procedure or information which will make the procedure easier to understand. A **"Caution"** outlines a special procedure or special steps which must be taken when completing the procedure where the Caution is found. Failure to pay attention to a Caution can result in damage to the component being repaired or the tools being used. A **"Warning"** is included where personal injury can result if the instructions aren't followed exactly as described.

Even though extreme care has been taken during the preparation of this manual, neither the publisher nor the author can accept responsibility for any errors in, or omissions from, the information given.

Chapter 1

Hydraulic systems

In the early days of motorised transportation, the entire brake system on a horseless carriage consisted of nothing more than a lever that the driver pulled, causing it to rub against a tyre. Although some mechanical advantage could be built into the lever, braking power was largely determined by the strength of the driver. Of course, this was a very inadequate system and could quickly be rendered useless by driving through a little water or mud!

As cars evolved, the brakes at the wheels (drum brakes, which we'll cover in the next Section) were actuated by a linkage or a cable, or a combination of the two. This was usually sufficient for the vehicle weights and the relatively low speeds they were able to achieve. This worked, but cables and linkages were a source of high wear and a definite "weak link" in the brake system chain.

By the late 1920's/early 1930's, most cars were equipped with hydraulically actuated brakes. This greatly increased braking reliability and safety. Since mechanical advantage can easily be designed into a hydraulic system, driving a motor vehicle became a much less tiresome proposition.

Why use fluid in a brake system? Well, for three reasons:

Liquids can't be compressed
Liquids can transmit motion
Liquids can transmit force and can also increase or decrease force

This was discovered long before the automobile was even dreamed of (in 1647), by a French philosopher and mathematician named Blaise Pascal (1623 - 1662). He determined that in a confined fluid, pressure applied externally is transmitted equally in all directions. In a static fluid, force is transmitted at the speed of sound throughout the fluid and acts at right angles on all surfaces in or confining the fluid **(see illustration)**. Of course, this happens because liquids can't be compressed.

Liquids can also transmit motion because of this law of physics. If a piston in a hydraulic cylinder is pushed in a certain amount, a piston in another hydraulic cylinder of equal size, connected by a tube, will move out an equal amount **(see illustration)**.

By the use of different size pistons in a hydraulic system, liquids can increase or decrease force. If a force of 200 pounds is applied to a hydraulic cylinder with an area of one square inch, a pressure of 200 pounds per square inch (psi) will be generated. This pressure of 200 psi will be present in the entire system. If this cylinder is connected by a tube to another cylinder with a piston having a surface area of 20 square

1.1 Pascal's law states that "pressure, when applied to a confined liquid, is transmitted undiminished." In this example, a force of 20 pounds has been exerted on the piston, which has a surface area of one square inch. Notice that each pressure gauge registers 20 pounds per square inch (psi), regardless of the size, shape or location of its chamber.

1.2 The piston in the hydraulic chamber at the left has been depressed two inches - the piston in the cylinder on the right has moved out an equal amount. The pistons are of the same surface area and the force transmitted is equal, too.

1.3 Here's an example of how liquids can increase force: 200 pounds of effort applied to the piston on the left, which has a surface area of one square inch, will yield an output of 4000 pounds at the piston on the right, which has a surface area of 20 square inches.

inches, a force of 200 psi will push on every square inch of the larger piston. A mechanical advantage of twenty would be generated, and a force of 4000 pounds would be pushing on the piston **(see illustration)**. Therefore, a force of 200 pounds could actually lift or move 4000 pounds! If this particular hydraulic system was operated in reverse, the mechanical advantage would be greatly diminished. A force of 80,000 pounds would have to be applied to the large piston to have 4000 pounds available at the smaller one.

The hydraulic brake system in all motor vehicles is based on these principles. When the driver of a car pushes on the brake pedal, the force exerted on the master cylinder is converted into system pressure and is distributed through the brake lines to the wheel cylinders and/or brake calipers. This action is what applies the brake shoes to the drums or the brake pads to the discs, creating friction, which converts the kinetic energy of the moving vehicle to heat and slows the car down.

The components that make up a modern hydraulic system are only a little more complex than the examples shown in the previous illustrations. Lets take a look at the individual components and the jobs they do.

Master cylinder

The master cylinder converts mechanical input force into system hydraulic pressure. Force exerted by the driver is transmitted through the brake pedal and applied to the master cylinder piston through a pushrod. As the piston moves forward in the cylinder, brake fluid is forced from the master cylinder. Remember, though, that the entire system is filled with fluid, so this motion is transmitted, undiminished, through the brake lines and hoses to the wheel cylinders or calipers. Once all movement is taken up in the wheel cylinders or calipers, pressure in the system begins to rise. Further movement of the components is impossible, but pressure will increase within the system if the driver pushes harder on the brake pedal.

Master cylinders are constructed of either cast iron or aluminium. On most vehicles the master cylinder is mounted on the bulkhead or power brake servo. Some have integral (non-detachable) fluid reservoirs **(see illustration)**, others have detachable reservoirs made of plastic **(see illustration)**. Some have remote reservoirs that are connected to the master cylinder with hoses **(see illustration)**. A reservoir is necessary to provide additional fluid to compensate for brake lining wear and movement and, in the unfortunate event of a brake fluid leak, a small margin of safety (there will be enough fluid left in the reservoir to enable the driver to pump the brake pedal a few times, hopefully bringing the vehicle to a stop!). Reservoirs must be vented to allow the fluid level to move up and down without creating a vacuum in the system. A rubber diaphragm between the fluid and the cap or cover allows this to happen, while sealing off the brake fluid from outside elements.

Many older vehicles were equipped with single-piston master cylinders **(see illustration)**, but all late model vehicles are equipped with dual-piston master cylinders. The pistons are fitted with seals, or piston cups, which seal tightly against the walls of the cylinder when pressure is developed in the system. This prevents fluid from leaking past the pistons, and allows pressure to be maintained in the system without

1.4 Cutaway of a typical integral reservoir master cylinder

1.5 Exploded view of a typical detachable reservoir master cylinder

1 Fluid level sensor connector
2 Brake lines
3 Reservoir-to-master cylinder hoses
4 Master cylinder
5 Reservoir
6 Reservoir mounting bracket
7 Power brake servo

1.6 Details of a typical remote-reservoir master cylinder arrangement

1 Filler cap
2 Reservoir
3 Master cylinder body
4 Valve (bleeding control)
5 Valve seat
6 Return spring
7 Spring retainer
8 Primary cup
9 Cup protecting washer
10 Piston
11 Secondary cup
12 Dished washer
13 Snap-ring
14 Rubber boot
15 Pushrod

1.7 Cutaway of a typical single-piston master cylinder

1.8 This is how a dual master cylinder works during normal operation and in the event of a partial brake system failure:

A The master cylinder in the static (released) position. The chambers in front of the pistons are filled and ready for the application of the brake pedal.

B Pressure has been applied to the brake pedal and transferred to the master cylinder through the pushrod. The pistons move forward, creating pressure in the hydraulic circuits.

C The hydraulic circuit to the front brakes has sprung a leak! Don't fear, though; the primary piston has moved forward and has physically contacted the secondary piston, moving it forward and creating pressure in the rear brake circuit. The fluid will eventually drain from the primary side of the reservoir, but there's still plenty of fluid in the secondary side.

D Not again! The problem with the front brake circuit has been repaired, but now the rear circuit blew. Thankfully, the pressure from the primary piston has shoved the secondary piston all the way to the front, and plenty of pressure is available to the front brakes.

1.9 Here's an example of a hydraulic brake system with a front/rear split - this type of system is the kind most often found on rear-wheel drive vehicles

bleeding down (decreasing due to leakage past the seals). The pistons are retained in the master cylinder bore by a stop plate (washer) and a circlip.

The old single-piston master cylinder worked fine unless a problem developed in the hydraulic system (a leak in a hose or failed piston cup in the master cylinder, for example), in which case the driver would completely lose his brakes and have to resort to the handbrake (have you ever tried to do this? Don't, unless you absolutely have to) or quickly try to find a place to make a fairly safe "crash landing"! On a dual-piston master cylinder brake circuit, each piston operates half of the system. With this design, if there is a problem in one half of the system, the other half of the system will still be functional (see illustration). On some vehicles the system is split from front-to-rear (see illustration). On others it's split diagonally - one half of the master cylinder operates the left front and right rear wheels and

1.10 Typical diagonally split hydraulic system

1 Master cylinder
2 Pressure differential
   warning valve

──── Primary circuit   ── ── ── Secondary circuit

1.11 Schematic of the triangular-split hydraulic system

1.12 Cutaway of a typical dual-piston master cylinder. Note: Some primary pistons have an O-ring instead of a secondary cup. Also, some secondary pistons have only one secondary cup, with the lips facing the primary piston

the other half operates the right front and the left rear wheels **(see illustration)**. On others still, it's split triangularly - each piston in the master cylinder operates separate pistons in the front brake calipers as well as one rear caliper **(see illustration)**. With this system, bringing the vehicle to a stop after a partial brake failure is a much less harrowing experience - the vehicle won't veer to one side as much as a diagonally split system, and the rear brakes won't lock-up easily (as would happen if the front brake circuit failed on a front-to-rear split system). In the event of a partial brake failure with any one of these designs, however, increased pedal travel and effort required to stop the vehicle will result.

Operation

When the pistons in the master cylinder are at rest, small passages located just in front of the primary cups of each piston are exposed. These are called compensating ports; they connect the master cylinder bore to the fluid reservoirs and allow the chamber in front of each piston to fill with brake fluid **(see illustration)**. When the driver depresses the brake pedal, the master cylinder pushrod forces the primary piston into the master cylinder bore and moves it toward the secondary piston. At this time, the primary compensating port is blocked off, which seals the

1	Spring seat	3	Washer (cup protector)	4	Secondary piston
2	Primary cup			5	Secondary cup

6	Spring seat	8	Washer (cup protector)
7	Primary cup		

1.13 Master cylinder piston details - typical

master cylinder bore. The pressure developed by the primary piston not only sends pressure through the primary system, it forces the secondary piston forward in the bore, blocking off the secondary compensating port, causing pressure to rise in the secondary system, too.

Behind each compensating port is a breather port (sometimes called a filler port). This port allows fluid from the reservoir to fill the area behind the primary cup, preventing air bubbles from travelling around the lips of the primary cups on the pistons when the brakes are released. This fluid also flows past the lips of the primary cups of the pistons when the brakes are released, filling the chambers in front of the pistons, readying them for the next pedal application. A spring fitted to the end of each piston helps return them to their "at rest" positions when the driver releases pressure on the brake pedal.

Now a brief explanation of piston cup terminology. Even though there is a primary piston and a secondary piston in a dual-piston master cylinder, each piston has a primary cup - it's the one that pushes the fluid and creates the pressure **(see illustration)**. Each piston also has a secondary cup. The secondary cup on the secondary piston is the one on the end of the piston closest to the primary piston of the master cylinder. Pressure generated by the primary cup of the primary piston pushes against the secondary cup of the secondary piston, which forces the secondary piston forward. The secondary cup on the primary piston prevents fluid from leaking out of the master cylinder. Most primary pistons are also equipped with an O-ring at the pushrod end of the piston, which acts as a "wiper ring," preventing contaminants from entering the bore of the master cylinder.

On some (but not all) brake circuits that feed drum brakes, a check valve is fitted in the outlet of the master cylinder **(see illustration)**. This valve maintains a little residual pressure (about 8 to 16 psi) in the lines and wheel cylinders. This pressure keeps the cups in the wheel cylinders sealed against the bores of the cylinders. In doing so, the cups seal the brake fluid in

1.14 Here's a typical master cylinder from an old four-wheel drum brake system. Notice the check valves fitted in the brake line outlets - they maintain a little residual pressure in the brake system, which keeps the lips of the wheel cylinder seals from leaking fluid or admitting air into the hydraulic system

1.15 Most pistons have bleed holes drilled through their heads, right behind the primary cup. When the brake pedal is released and the pistons retract, fluid rushes through these holes and helps push the lips of the cup off the cylinder wall. This action ensures rapid filling of the pressure chamber in front of the piston.

1.16 Exploded view of a typical double-piston wheel cylinder

and don't allow air to infiltrate the system.

When the driver lifts his or her foot from the brake pedal, the pistons begin to return to their "at rest" position. As this happens, brake fluid flows through the bleeder holes in the head of each piston **(see illustration)**, forcing the piston cups away from the cylinder wall and allowing fluid to flow into the chamber ahead of each piston. The compensating ports are uncovered when the pistons are fully retracted, and pressure will equalise between the fluid in the cylinder bore and the fluid in the reservoir.

Wheel cylinders

Wheel cylinders are used in drum brake assemblies. They convert the hydraulic pressure created by the master cylinder into mechanical force, which pushes outward on the brake shoes, expanding the shoes against the brake drum.

Wheel cylinders are usually made from cast iron. The most common type is the double-piston wheel cylinder, which uses two pistons (usually aluminium), two rubber cups, cup expanders and a coil spring between the two piston assemblies **(see illustration)**. Some designs use pushrods connected to the brake shoes. Other styles use slotted or notched pistons, in which the ends of the brake shoes ride. At each end of the wheel cylinder is a rubber boot, which seals the unit from brake dust and other elements.

Wheel cylinders are drilled and tapped for the brake line connection and bleeder screw. They are retained to the brake backing plate with one or two bolts, or a spring steel clip.

Other types of wheel cylinders include the single-piston cylinder **(see illustration)** and the stepped cylinder. The single-piston cylinder is usually used in pairs; each cylinder actuates one brake shoe. Stepped cylinders are essentially the same as double-piston cylinders, except that one half of the cylinder bore is larger than the other. The larger piston is capable of exerting more force than the smaller one. So, stepped cylinders are only used in drum brake designs where it is necessary to apply more pressure to one of the brake shoes than the other.

Calipers

The brake calipers, used on disc brake set-ups, are basically frames that house the brake pads and the hydraulic cylinders, which convert the system pressure from the master cylinder into mechanical force. This force squeezes the brake pads against the disc, which causes friction and heat dissipation, which in turn slows the vehicle. Calipers will be explained in greater detail under the Disc brakes heading.

1 Trailing shoe seat/adjuster screw
2 Adjuster star wheel
3 Adjuster detent
4 Washer
5 Screw
6 Bleeder screw
7 Cover
8 Cup
9 Piston
10 Dust boot

1.17 Here's an exploded view of a typical single-piston wheel cylinder (this one's from a front brake)

Pressure differential warning switch

This device **(see illustration)**, used on some systems with dual-piston master cylinders, alerts the driver of a partial brake failure by illuminating a warning light on the instrument panel. Most pressure differential warning switches are mounted in the hydraulic system downstream of the master cylinder, but some are mounted in the master cylinder housing **(see illustration)**.

1 Warning switch
2 End plugs
3 Piston
4 Springs
5 Seals

1.18 Cutaway of a pressure differential warning switch

1 Warning switch
2 O-ring
3 Plug
4 O-ring
5 Switch piston assembly
6 Master cylinder body

1.19 Here's an example of a pressure differential warning switch housed in the master cylinder (this one's from a mid-80's General Motors/Vauxhall vehicle)

As stated earlier in this chapter, if a portion of a dual-circuit brake system fails, half of the brake system is rendered inoperative, but the other half will still function. The result will be increased effort required to stop the vehicle, and the pedal will travel closer to the floor.

A hydraulically activated switch will alert the driver of this condition. Both circuits of the hydraulic brake system travel through this switch. A small hydraulic piston is situated between the primary circuit and the secondary circuit. As long as there are no leaks in either circuit, the piston will remain centred in the switch body. But if a brake line in one half of the system springs a leak, which will cause a pressure drop in that half of the system, the piston in the pressure differential warning switch will be forced to the side with less pressure. It takes approximately 80 to 150 pounds of pressure difference to move the piston. This action depresses a plunger on the switch terminal, or allows the plunger on the switch to fall into a cut-out in the piston, depending on the design of the switch. In either case, the switch grounds the warning circuit and the light on the dash comes on. Some pressure differential warning switches are self-centering. This means that after a brake system failure has taken place and the problem has been fixed, it isn't necessary to reset the switch. Other types of switch must be reset manually. Turn the ignition switch to On or Accessory. Slowly press the brake pedal down and the piston will centre itself, causing the warning light to go out. This will work with some switches. If it does not cause the light to go out, while an assistant is depressing the brake pedal, loosen the bleeder screw in the circuit that did NOT have the problem. Close the bleeder screw as soon as the light goes out, or you'll have to reset the switch again by opening a bleeder screw in the other hydraulic circuit.

Metering valve

The metering valve, sometimes referred to as the hold-off valve, is used only on vehicles with disc brakes in the front and drum brakes in the rear. It prevents the disc brakes from applying before the drum brakes. This permits a more even, controllable braking action because the front and rear brakes will apply at the same time. This will also ensure that the drum brakes do an equal amount of work during light braking; if a metering valve wasn't used, the front brakes would do all the braking during light stops.

This valve, located in the hydraulic circuit to the front brakes **(see illustration)**, prevents brake fluid movement to the calipers until a sufficient amount of pressure has built up in the system - enough to overcome the resistance of the drum brake shoe retracting springs and begin to apply the shoes to the drum. At this designated pressure, the valve opens and allows pressure through to the disc brakes.

Metering valves are usually combined with the pressure differential warning switch and, on models so equipped, the proportioning valve.

Proportioning valve

This valve was once found only on vehicles with drum brakes on the rear wheels, but now most cars with four-wheel disc brakes use them, too. It's located in the hydraulic circuit to the rear wheels and limits the amount of hydraulic pressure to the wheel cylinders or calipers to prevent rear wheel lockup during panic stops **(see illustration)**. The proportioning valve is sometimes remotely mounted (like the metering valve in the

1.20 The metering valve is used on vehicles with disc brakes in the front and drum brakes in the rear. It delays pressure to the front brakes until the rear brakes begin to apply, resulting in a more balanced braking action. It's located in the hydraulic line to the front brakes (arrow). In this example, it's integrated into the combination valve

1.21 This proportioning valve is built into the pressure differential warning switch

1.22 These pressure control valves, similar to proportioning valves, are screwed right into the rear brake outlets of the master cylinder (the outlets for the front brakes aren't shown in this illustration - they're on the other side of the master cylinder body)

previous illustration, or at the rear of the vehicle), but on some brake systems is built right into the master cylinder **(see illustration)**.

On some vehicles, the proportioning valve has a fixed setting. It will regulate system pressure at the same rate, regardless of any other conditions. On other vehicles, especially (but not limited to) pick-up trucks, a variable proportioning valve is used **(see illustrations).** Sometimes it's called a pressure control valve or load-sensing proportioning valve, but it does the same thing - it limits pressure to the rear brakes just as a normal proportioning valve does, but it's connected to a portion of the rear suspension by a linkage, which allows the

1.23 This variable-rate proportioning valve is mounted to the underside of this vehicle and is connected by a rod to a rear suspension arm. When the rear of the vehicle is loaded, the valve will allow normal pressure to the rear brakes. During hard stops, the rear of the car will tend to rise, shifting weight to the front. The valve will then reduce pressure to the rear brakes, preventing the rear wheel from locking up

1.24 A typical example of a Load Sensing Proportioning Valve (LSPV)

valve to monitor ride height and the amount the rear end of the vehicle rises during hard stops. By doing so, the valve can more accurately regulate pressure to the rear brakes. If the vehicle is carrying a heavy load, the valve will allow more pressure to the rear brakes, since the rear of the vehicle won't tend to rise as much during a hard stop as the same vehicle with no load at all (which means there's more weight on the rear wheels, so they won't lock up too easily). It also helps the valve distinguish between a fairly hard stop and an all-out panic stop.

1.25 Cutaway of a typical combination valve - this one incorporates all three functions:
Metering - Delays pressure application to the front brake calipers until the rear drum brake shoes have overcome the tension of their retracting springs

Pressure differential warning - Warns the driver of a failure in the brake hydraulic system
Proportioning - Controls, and on some versions ultimately limits, pressure to the rear drum brakes, to prevent the rear wheels from locking up during hard stops

Combination valve

The combination valve combines the pressure differential warning switch, the metering valve and/or the proportioning valve into one unit **(see illustration)**. Each of the separate components works in the same way as described previously, but they're centralised instead of scattered throughout the vehicle. Combination valves are usually located near the master cylinder **(see illustration)**.

Some combination valves only consist of a pressure differential warning switch and a metering valve. This allows the use of a load sensing type of proportioning valve at the rear of the vehicle. On models with four-wheel drum brakes, the combination valve is made up of a pressure differential warning switch and a proportioning valve.

Brake hoses and lines

Brake lines and hoses are the conduit in which the hydraulic pressure from the master cylinder is transferred to the hydraulic cylinders at the wheel brakes. Non-flexible, steel tubing is used wherever possible. Where the brake lines must span a gap that moves - between the chassis and suspension or steering, for example - flexible brake hoses must be used.

Metal brake lines

Rigid brake lines are constructed from high-quality seamless, double-thickness steel tubing. They are coated (usually with a copper-lead alloy) to prevent

1.26 On many vehicles, the combination valve is mounted on a bracket adjacent to the master cylinder - on others, it's mounted further down

corrosion. If it becomes necessary to renew a brake line, only use original-equipment line or brake line of equal quality. Never use copper, aluminium, brass or inferior steel tubing - these materials can't withstand the normal vibration present in a motor vehicle and will fatigue, leading to cracks and subsequent brake failure.

Because of this vibration, the brake lines must be secured to the frame or underbody of the vehicle with clips. Even the high-quality materials used for brake lines will eventually work-harden and break if subjected to vibration for a long enough period of time.

Since relatively high pressures are created in a brake hydraulic system, double-lap flares are used on the ends of the lines where they connect to a brake hose or other component. Even though flaring tools and blank brake lines are readily available, don't be tempted to fabricate your own brake lines. Brake lines, with the union nuts fitted, the fittings flared and the lines pre-bent to the proper shapes, are available, which makes brake line renewal much easier and safer. It isn't easy to make a good, clean, double-lap flare in double-wall steel tubing!

Flexible brake hose

Brake hoses, too, are constructed to stand up to the harshest of conditions. Continually subjected to movement, heat, cold, pressure, road debris, water, mud, etc., it's amazing they last as long as they do. In fact, on modern vehicles, brake hoses will typically last the lifetime of the vehicle.

Flexible brake hoses on most passenger cars and light trucks are made from numerous layers, or plies, of fabric impregnated with a synthetic rubber compound. They are then wrapped with a tough sheath of synthetic rubber or plastic material, and the metal fittings are crimped to the ends.

Some exotic cars and most racing cars use Teflon-lined, stainless steel braided hose. These lines are great for high-performance use, mainly because they resist swelling under pressure and give a more precise brake pedal feel, but they are very expensive and require special fittings.

Brake hoses, where they connect to the rigid metal lines, must be securely fastened in a bracket. This is most commonly accomplished by passing the hose end through the bracket first, securing the hose end to the bracket with a narrow nut or a spring-steel clip, then attaching the metal line with a flare-nut fitting **(see illustrations).** On some designs, the fitting on the hose is shaped to fit a similar shape in its mounting bracket; this prevents the hose from twisting. If the hose isn't secured to the bracket, vibration will eventually take its toll on the metal line, causing it to fail.

When replacing brake hoses, it's a good idea to take

1.27 Here's one method of securing a flexible brake hose to its bracket. The star shape on the hose fitting interlocks with the star shape in the bracket - this will prevent the hose from slipping in its bracket and twisting. The clip will keep the hose fitting from backing out of the bracket, which will prevent the rigid metal line from vibrating.

1.28 Instead of a clip, this hose is secured to its bracket with a locknut

the old one with you to the accessory shop or dealer. Compare the length of the hoses and the fittings to make sure the new hose is exactly the same as the original.

Brake fluid

Brake fluid can be considered the "life blood" of the brake hydraulic system. Most vehicles on the road today use brake fluid conforming to DOT 3 or DOT 4 safety standards. DOT stands for (US) Department Of Transportation, the governing body that sets the standards for brake fluid, among other things.

Never introduce any other liquid into the brake hydraulic system. Only a very small percentage of car manufacturers use anything other than brake fluid in their vehicles. Notably, some Citroëns use a type of mineral oil known as LHM in their brake systems. Brake fluid and mineral oil don't mix.

If any other kind of fluid contaminates your brake system, the entire system must be drained, flushed and refilled with clean brake fluid. But, since it isn't possible to completely remove all fluid from the brake system, this means that every hydraulic component in the system must be removed, disassembled and fitted with new seals. No shortcuts. Mineral oil or petroleum products are not compatible with the material that the brake system seals are made of. These liquids can cause the seals to swell and/or soften - either way, a very dangerous situation would be present.

As you can see, it is important that clean, uncontaminated brake fluid be used in the hydraulic system. It's a unique fluid, with more to its job than you might think. In addition to transmitting pressure, brake fluid must be able to:

a) Maintain a constant viscosity.
b) Be compatible with the lines and seals (i.e. all rubber/synthetic rubber components) in the hydraulic system.
c) Withstand heat - DOT 3 brake fluid has a 460-degree boiling point.
d) Resist freezing.
e) Lubricate the sliding parts in the system.
f) Resist compression.
g) Flow through small orifices with minimum resistance.
h) Resist the formation of sludge or gum deposits, regardless of temperature or pressure.
i) Prevent corrosion of metal parts.
j) Mix with other approved brake fluids.
k) Last, but certainly not least, last! Brake fluid must be able to do all of the above even after being in the system for an extended period of time (years).

When adding brake fluid to the brake fluid reservoir, always use brake fluid from a small, sealed brake fluid container. Since brake fluid is hygroscopic (meaning it is able to absorb moisture), fluid stored in an open container, or even in a sealed large container (if it's been sitting on the shelf for a long time) may contain too much moisture. If the fluid is laden with too much moisture, its boiling point is lowered. When the moisture-tainted brake fluid is subjected to the high heat of a modern brake system, the water molecules turn to gas, forming bubbles. This will cause a spongy feeling brake pedal. If the problem is serious enough it can cause complete brake failure. If this happens, the hydraulic system must be purged of all old brake fluid and filled with new fluid.

Take care when handling brake fluid. Some important points to remember are listed in the 'Hints & Tips' box.

HINTS & TIPS

- Brake fluid is poisonous. If it is accidentally ingested, call a poison control centre or seek medical attention immediately.
- For the above reason, never store or dispose of brake fluid in a beverage container (when bleeding brakes, for example).
- If you get brake fluid on your skin, wash it off immediately with soap and water. It's a good idea to wear latex gloves when there's a possibility of coming into contact with brake fluid.
- Wear eye protection whenever bleeding the brakes or working around brake fluid. If you get brake fluid in your eyes, rinse them out with plenty of water, then seek medical attention.
- Brake fluid will damage paint. Be careful when working on the hydraulic system near painted components. Cover all exposed bodywork in the surrounding area. Immediately rinse off brake fluid spills with lots of water

Wheel brakes

Now that we know how hydraulic power is generated and transmitted, let's take a look at the different kinds of brake set-ups at the wheels - the components that bear the brunt of the braking force and bring your vehicle to a stop.

Regardless of the type of brakes a vehicle may be equipped with, all brakes do the same thing; convert the energy of the moving vehicle into another form of energy - heat. They do this by rubbing parts together, and the resulting friction between the moving parts creates heat. The faster the brakes can create, absorb and dissipate heat, the faster the vehicle will slow down.

There are several factors that determine the efficiency of a brake. These are:

a) *The amount of pressure applied to the brake pads or shoes (more pressure = more friction).*
b) *The total area of the brake lining (greater area = more friction).*
c) *The diameter of the brake disc or drum (larger diameter = more powerful brake - like using a long lever to move a big rock).*
d) *The diameter of the vehicle's tyres (a tall tyre acts like a long lever turning the brake - the larger the diameter of the tyre, the more powerful the brake must be).*
e) *The coefficient of friction between the brake pads and disc or brake shoes and drum.*
f) *The ability of the brake to dissipate heat.*
g) *The coefficient of friction between the tyre contact patch and the earth.*

Creating friction is no problem, but dealing with the resulting heat has kept engineers busy for years, constantly searching for ways to improve braking efficiency. Even the brakes of years ago were pretty good at stopping a vehicle from a high rate of speed one or two times before allowing them to cool off, but as the brakes heated up, their ability to dissipate heat decreased, which reduced braking power. This frequently lead to brake fade, a condition that, when mild, requires more pedal effort from the driver to slow the vehicle. When severe, brake fade can lead to a complete loss of braking ability.

While the brakes fitted on modern vehicles are certainly not immune to brake fade, they are able to safely handle many more hard stops, one after the other, than the brakes on older vehicles. This is due to improved materials used in the construction of braking components and, to an even greater degree, advances in the design of wheel brakes, enabling them to disperse heat faster.

Brake fade

Brake fade is a condition that can occur when the brakes have become overheated and lose their ability to create friction and dissipate heat. The driver of a vehicle experiencing complete brake fade finds himself/herself pushing on a hard brake pedal with no stopping ability. Eventually, glazed brake linings occur, which adds to the loss of braking power.

This problem is compounded on a drum brake set-up. The drums expand when they get hot, which adds to the distance the shoes must travel before they contact the friction surface. They also lose some of their rigidity and tend to flex outward when the brake shoes start pushing against them.

There's another danger associated with overheated brakes. If the brake fluid is not in top condition (if it's old and has absorbed a lot of moisture), the heat created by the brakes can be conducted to the hydraulic components, resulting in boiling brake fluid. If this happens, the driver is in even more trouble, because even if the brakes cool off enough to allow some degree of operation, the bubbles in the brake fluid will remain - the brake pedal will be soft and mushy and probably travel to the floor, unable to produce any pressure in the hydraulic system. This is because the gas bubbles in the brake fluid are compressible. The only way to get rid of them is to bleed the hydraulic system (at which time all of the old fluid should be purged and replaced with fresh brake fluid).

Brake fade is not only a heat problem - it can be brought on by water, too. While this condition isn't quite as dangerous as heat-induced fade (provided there isn't a parked car directly in front of you as you're trying to stop), it can take a driver by surprise.

The stopping capability of disc brakes isn't affected much by water; the spinning disc throws off the water, and any remaining moisture on the disc or pads is quickly vaporised shortly after the brakes are applied. Drum brakes, however, are very susceptible to water-induced fade.

When water enters a drum brake assembly (usually through the gap between the brake drum and the backing plate) it becomes trapped. It gets thrown outward by the centrifugal force of the spinning drum and acts like a lubricant between the shoes and the drum's friction surface. The problem is made worse when the water mixes with accumulations of brake dust. The resulting mud-like mixture takes longer to burn off than plain water.

If you find yourself experiencing water-induced brake fade, hold your foot down hard on the brake pedal - if there's no immediate change in braking action, release the brakes and apply them again (all the while trying to avoid any obstacles in your path). A couple of repeated applications of the pedal like this should clear up the problem.

There are two basic designs of brakes in use today - disc brakes and drum brakes. There are many different variations of each, but they all operate in a similar manner, using friction to generate heat. The following sections examine the design, components and operation of these brake designs.

Drum brakes

The first wheel brakes fitted to early cars were drum brakes. They weren't like the drum brakes on a modern vehicle, though. They worked much like a band in an automatic transmission. The friction material surrounded the outside surface of the drum and clamped tight around the spinning drum when the brakes were applied. It was a very simple arrangement, but had a couple of drawbacks; they couldn't get rid of heat very well and were almost useless if they got wet.

A major breakthrough in braking effectiveness came about when engineers placed the friction surface on the *inside* of the drum. This helped to seal the brake from the elements a little better, and allowed a much greater surface area of the drum to be in contact with the surrounding air, which allowed the brake drum to dissipate the heat it had absorbed much quicker.

The major components of a drum brake assembly are the brake drum, the brake shoes, the backing plate, the wheel cylinder(s), and all the hardware necessary to mount and connect the components **(see illustrations).** Most rear drum brake assemblies also have self-adjusting mechanisms to keep the shoes within a predetermined distance from the drum, even as

Chapter 1

WHEEL CYLINDER LINKS
SECONDARY SHOE & LINING
SHOE GUIDE
PARKING BRAKE STRUT
STRUT SPRING
ADJUSTER LEVER
ACTUATING LINK

WHEEL CYLINDER SCREWS
BACKING PLATE

HOLD DOWN PINS

PARKING BRAKE LEVER
WHEEL CYLINDER
PRIMARY SHOE AND LINING

HOLD DOWN SPRING & CUP
HOLD DOWN SPRING
ADJUSTING SCREW SPRING
ADJUSTING SCREW
LEVER RETURN SPRING
BRAKE SHOE RETURN SPRING

1.29 Exploded view of a typical duo-servo drum brake

Backing Plate

Shoe Adjusting
Hole Plug

Front Shoe

Wheel Cylinder
Adjuster
Rear Shoe
C-Washer
Adjusting Shim
Automatic Adjusting Lever
C-Washer

Return Spring

Pin
Retainer
Hold-Down Spring
Anchor Spring
Parking Brake Lever
Spring

1.30 Exploded view of a typical leading/trailing drum brake the lining material wears down.

The following is a description of each major component and its function.

Backing plate - Bolted to the axle housing (rear brake) or steering knuckle (front brake), the backing plate provides a mounting place for the brake shoes and wheel cylinders. It's usually made of heavy-gauge stamped steel. It has raised areas, or lands, for the edges of the brake shoes to ride on. One of the most important parts of the backing plate is the anchor, or on some designs, the anchor pin. The anchor or anchor pin is the immovable rest that the end of the brake shoes rest on, and the point that all braking force for that brake (not heat dissipation, but the portion of the energy of the moving vehicle that the brake is responsible for) is transmitted through. The anchor on some vehicles is riveted to the backing plate. On others, it's bolted to the axle housing or steering knuckle.

Wheel cylinder(s) - This is the component that converts hydraulic pressure into mechanical energy. Wheel cylinders are explained in detail under the *Hydraulic systems* heading.

Brake shoes - The brake shoe assembly usually consists of two brake shoes. A friction material is fastened to each shoe by means of rivets or by a process called bonding - a form of gluing under a heated drying process. The brake shoes are the components that the wheel cylinder pistons push out on, expanding them to rub against the friction surface of the brake drum. Brake shoes have been designed for maximum rigidity.

On a duo-servo design (we'll get to that) the shoe that faces the front of the vehicle is referred to as the primary shoe. The other one is the secondary shoe. The primary shoe is shorter (or at least the lining is) than the secondary.

On a leading/trailing brake, the front shoe is called the leading shoe; the rear shoe is called the trailing shoe.

In a drum brake set-up that has separate wheel cylinders for each brake shoe, both shoes are primary or leading shoes. This is known as a twin leading shoe arrangement.

Brake lining - The job of the brake lining is to create friction (heat) when it's pressed against the brake drum. As previously stated, the linings are riveted or bonded to the brake shoe. Most brake linings are made of asbestos, held together with special compounds; asbestos-free linings are also available. Some have brass or copper wires impregnated in the lining. Some linings are grooved, slotted or woven to improve cooling. Brake lining wears down in use, and must be changed when it becomes too thin (approximately 1/16-inch from the shoe [bonded linings] or the rivet heads [riveted linings]).

Brake drum - The brake drum spins with the wheel and absorbs and dissipates heat when the brakes are applied and the shoes rub against it. Brake drums are usually made from cast iron, but some are made of aluminium, fitted with cast iron liners for a friction surface. Some drums have cooling vanes cast into their outer surfaces to increase area and aid in cooling.

After a considerable amount of use, brake drums normally will become a little out-of-round. This is due to the intense temperature changes the drum is subjected to. Drums can be machined to get rid of an out-of-round condition or score marks, but all brake drums have a maximum allowable diameter, sometimes cast or stamped somewhere on the drum's surface. This dimension must not be exceeded, because the drum wouldn't be able to dissipate heat well enough, and could even fatigue and crack.

Attaching hardware and other components - A variety of bits and pieces are required to secure the brake shoes to the backing plate and, on rear drum brakes, actuate the handbrake and ensure that the brake shoes self-adjust during operation. Not all of the following components are found on every drum brake set-up.

Hold-down pin, spring and cup - This simple device retains the brake shoe to the backing plate, but allows the brake shoe to move side-to-side a little, if necessary, to better conform to the friction surface of the brake drum. The hold-down pin is inserted from the backside of the backing plate and passes through a hole in the brake shoe. A spring is then placed over the pin and is retained by a cup, or retainer.

Shoe retracting (or return) springs - These springs pull the shoes away from the brake drum after the brake has been released. They're strong enough to overcome the residual pressure in the hydraulic system, so they push the pistons back into the wheel cylinders a little bit, preventing the shoes from dragging against the brake drum.

Handbrake lever and strut - Connected by a cable to the handbrake lever inside the vehicle, the handbrake lever inside of a drum brake assembly expands the shoes, with the help of the handbrake strut, out against the drum when the handbrake lever inside the vehicle is lifted. The handbrake lever and strut operate like a "mechanical wheel cylinder."

Self-adjusting mechanism - Self-adjusting mechanisms come in many forms, but they all work to keep the lining on the brake shoes reasonably close to the friction surface of the brake drum, as the lining wears down. On most set-ups, a small lever, actuated by a cable or linkage, turns an adjuster, or "star" wheel, located between the brake shoes. As the adjuster is turned, the shoes are expanded outward a little bit.

Some self-adjusters are activated during normal braking, while others operate when the handbrake is used or the vehicle is driven in reverse and the brakes are applied.

Operation

We've covered the master cylinder and how it creates pressure in the hydraulic system, and how this pressure is converted into mechanical energy by the wheel cylinder. The pistons in the wheel cylinder then push outward on the brake shoes, forcing them against the brake drum, which creates the friction. The heat caused by this friction is then stored in the brake drum and dissipated to the air.

All modern drum brakes are self-energising, which means the braking force is multiplied by the spinning action of the drum as the brake shoe is applied to it. This self-energising action is accomplished by the toe (top) of the leading or primary shoe moving out and making contact with the rotating drum. The drum attempts to take the shoe with it - the shoe tends to stick to the drum along its entire span. Of course, it can't begin to spin with the drum, because it's prevented from doing so by the anchor plate or pin.

A duo-servo design drum brake takes this self-energising action one step further **(see illustration)**. Since there is only one anchor pin in this type of brake, the self-energising force imposed on the primary shoe is transferred to the secondary shoe through a link, or more commonly, the adjusting screw. This forces the bottom of the secondary shoe onto the spinning drum, and the self-energising process is applied to the secondary shoe to an even greater extent, forcing the top of the secondary shoe into the anchor pin (this is why secondary shoes have more lining material on them). At the same time, the wheel cylinder is also pushing against the secondary shoe. As you can imagine, braking force is greatly multiplied. With this design, the self-energising action takes place when the brakes are applied when the vehicle is moving forwards or reversing - it doesn't matter. Brake designs that have a similar brake shoe/anchor pin layout, but use a single-sided wheel cylinder, are called uni-servo brakes (and only have servo-action brakes when going forwards).

There's one drawback to the duo-servo design - sometimes they work too well, and can lock up the rear wheels. For the most part, duo-servo brakes are used on heavier, rear-wheel drive vehicles. Many other vehicles use self-energising brakes, but without the duo-servo action. In these designs, the wheel cylinder acts on one end of the brake shoe, but the other end rests against an anchor plate or pin.

One variation of this set-up arranges the brake shoes and wheel cylinder in a similar manner to that of the duo-

1.31 The self-energising, or servo-action drum brake uses the rotation of the brake drum to increase the pressure on the brake shoes, making the driver's job easier

1.32 Double-anchor, double-cylinder design drum brake. This set-up makes for a powerful brake, as long as the vehicle is travelling forward

servo design, but instead of the anchor pin at the top and a connecting link between the shoes at the bottom, the bottom of each shoe resting against an anchor (sometimes each shoe has its own anchor pin). This type of brake is commonly referred to as a leading/trailing or double-anchor design **(see illustration 1.30)**. When the vehicle is travelling forward, only the leading shoe will be self-energised. When the vehicle is braked in reverse, the trailing shoe will be self-energised.

A less common design uses two leading, or primary, shoes. This is called a double-anchor, double-cylinder brake, also called a leading/leading or twin leading shoe brake **(see illustration)**. Each shoe has its own wheel cylinder, and each shoe is self-energising when the brakes are applied, but only when the vehicle is travelling forwards. In reverse there is no self-energising action at all, and much more muscle power is required to stop the vehicle.

Braking ratio

When the brakes are applied, the natural tendency of the vehicle is to dip forward, placing the greater stopping requirement on the front wheels and less on the rear wheels.

Through increased friction area and a larger cylinder bore on the front brakes (whether they are disc or drum brakes, it doesn't matter), a greater capacity for braking is the result.

Most modern vehicles split the ratio of braking to 60-percent on the front wheels and 40-percent on the rear wheels (this is why most vehicles have disc brakes up front). Under severe braking this ratio can become even more imbalanced, but thanks to the proportioning valve (or pressure control valve), pressure is limited to the rear brakes to keep them from locking up as the rear of the vehicle lightens up.

Disc brakes

Once considered an item for sports cars and racers, it didn't take the disc brake long to find a home amongst the most domesticated of vehicles. The disc brake represents the most important advancement in brake design since self-energising servo-action.

The disc brake differs from the drum brake in that the friction surface is external, allowing it to cool much more rapidly. There is little deflection or bending in a disc brake assembly, unlike in a drum brake. Friction is created by forcing two brake pads against a rotating disc **(see illustration)**. The disc is pinched between the pads, so the only part that could possibly flex is the caliper, but calipers don't flex very much. The result is a very efficient brake.

1.33 Cutaway of a typical front disc brake (sliding caliper shown)

Most modern vehicles are equipped with disc brakes on the front wheels, at least. Many are equipped with discs at the rear, too. Since weight transfers to the front of the vehicle under braking, it is important to have more powerful brakes up front - they do most of the work.

Disc brakes have many advantages over drum brakes:

a) Resistance to heat fade - disc brakes dissipate heat more rapidly because more of the braking surface is exposed to air. Heat also makes the discs a little thicker, which has no ill effects on braking (with a drum brake, heat tends to allow the drum to expand and flex).

b) Resistance to water fade - rotation of the disc tends to throw off the water.

c) Better straight-line stops - because of their clamping action, disc brakes are less likely to pull.

d) Ease of serviceability - disc brake pads, in almost all cases, are easier to renew that drum brake shoes.

e) Lighter weight.

f) Cheaper to manufacture.

The major components of a disc brake assembly are:

The brake disc, or rotor - This part is attached to the hub and turns with the wheel. The thickness and diameter of the disc determine how much heat the brake can absorb and dissipate. Some discs are vented to improve cooling.

The brake pads - These are composed of a steel backing plate to which the brake lining (friction material) is attached. Brake pad linings are attached by rivets or are bonded to the backing plate, just like the brake

1. Piston seal
2. Piston
3. Dust boot
4. Dust boot retaining ring
5. Fluid transfer channel
6. Caliper (outer half)
7. Bleeder screw
8. Bolt (retains caliper halves)
9. Retaining clip
10. Brake pad
11. Bleeder screw
12. Anti-rattle spring
13. Pad retaining pin
14. Caliper (inner half)

1.34 Cutaway of a typical fixed caliper

mechanical energy. Calipers can have up to four pistons, or even more on exotic designs. The caliper is affixed to a mounting bracket that is bolted to the steering knuckle or suspension arm, or fastened to bosses that are integral with the knuckle.

Designs

There are three general designs of disc brakes, determined by caliper arrangement: Fixed caliper, floating calipers and sliding calipers.

Fixed caliper - In this design, the caliper is attached to the steering knuckle (or a bracket attached to the knuckle) and is stationary **(see illustrations).** A minimum of two opposing pistons must be used on this design - one to apply each pad. Some fixed calipers use four pistons (two per pad) and some even use three pistons (a large piston in one half of the caliper and two smaller ones in the other half).

As the brake pedal is applied, pressure from the master cylinder is distributed equally to the pistons, which are forced against the brake pads, which squeeze the disc. The caliper doesn't move. Brake pads are usually retained by a pin (or pins) in this set-up.

Most fixed calipers are constructed of two castings containing the hydraulic pistons. The halves are bolted together, some having fluid passages leading from one half to the other. On other designs a fluid transfer tube leads from one side of the caliper to the other to supply the outer piston(s) with hydraulic pressure.

Some fixed calipers are equipped with springs behind the pistons, to keep the pistons from retracting more

shoes in a drum brake. The composition of the lining is similar to a drum brake shoe, also.

The brake caliper - This is the component that squeezes the pads against the disc. It is a U-shaped casting that fits over the disc and pads. It contains at least one hydraulic cylinder, which converts the pressure developed by the master cylinder into

1. Caliper body
2. Outer pistons
3. Inner piston
4. Piston seals
5. Dust boot
6. Piston seal
7. Dust boot
8. Brake pad
9. Pad retaining pin
10. Clip
11. Bleeder screw
12. Dust cap
13. Mounting shim
14. Anti-rattle spring

1.35 Exploded view of a three-piston fixed caliper

1.36 An exploded view of a typical single-piston floating caliper

than just enough to relieve pressure on the disc. This ensures the pads stay right next to the disc (they actually rub against the disc, but with no pressure applied). The result is a firm brake pedal without an excessive amount of travel.

Floating caliper - The floating caliper uses a piston (two in some designs) only in one side of the caliper **(see illustration)**. The caliper is mounted on guide pins that ride in bushings or sleeves, so it is free to move back and forth. As hydraulic pressure builds up behind the caliper piston, the piston pushes on the inner brake pad, forcing it against the disc. As this happens, the inside of the caliper is pushed away from the disc, which simultaneously pulls the outside of the caliper into the outer brake pad, forcing it against the disc **(see illustration)**. The result is the same powerful clamping action without the complexity of multiple pistons.

Another advantage of the floating caliper is the tendency to absorb pulsations caused by disc runout (wobble). With a fixed caliper, a warped disc will push the pistons back slightly with every rotation of the disc (this is called knockback). Under braking, this will be transmitted back through the hydraulic system to the brake pedal, causing it to pulsate under the driver's foot. In a floating caliper set-up, the caliper will move back and forth with the pads as the warped disc moves them back and forth, eliminating almost all of the pulsating at

1.37 In a floating caliper, the action of the piston not only pushes the inner brake pad against the disc, it also pulls the outer brake pad against the disc (sliding calipers work like this, too)

1.38 Exploded view of a typical sliding caliper

A   Caliper mounting bracket
B   Retaining pins
C   Outer brake pad
D   Anti-rattle clip
E   Tension spring
F   Caliper retaining key
G   Dust boot
H   Piston seal
I   Not used
J   Piston
K   Caliper housing
L   Dust cap
M   Bleeder screw
N   Brake hose
O   Caliper retaining key
P   Tension spring
Q   Anti-rattle clip
R   Inner brake pad

the brake pedal.

The outer brake pad in a floating caliper set-up is usually affixed to the caliper housing by a retaining spring or tangs. The inner pad is sometimes fastened to the caliper piston or is retained by the caliper mounting bolts. There are exceptions, though. On some designs, both pads ride in the caliper bracket.

In addition, floating calipers are much easier to service than fixed calipers, and are cheaper to manufacture.

Sliding caliper - The sliding caliper is a variation of the floating caliper. Unlike the floating caliper, however, the sliding caliper uses no guide pins; instead, a pair of machined abutments on the caliper adapter position and align the caliper. Retaining clips, springs, keys or "wedge"-type pins keep the caliper on machined guides (sometimes called "ways") on the adapter, allowing lateral movement of the caliper **(see illustrations).**

In a sliding caliper set-up, the brake pads sometimes ride on the machined abutments of the caliper adapter. In other designs, one of the pads rides on the adapter and the other pad is affixed to the caliper - either the

1.39 Here's another kind of sliding caliper - the caliper pins in this set-up are spring steel filled with rubber to ensure a tight fit after they're driven into place

frame or the piston.

Apart from the way the caliper is mounted and the method of retaining the brake pads, operation of the sliding caliper is the same as the floating caliper.

Operation

We've actually discussed how the caliper works, but there's an important feature of brake calipers that we haven't covered yet, and that is the self-adjusting capability of the brake caliper.

The piston in a brake caliper fits in its bore with very little clearance (no more than 0.005-inch). To hold the hydraulic fluid in the caliper under pressure, the piston is surrounded by an O-ring near the opening in the piston bore. There's also a dust boot at the top of the piston, and on some calipers the boot seats in a groove just like the piston seal, but serves no purpose in fluid sealing at all. The O-ring seal is much larger than it needs to be for sealing purposes alone. It plays the main role in the self-adjusting feature of disc brakes.

When pressure from the master cylinder builds up behind the caliper piston, the piston is forced out and applies the brake pads. As the piston travels outward, the piston seal is distorted - it bends out with the piston **(see illustration)**. When the brakes are released, pressure behind the piston subsides and the seal pulls the piston back home (remember, we're only talking about a fraction of an inch). As the pads wear down, the piston travels out a little farther, and even though the seal bends out with the piston, it can only go so far. So,

1.40 These drawings illustrate the seal retraction action that takes place after the brakes are released. In the top drawing, pressure has pushed the piston from the bore a little. The piston seal has distorted and "followed" the piston. In the bottom drawing, the brakes have been released, and the seal has pulled the piston back into the caliper

the piston slides through the seal enough to take up the slack caused by the thinner brake pads. In doing so, the brake pedal remains firm and doesn't travel to the floor as the brake pads wear down.

Some older multi-piston calipers achieve the same self adjusting action by placing coil springs behind each piston.

As you can see, the disc brake has many advantages over the drum brake, but it has one disadvantage - there's no self-energising action. It could be compared to a drum brake with two trailing shoes. There are two ways to compensate for this: large caliper pistons and some form of power assist to help the driver supply the necessary pressure to the master cylinder.

Handbrakes

All vehicles are equipped with some form of handbrake (also called a parking brake) to prevent the vehicle from moving when it's parked. This is sometimes referred to as an emergency brake. Although it'll help you slow down your vehicle in the unlikely event of a complete brake failure, chances are the handbrake will fade out or just be incapable of supplying enough

pressure to apply the brakes hard enough to slow the vehicle in a reasonable amount of time.

Most handbrakes simply utilise the service brakes on the rear wheels, through cable actuation, although some vehicles are equipped with a separate handbrake. A few manufacturers place the handbrake on the front wheels.

In a typical drum brake assembly, the cable pulls on a handbrake lever attached to the secondary or trailing shoe. The lever bears against a strut connected to the primary or leading shoe, forcing the shoes against the brake drum.

In some disc brake assemblies, the handbrake cable is attached to a lever on the rear caliper. The lever is connected to an actuating screw that is threaded into the caliper piston. When the handbrake is applied, the lever turns the actuating screw, which forces the piston out, applying the brake pads.

Another version of this handbrake uses a lever that, when pulled by the handbrake cable, forces a small pushrod into an adjuster spindle threaded into the caliper piston. This pushes the caliper piston from the caliper and applies the brake **(see illustration)**.

In other disc brake set-ups, a separate set of brake

1.41 Exploded view of a typical rear caliper with an adjuster spindle-type handbrake pads (much smaller than the regular pads) are clamped against the disc when actuated by the handbrake cable **(see illustration)**. These pads are usually so small that they are good for nothing more than holding the vehicle stationary - they're almost useless for slowing the vehicle down in the event of a total brake failure (thank goodness total brake failures are extremely rare occurrences!).

The other handbrake arrangement on a rear disc brake set-up places a pair of handbrake shoes inside the "hat," or inner diameter, of the disc. These work like a miniature drum brake set-up **(see illustration)**.

The least common handbrake arrangement places a drum on the output shaft of the transmission, with the backing plate and brake shoes connected to the transmission housing. With the exception of some Land Rover models, this type of arrangement hasn't been used by automobile manufacturers for years.

Servos

The brake servo is a device that helps the driver apply pressure to the master cylinder. On older vehicles with four wheel drum brakes, power assistance was not too important because of the self-energising action inherent to the design of drum brakes. As disc brakes gained

1	Operating lever	4	Adjuster nut
2	Pad carrier assembly	5	Adjuster bolt
3	Pawl assembly	6	Handbrake pads

1.42 Here's a cutaway view of a handbrake mechanism on a Jaguar. The small pads are lever operated and self adjusting.

1.43 An exploded view of the "drum-type" handbrake set-up on a rear disc brake

1.44 Fitting details of a typical vacuum-operated power brake servo

popularity, servos became much more common. In fact, they are almost a necessity on systems with disc brakes, since so much pressure is required to successfully clamp a spinning disc between the brake pads. Without a servo, the cylinders in the brake calipers would have to be bigger, requiring a longer travel master cylinder or more mechanical advantage built into the brake pedal to develop the necessary pressure. Either way, brake pedal travel would be excessive.

There are two general types of servos available: Vacuum-operated and hydraulically operated. The most common is the vacuum-operated type, but the hydraulically-operated type was used on a few older vehicles.

Vacuum-operated servos

There are two basic kinds of vacuum-operated servos: vacuum suspended and air-suspended. Both kinds use a diaphragm, or diaphragms, to separate two or four chambers. They each create a pressure differential situation inside to aid in pushing the pushrod into the master cylinder **(see illustrations).**

In the event of a fault developing inside the servo, enough vacuum is stored to provide sufficient assistance for two or three brake applications and after

that, the performance of the hydraulic part of the braking system is only affected in that the need for higher pedal pressures will be noticed.

Vacuum-operated servos are constructed of stamped steel housings that lock together. The internals are replaceable, but doing so just isn't feasible. When a servo fails, it's much easier to simply exchange the old unit for a new or rebuilt one, since special tools and expertise are required to overhaul one.

Operation

Note: *The following description details the operation of a typical vacuum suspended brake servo. The air suspended servo operates in a similar manner, but instead of vacuum being present on both sides of the diaphragm and introducing atmospheric pressure into the brake pedal side of the unit, air is present on both sides of the diaphragm and vacuum is introduced to the master cylinder side of the servo.*

Brakes released - In the "at rest" condition with the engine running, vacuum is present on both sides of the power piston. Air at atmospheric pressure, entering through the filter behind the pushrod, is shut off at the air valve. The floating control valve is held away from the seat in the power piston insert. Any air in the system is drawn through a small passage in the power piston,

1.45 Cutaway view of a typical vacuum-operated servo (vacuum-suspended type)

past the power piston insert valve seat to the insert itself. It then travels through a drilling in the support plate, into the space in front of the power piston then to the intake manifold via a check valve. Vacuum therefore exists on both sides of the power piston which is held against the rear of the housing under spring action.

Brakes applied - When the brake pedal is depressed, the pushrod carries the air valve away from the floating control valve. The floating control valve will follow until it contacts the raised seat in the power piston insert; vacuum is now shut off to the rear power piston and atmospheric pressure (air) enters the housing at the rear of the power piston. The power piston therefore moves forward to operate the floating piston assembly of the hydraulic master cylinder. As pressure increases on the end of the master cylinder piston, the reaction plate is moved off its seat on the lower piston and contacts the reaction levers. These levers swing on their pivots and bear against the end of the air valve operating rod assembly to provide a feedback (approximately 30-percent of the master cylinder load) to the pedal. This enables the driver to "feel" the degree of brake application.

Brake holding - When the desired braking force is

achieved, the power piston moves forward until the floating control valve again seats on the air valve. The power piston will now remain stationary until there is a change in applied pedal pressure.

Brakes released - When the pedal pressure is released, the air valve is forced back to contact the power piston under spring action. As it moves, the floating control valve is pushed off its seat on the power piston insert by the air valve. Atmospheric pressure (air) is shut off by the air valve seating on the floating control valve. As the floating control valve lifts from its seat, it opens the rear of the power piston to intake manifold vacuum, and the power piston returns to the rear housing. The hydraulic pressure in the brake system is released as the floating piston assembly returns to the normal position.

Vacuum failure - In the event of vacuum failure, i.e. the engine dies, the vacuum line cracks or the diaphragm inside the booster ruptures, application of the brake pedal moves the pedal pushrod which in turn contacts the master cylinder pushrod and the brakes are applied. This gives a condition as found in a standard, non-power assisted brake system, and a correspondingly higher pedal pressure is required.

1 Nuts
2 Master cylinder
3 Servo unit
4 Nut
5 Gasket

1.46 Mounting details of a hydraulically operated brake servo. This unit uses pressure from the power steering pump to assist the driver in applying the brakes.

Hydraulically operated servos

Some power boosters are operated by hydraulic pressure instead of intake manifold vacuum **(see illustration)**. Most of these systems use pressure generated by a belt-driven pump which also supplies the power steering gear. When the engine is running, the pump supplies hydraulic pressure to a power flow regulator/accumulator. The regulator/accumulator

1 Pushrod
2 Electrical connector
3 Electrical connector
4 Brake lines
5 Nut
6 Master cylinder
7 Electro-hydraulic pump
8 Accumulator
9 Pressure switch

1.47 Electro-mechanical brake servo assembly

stores and regulates the pressure to the hydraulic servo unit, which is mounted between the master cylinder and the bulkhead, just like a vacuum brake servo. When the brake pedal is depressed, a pressure regulating valve opens, admitting power steering fluid under pressure into a chamber. This pressure helps actuate the master cylinder, reducing pedal effort. In the event of a failure in the power steering pump (or if the engine dies), the accumulator stores enough pressure in it for one or two reserve stops. Braking will then revert to non-power assist.

Another kind of hydraulic servo **(see illustration)** is integral with the master cylinder. In addition to the master cylinder, it consists of an electro-hydraulic pump, a nitrogen-charged fluid accumulator, a pressure switch and the servo unit.

The accumulator stores brake fluid at pressures of 500 to 700 psi. When pressure drops below this value, the pressure switch signals the pump to activate, which charges up the accumulator. When the driver depresses the brake pedal, pressurised fluid from the accumulator pushes on the power piston in the servo to help apply the master cylinder pistons.

A third type of hydraulic operation is found in some Citroën models. In this system a belt-driven pump provides hydraulic pressure to activate the braking, suspension and (where applicable) power steering systems. Detailed examination of such systems is beyond the scope of this book, but it is worth remembering that the basic principle of operation - the transmission of force via an incompressible fluid - remains the same.

Chapter 2
Tools and Equipment

A place to work

Establish a place to work. It doesn't have to be particularly large, but it should be clean, safe, well-lit, organised and adequately equipped for the job. True, without a good workshop or garage, you can still service and repair brakes, even if you have to work outside. However, major repairs should be carried out in a sheltered area with a roof. Some of the procedures in this book require an environment totally free of dirt, which could cause contamination and subsequent failure if it finds its way into the brake system.

The workshop

The size, shape and location of a workshop building is usually dictated by circumstance rather than personal choice. Every do-it-yourselfer dreams of having a spacious, clean, well-lit building specially designed and equipped for working on everything from small engines on lawn and garden equipment to cars and other vehicles. In reality, however, most of us must content ourselves with a garage, basement or shed in the backyard.

Spend some time considering the potential - and drawbacks - of your current facility. Even a well-established workshop can benefit from intelligent design. Lack of space is the most common problem, but you can significantly increase useful space by carefully planning the locations of work and storage areas. One strategy is to look at how others do it. Ask local garage owners if you can see their workshops. Note how they've arranged their work areas, storage and lighting, then try to scale down their solutions to fit your own workshop space, finances and needs.

General workshop requirements

A solid concrete floor is the best surface for a workshop area. The floor should be even, smooth and dry. A coat of paint or sealant formulated for concrete surfaces will make oil spills and dirt easier to remove and help cut down on dust - always a problem with concrete.

Paint the walls and ceiling white for maximum reflection. Use gloss or semi-gloss enamel. It's washable and reflective. If your workshop has windows, situate workbenches to take advantage of them. Skylights are even better. You can't have too much natural light. Artificial light is also good, but you'll need a lot of it to equal ordinary daylight.

Make sure the building is adequately ventilated. This is critical during the winter months, to prevent condensation problems. It's also a vital safety consideration where solvents, fuel and other volatile liquids are being used. You should be able to open one or more windows for ventilation. In addition, opening vents in the walls are desirable.

Electricity and lights

Electricity is essential in a workshop. It's relatively easy to refit if the workshop is part of the house, but it can be difficult and expensive to refit if it isn't. Safety should be your primary consideration when dealing with electricity. Unless you have a very good working knowledge of electrical fittings, have an electrician do any work required to provide power and lights in the workshop.

Consider the total electrical requirements of the workshop, making allowances for possible later additions of lights and equipment. Don't substitute extension cords for legal and safe permanent wiring. If the wiring isn't adequate, or is substandard, have it upgraded.

Give careful consideration to lights for the workshop. A pair of 150-watt incandescent bulbs, or two 48-inch long, 40-watt fluorescent tubes, suspended approximately 48 inches above the workbench, are the minimum you can get by with. As a rule, fluorescent lights are probably the best choice. Their light is bright, even, shadow-free and fairly economical, although some people don't care for the bluish tinge they cast on everything. The usual compromise is a good mix of fluorescent and incandescent fixtures.

The position of the lights is important. Don't place a fixture directly above the work area. It will cause shadows, even with fluorescent lights. Attach the light(s) slightly to the rear - or to each side - of the workbench or garage to provide shadow-free lighting. A portable inspection light is very helpful for use when overhead lights are inadequate. If fuel, solvents or other flammable liquids are present - not an unusual situation in a workshop - use special fittings to minimise the risk of fire. And don't use fluorescent lights above machine tools (like a drill press). The flicker produced by alternating current is especially pronounced with this type of light and can make a rotating chuck appear stationary at certain speeds - a very dangerous situation.

2.1 Home-made wood shelves are relatively inexpensive to build and you can design them to fit the available space, but all that wood can be a fire hazard

Storage and shelves

Set up an organised storage area to avoid losing parts. You'll need storage space for hardware, lubricants and other chemicals, rags, tools and equipment.

If space and finances allow, refit metal shelves along the walls. Arrange the shelves so they're widely spaced near the bottom to take large or heavy items. Metal shelf units are pricey, but they make the best use of available space. And the shelf height is adjustable on most units.

Wood shelves **(see illustration)** are sometimes a cheaper storage solution. But they must be built - not just assembled. They must be much heftier than metal shelves to carry the same weight, the shelves can't be adjusted vertically and you can't just disassemble them and take them with you if you move. Wood also absorbs oil and other liquids and is obviously a much greater fire hazard.

Store small parts in plastic drawers or bins mounted on metal racks attached to the wall. They're available from most hardware, home and lumber stores. Bins come in various sizes and usually have slots for labels.

Workbenches

A workbench is essential - it provides a place to lay out parts and tools during repair procedures, and it's a lot more comfortable than working on a floor or the driveway. The workbench should be as large and sturdy as space and finances allow. If cost is no object, buy industrial steel benches. They're more expensive than home-built benches, but they're very strong, they're easy to assemble, and - if you move - they can be disassembled quickly and you can take them with you. They're also available in various lengths, so you can buy the exact size to fill the space along a wall.

If steel benches aren't in the budget, fabricate a bench frame from slotted angle-iron or timber **(see**

HINTS & TIPS

- All kinds of containers are useful in a workshop. Glass jars are handy for storing fasteners, but They're easily broken. Cardboard boxes are adequate for temporary use, but if they become damp, the bottoms eventually weaken and fall apart if you store oily or heavy parts in them. Plastic containers come in a variety of sizes and colours for easy identification. Egg cartons are excellent organisers for tiny parts. Large ice cream tubs are suitable for keeping small parts together. Get the type with a snap cover. Old metal cake pans, bread pans and muffin tins also make good storage containers for small parts.

2.2 You can build a sturdy, inexpensive workbench with 4 x 4s, 2 x 6s and a solid core door with hardboard laminations - or build a bench using the wall as an integral member as shown

illustration). Cut the pieces of the frame to the required size and bolt them together with carriage bolts. A 30 or 36 by 80-inch, solid-core door with hardboard surfaces makes a good bench top. And you can flip it over when one side is worn out.

An even cheaper - and quicker - solution? Assemble a bench by attaching the bench top frame pieces to the wall with angled braces and use the wall studs as part of the framework.

Regardless of the type of frame you decide to use for the workbench, be sure to position the bench top at a comfortable working height and make sure everything is level. Shelves refitted below the bench will make it more rigid and provide useful storage space.

Tools and equipment

For some home mechanics, the idea of using the correct tool is completely foreign. They'll cheerfully tackle the most complex procedures with only a set of cheap open-end spanners of the wrong type, a single screwdriver with a worn tip, a large hammer and an adjustable spanner. Though they often get away with it, this cavalier approach is stupid and dangerous. It can result in relatively minor annoyances like stripped fasteners, or cause catastrophic consequences like brake failure. It can also result in serious injury.

A complete assortment of good tools is a given for anyone who plans to work on cars. If you don't already have most of the tools listed below, the initial investment may seem high, but compared to the spiralling costs of routine maintenance and repairs, it's worth while.

Besides, you can use a lot of the tools around the house for other types of mechanical repairs. While some of the tools we'll describe aren't necessary to complete most brake repair operations, they are representative of the kinds of tools you would expect to find in a well-equipped workshop.

Buying tools

There are two ways to buy tools. The easiest and quickest way is to simply buy an entire set. Tool sets are often priced substantially below the cost of the same individually priced tools - and sometimes they even come with a tool box. When purchasing such sets, you often wind up with some tools you don't need or want. But if low price and convenience are your concerns, this might be the way to go. Keep in mind that you're going to keep a quality set of tools a long time (maybe the rest of your life), so check the tools carefully; don't skimp too much on price, either. Buying tools individually is usually a more expensive and time-consuming way to go, but you're more likely to wind up with the tools you need and want. You can also select each tool on its relative merits for the way you use it.

You can get most of the hand tools on our list from the tool department of any car accessory shop or similar chain that sells hand tools. Special tools are available from companies supplying the needs of professional mechanics. These companies can also supply the other tools you need, but they'll probably be more expensive.

Also consider buying second-hand tools from auctions or similar outlets. You may have limited choice in sizes, but you can usually determine from the condition of the tools if they're worth buying. You can end up with a number of unwanted or duplicate tools, but it's a cheap way of putting a basic tool kit together, and you can always sell off any surplus tools later.

Until you're a good judge of the quality levels of tools, avoid mail order firms, flea markets and car boot sales. Some of them offer good value for the money, but many sell cheap, imported tools of dubious quality. Like other consumer products counterfeited in the Far East, these tools run the gamut from acceptable to unusable.

If you're unsure about how much use a tool will get, the following approach may help. For example, if you need a set of combination spanners but aren't sure which sizes you'll end up using most, buy a cheap or medium-priced set (make sure the jaws fit the fastener sizes marked on them). After some use over a period of time, carefully examine each tool in the set to assess its condition. If all the tools fit well and are undamaged, don't bother buying a better set. If one or two are worn, renew them with high-quality items - this way you'll end up with top-quality tools where they're needed most and the cheaper ones are sufficient for occasional use. On rare occasions you may conclude the whole set is poor quality. If so, buy a better set, if necessary, and remember never to buy that brand again.

In summary, try to avoid cheap tools, especially when you're purchasing high-use items like screwdrivers, spanners and sockets. Cheap tools don't last long. Their initial cost plus the additional expense of replacing them will exceed the initial cost of better-quality tools.

Hand tools

Note: *The information that follows is for early-model vehicles with only Imperial (inch) fastener sizes. On most late-model vehicles, you'll need metric spanners, sockets and Allen keys. Generally, manufacturers began integrating metric fasteners into their vehicles around 1975.*

A list of general-purpose hand tools you should have in your workshop

Adjustable spanner - 10-inch
Allen key set (1/8 to 3/8-inch or 4 mm to 10 mm)
Ball peen hammer - 12 oz (any steel hammer will do)
Brake bleeding kit
Brass hammer
Brushes (various sizes, for cleaning small parts)
Combination (slip-joint) pliers - 6-inch
Centre punch
Cold chisels - 1/4 and 1/2-inch
Combination spanner set (1/4 to 1-inch or 7mm to 19mm)
Dial indicator and base
Extensions - 1-, 6-, 10- and 12-inch
Feeler gauge set
Files (assorted)
Flare-nut (split ring) spanners

Floor jack
Gasket scraper
Hacksaw and assortment of blades
Impact screwdriver and bits
Locking pliers
Micrometer(s) (a one-inch micrometer is suitable for most work)
Phillips screwdriver (no. 2 x 6-inch)
Phillips screwdriver (no. 3 x 8-inch)
Phillips screwdriver (stubby - no. 2)
Pin punches (1/16, 1/8, 3/16-inch)
Pliers - electrician's
Pliers - needle-nose
Pliers - circlip (internal and external)
Pliers - vice-grip
Pliers - diagonal cutters
Ratchet
Scraper (made from flattened copper tubing)
Scribe
Socket set (6-point sockets are preferred, but some fasteners require the use of 12-point sockets)
Soft-face hammer (plastic/rubber)
Spark plug socket (with rubber insert)
Spark plug gap adjusting tool
Standard screwdriver (1/4-inch x 6-inch)
Standard screwdriver (5/16-inch x 6-inch)
Standard screwdriver (3/8-inch x 10-inch)
Standard screwdriver (5/16-inch - stubby)
Steel ruler - 6-inch
Stud extractor set
Tap and die set
Thread gauge
Torque spanner (same size drive as sockets)
Torx socket(s)
Universal joint
Vacuum gauge/pump (hand-held)
Wire brush (large)
Wire cutter pliers

What to look for when buying hand tools and general purpose tools

Spanners and sockets

Spanners vary widely in quality. One indication of their quality is their cost: The more they cost, the better they are. Buy the best spanners you can afford. You'll use them a lot.

Start with a set containing spanners from 1/4 to 1-inch (or from 8 to 19 mm) in size. The size, stamped on the spanner **(see illustration)**, indicates the distance across the nut or bolt head, or the distance between the spanner jaws - not the diameter of the threads on the fastener - in inches. For example, a 1/4-inch bolt usually

2.3 The size stamped on a spanner indicates the distance across the nut or bolt head (or the distance between the spanner jaws) in inches or mm, not the diameter of the threads on the fastener

has a 7/16-inch hex head - the size of the spanner required to loosen or tighten it. However, the relationship between thread diameter and hex size doesn't always hold true. In some instances, an unusually small hex may be used to discourage over-tightening or because space around the fastener head is limited. Conversely, some fasteners have a disproportionately large hex-head.

Spanners are similar in appearance, so their quality level can be difficult to judge just by looking at them. There are bargains to be had, just as there are overpriced tools with well-known brand names. On the other hand, you may buy what looks like a reasonable value set of spanners only to find they fit badly or are made from poor-quality steel.

With a little experience, it's possible to judge the quality of a tool by looking at it. Often, you may have come across the brand name before and have a good idea of the quality. Close examination of the tool can often reveal some hints as to its quality. Prestige tools are usually polished and chrome-plated over their entire surface, with the working faces ground to size. The polished finish is largely cosmetic, but it does make them easy to keep clean. Ground jaws normally indicate the tool will fit well on fasteners.

A side-by-side comparison of a high-quality spanner with a cheap equivalent is an eye opener. The better tool will be made from a good-quality material, often a forged/chrome-vanadium steel alloy **(see illustration)**. This, together with careful design, allows the tool to be kept as small and compact as possible. If, by comparison, the cheap tool is thicker and heavier, especially around the jaws, it's usually because the extra material is needed to compensate for its lower quality. If the tool fits properly, this isn't necessarily bad - it is, after all, cheaper - but in situations where it's necessary to work in a confined area, the cheaper tool may be too bulky to fit.

Open-end spanners

Because of its versatility, the open-end spanner is the most common type of spanner. It has a jaw on either end, connected by a flat handle section. The jaws either vary by a size, or overlap sizes between consecutive spanners in a set. This allows one spanner to be used to

2.4 One quick way to determine whether you're looking at a quality spanner is to read the information printed on the handle - if it says "chrome vanadium" or "forged", it's made out of the right material

2.5 Open-end spanners can do several things other spanners can't - for example, they can be used on bolt heads with limited clearance (above) and they can be used in tight spots where there's little room to turn a spanner by flipping the offset jaw over every few degrees of rotation

2.6 Ring spanners have a ring-shaped "box" at each end - when space permits, they offer the best combination of "grip" and strength

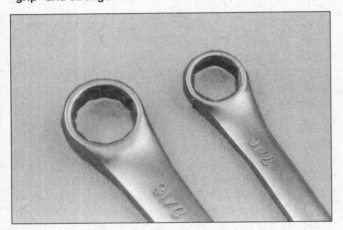

2.7 Ring spanners are available in 12 (left) and 6-point (right) openings; even though the 12-point design offers twice as many spanner positions, buy the 6-point first - it's less likely to strip off the corners of a nut or bolt head

2.8 Buy a set of combination spanners from 1/4 to 1-inch or 7mm to 19mm

hold a bolt head while a similar-size nut is removed. A typical fractional size spanner set might have the following jaw sizes: 1/4 x 5/16, 3/8 x 7/16, 1/2 x 9/16, 9/16 x 5/8 and so on.

Typically, the jaw end is set at an angle to the handle, a feature which makes them very useful in confined spaces. By turning the nut or bolt as far as the obstruction allows, then turning the spanner over so the jaw faces in the other direction, it's possible to move the fastener a fraction of a turn at a time **(see illustration)**. The handle length is generally determined by the size of the jaw and is calculated to allow a nut or bolt to be tightened sufficiently by hand with minimal risk of breakage or thread damage (though this doesn't apply to soft materials like brass or aluminium).

Common open-end spanners are usually sold in sets and it's rarely worth buying them individually unless it's to renew a lost or broken tool from a set. Single tools invariably cost more, so check the sizes you're most likely to need regularly and buy the best set of spanners you can afford in that range of sizes. If money is limited, remember that you'll use open-end spanners more than any other type - it's a good idea to buy a good set and cut corners elsewhere.

Ring spanners

Ring spanners **(see illustration)** have ring-shaped ends with a 6-point (hex) or 12-point (double hex) opening **(see illustration)**. This allows the tool to fit on the fastener hex at 30 (12-point) or 60-degree (6-point) intervals. Normally, each tool has two ends of different sizes, allowing an overlapping range of sizes in a set, as described for open-end spanners.

Although available as flat tools, the handle is usually offset at each end to allow it to clear obstructions near the fastener, which is normally an advantage. In addition to normal length spanners, it's also possible to buy long handle types to allow more leverage (very useful when trying to loosen rusted or seized nuts). It is, however, easy to shear off fasteners if not careful, and sometimes the extra length impairs access.

As with open-end spanners, ring spanners are available in varying quality, again often indicated by finish and the amount of metal around the ring ends. While the same criteria should be applied when selecting a set of ring spanners, if your budget is limited, go for better-quality open-end spanners and a slightly cheaper set of rings.

Combination spanners

These spanners **(see illustration)** combine a ring and open-end of the same size in one tool and offer

2.9 Adjustable spanners can handle a range of fastener sizes - they're not as good as single-size spanners but they're handy for loosening and tightening those odd-sized fasteners for which you haven't yet bought the correct spanner

2.10 When you use an adjustable spanner, make sure the movable jaw points in the direction the spanner is being turned (arrow) so the spanner doesn't distort and slip off the fastener head

many of the advantages of both. Like the others, they're widely available in sets and as such are probably a better choice than ring spanners only. They're generally compact, short-handled tools and are well suited for tight spaces where access is limited.

Adjustable spanners

Adjustable spanners **(see illustration)** come in

2.11 Split ring spanners should always be used when loosening or tightening line fittings (tube nuts) - the two odd-shaped items on the right are split ring crows' feet, which are useful for loosening hard-to-reach fittings when used with a long extension

several sizes. Each size can handle a range of fastener sizes. Adjustable spanners aren't as effective as one-size tools and it's easy to damage fasteners with them. However, they can be an invaluable addition to any tool kit - if they're used with discretion.

The most common adjustable spanner is the open-end type with a set of parallel jaws that can be set to fit the head of a fastener. Most are controlled by a threaded spindle, though there are various cam and spring-loaded versions available. Don't buy large tools of this type; you'll rarely be able to find enough clearance to use them.

Split ring spanners

These spanners, sometimes called flare nut spanners, are used for loosening and tightening hydraulic line fittings (tube nuts). Construction is similar to a six-point ring spanner, but a portion of one of the flats is cut out to allow the spanner to pass over a line or hose **(see illustration)**. This design offers much more surface area of the spanner to be in contact with the flats on the fitting, which will prevent the fittings from being rounded off because the load is distributed over as much area as possible. They are also thicker than most open or ring spanners, which adds to the surface area in contact with the tube nut. **Caution:** *When loosening a tube nut on a fitting connected to a flexible hose, always use a second spanner to hold the larger, female fitting stationary. This will prevent the hydraulic line from twisting.*

2.12 A typical socket set includes a ratchet, a set of sockets, a long and a short extension, a universal joint and a spark plug socket

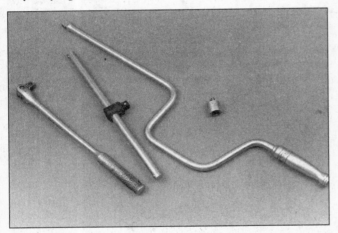

2.13 Lots of other accessories are available for ratchets; From left to right, an extension handle, a sliding T-handle, a speed handle and a 3/8-to-1/4-inch adapter

2.14 Deep sockets enable you to loosen or tighten an elongated fastener, or to get at a nut with a long bolt protruding from it

Ratchet and socket sets

Ratcheting socket spanners **(see illustration)** are highly versatile. Besides the sockets themselves, many other interchangeable accessories - extensions, U-drives, step-down adapters, screwdriver bits, Allen bits, crow's feet, etc. - are available. Buy six-point sockets - they're less likely to slip and strip the corners off bolts and nuts. **Note:** *Some brake system fasteners (caliper mounting bolts on some vehicles, for example) require the use of 12-point sockets.* Don't buy sockets with extra-thick walls - they might be stronger but they can be hard to use on recessed fasteners or fasteners in tight quarters.

A 3/8-inch drive set is adequate for most work. Sometimes a 1/2-inch drive set is required when working with large fasteners. Although the larger drive is bulky and more expensive, it has the capacity of accepting a very wide range of large sockets. Later, you may want to consider a 1/4-inch drive for little stuff like ignition and carburettor work.

Interchangeable sockets consist of a forged-steel alloy cylinder with a hex or double-hex formed inside one end. The other end is formed into the square drive recess that engages over the corresponding square end of various socket drive tools.

Sockets are available in 1/4, 3/8, 1/2 and 3/4-inch drive sizes. A 3/8-inch drive set is most useful for engine repairs, although 1/4-inch drive sockets and accessories may occasionally be needed.

The most economical way to buy sockets is in a set. As always, quality will govern the cost of the tools. Once again, the 'buy the best' approach is usually advised when selecting sockets. While this is a good idea, since the end result is a set of quality tools that should last a lifetime, the cost is so high it's difficult to justify the expense for home use.

As far as accessories go, you'll need a ratchet, at least

2.15 Standard and Phillips bits, Allen-head and Torx drivers will expand the versatility of your ratchet and extensions even further

one extension (buy a three or six-inch size), a spark plug socket and maybe a T-handle or breaker bar. Other desirable, though less essential items, are a speeder handle, a U-joint, extensions of various other lengths and adapters from one drive size to another **(see illustration)**. Some of the sets you find may combine drive sizes; they're well worth having if you find the right set at a good price, but avoid being dazzled by the number of pieces.

Above all, be sure to completely ignore any label that reads (for instance) '86-piece Socket Set', which refers to the number of pieces, not to the number of sockets (sometimes even the metal box and plastic insert are counted in the total!).

Apart from well-known and respected brand names, you'll have to take a chance on the quality of the set you buy. If you know someone who has a set that has held up well, try to find the same brand, if possible. Take a pocketful of nuts and bolts with you and check the fit in some of the sockets. Check the operation of the ratchet. Good ones operate smoothly and crisply in small steps; cheap ones are coarse and stiff - a good basis for guessing the quality of the rest of the pieces.

One of the best things about a socket set is the built-in facility for expansion. Once you have a basic set, you can purchase extra sockets when necessary and renew worn or damaged tools. There are special deep sockets for reaching recessed fasteners or to allow the socket to fit over a projecting bolt or stud **(see illustration)**. You can also buy screwdriver, Allen and Torx bits to fit various drive tools (they can be very handy in some applications) **(see illustration)**. Most socket sets include a special deep socket for 14 millimetre spark plugs. They have rubber inserts to protect the spark plug porcelain insulator and hold the plug in the socket to avoid burned fingers.

Torque wrenches

Torque wrenches **(see illustration)** are essential for tightening critical fasteners. A fastener that's not tight enough may eventually escape from its hole. An overtightened fastener, on the other hand, could break under stress.

There are two types of torque wrenches - the 'beam' type, which indicates torque loads by deflecting a flexible shaft and the 'click' type (see illustrations), which emits an audible click when the torque resistance reaches the specified resistance.

Torque wrenches are available in a variety of drive sizes and torque ranges for particular applications. For most work, 10 to 150 Nm (8 to 100 lbf ft) should be adequate. Keep in mind that 'click' types are usually more accurate (and more expensive).

2.16 Torque wrenches (click-type on left, beam-type on right) are the only way to accurately tighten critical fasteners like connecting rod bolts, cylinder head bolts, etc.

2.17 The deflecting beam-type torque wrench is inexpensive and simple to use - just tighten the fastener until the pointer points to the specified torque setting

2.18 "Click" type torque wrenches can be set to "give" at a pre-set torque, which makes them very accurate and easy to use

2.19 The impact driver converts a sharp blow into a twisting motion - this is a handy addition to your socket arsenal for those fasteners that won't let go - you can use it with any bit that fits a 3/8 inch drive ratchet

Impact drivers

The impact driver **(see illustration)** belongs with the screwdrivers, but it's mentioned here since it can also be used with sockets (impact drivers normally are 3/8-inch square drive). As explained later, an impact driver works by converting a hammer blow on the end of its handle into a sharp twisting movement. While this is a great way to jar a seized fastener loose, the loads imposed on the socket are excessive. Use sockets only with discretion and expect to have to renew damaged ones on occasion.

Using spanners and sockets

Although you may think the proper use of tools is self-evident, it's worth some thought. After all, when did you last see instructions for use supplied with a set of spanners?

Which spanner?

Before you start working, figure out the best tool for the job; in this instance the best spanner for a hex-head fastener. Sit down with a few nuts and bolts and look at how various tools fit the bolt heads.

A golden rule is to choose a tool that contacts the largest area of the hex-head. This distributes the load as evenly as possible and lessens the risk of damage. The shape most closely resembling the bolt head or nut is another hex, so a 6-point socket or ring spanner is usually the best choice **(see illustrations)**. Many sockets and ring spanners have double hex (12-point) openings. If you slip a 12-point ring spanner over a nut, look at how and where the two are in contact. The corners of the nut engage in every other point of the spanner. When the spanner is turned, pressure is applied evenly on each of the six corners. This is fine unless the fastener head was previously rounded off. If so, the corners will be damaged and the spanner will slip. If you encounter a damaged bolt head or nut, always use a 6-point spanner or socket if possible. If you don't have one of the right size, choose a spanner that fits securely and proceed with care.

If you slip an open-end spanner over a hex-head fastener, you'll see the tool is in contact on two faces only **(see illustration)**. This is acceptable provided

2.20 Try to use a six-point ring spanner (or socket) whenever possible - its shape matches that of the fastener, which means maximum grip and minimum slip

2.21 Sometimes a six-point tool just doesn't offer you any grip when you get the spanner at the angle it needs to be in to loosen or tighten a fastener - when this happens, pull out the 12-point sockets or spanners - but remember; they're much more likely to strip the corners off a fastener

the tool and fastener are both in good condition. The need for a snug fit between the spanner and nut or bolt explains the recommendation to buy good-quality open-end spanners. If the spanner jaws, the bolt head or both are damaged, the spanner will probably slip, rounding off and distorting the head. In some applications, an open-end spanner is the only possible choice due to limited access, but always check the fit of the spanner on the fastener before attempting to loosen it. If it's hard to get at with a spanner, think how hard it will be to remove after the head is damaged.

The last choice is an adjustable spanner or self-locking pliers (Mole wrench). Use these tools only when all else has failed. In some cases, self-locking pliers may be able to grip a damaged head that no spanner could deal with, but be careful not to make matters worse by damaging it further.

Bearing in mind the remarks about the correct choice of tool in the first place, there are several things worth noting about the actual use of the tool. First, make sure the spanner head is clean and undamaged. If the fastener is rusted or coated with paint, the spanner won't fit correctly. Clean off the head and, if it's rusted, apply some penetrating oil. Leave it to soak in for a while before attempting removal.

It may seem obvious, but take a close look at the fastener to be removed before using a spanner. On many mass-produced machines, one end of a fastener may be fixed or captive, which speeds up initial assembly and usually makes removal easier. If a nut is fitted on a stud or a bolt threads into a captive nut or tapped hole, you may have only one fastener to deal with. If, on the other hand, you have a separate nut and

2.22 Open-end spanners contact only two sides of the fastener and the jaws tend to open up when you put some muscle on the spanner handle - that's why they should only be used as a last resort

bolt, you must hold the bolt head while the nut is removed. In some areas this can be difficult, particularly where engine mountings are involved. In this type of situation you may need an assistant to hold the bolt head with a spanner while you remove the nut from the other side. If this isn't possible, you'll have to try to position a ring spanner so it wedges against some other component to prevent it from turning.

Be on the lookout for left-hand threads. They aren't common, but are sometimes used on the ends of rotating shafts to make sure the nut doesn't come loose during operation. If you can see the shaft end, the thread type can be checked visually. If you're unsure, place your thumbnail in the threads and see which way you have to turn your hand so your nail 'unscrews' from the shaft. If you have to turn your hand anti-clockwise, it's a conventional right-hand thread.

Beware of the upside-down fastener syndrome. If you're loosening a fastener from the under side of a something, it's easy to get confused about which way to turn it. What seems like anti-clockwise to you is actually clockwise (from the fastener's point of view). Even after years of experience, this can still catch you once in a while.

In most cases, a fastener can be removed simply by placing the spanner on the nut or bolt head and turning it. Occasionally, though, the condition or location of the fastener may make things more difficult. Make sure the spanner is square on the head. You may need to reposition the tool or try another type to obtain a snug fit. Make sure the engine you're working on is secure and can't move when you turn the spanner. If necessary, get someone to help steady it for you. Position yourself so you can get maximum leverage on the spanner.

If possible, locate the spanner so you can pull the end towards you. If you have to push on the tool, remember that it may slip, or the fastener may move suddenly. For this reason, don't curl your fingers around the handle or you may crush or bruise them when the fastener moves; keep your hand flat, pushing on the spanner with the heel of your thumb. If the tool digs into your hand, place a rag between it and your hand or wear a heavy glove.

If the fastener doesn't move with normal hand pressure, stop and try to figure out why before the fastener or spanner is damaged or you hurt yourself. Stuck fasteners may require penetrating oil, heat or an impact driver or air tool.

Using sockets to remove hex-head fasteners is less likely to result in damage than if a spanner is used. Make sure the socket fits snugly over the fastener head, then attach an extension, if needed, and the ratchet or breaker bar. Theoretically, a ratchet shouldn't be used for loosening a fastener or for final tightening because the ratchet mechanism may be overloaded and could slip. In some instances, the location of the fastener may mean you have no choice but to use a ratchet, in which case you'll have to be extra careful.

Never use extensions where they aren't needed. Whether or not an extension is used, always support the drive end of the breaker bar with one hand while turning it with the other. Once the fastener is loose, the ratchet can be used to speed up removal.

Pliers

Some tool manufacturers make 25 or 30 different types of pliers. You only need a fraction of this selection **(see illustration)**. Get a good pair of slip-joint pliers

2.23 A typical assortment of the types of pliers you need to have in your box - from the left; diagonal cutters, needle-nose pliers, water pump pliers, self-locking pliers, needle-nose self-locking pliers

2.24 To adjust the jaws on a pair of self-locking pliers, grasp the part you want to hold with the jaws, tighten them down by turning the knurled knob on the end of one handle and snap the handles together - if you tightened the knob all the way down, you'll probably have to open it up (back it off) a little before you can close the handles

for general use. A pair of needle-nose pliers is handy for reaching into hard-to-get-at places. A set of diagonal wire cutters is essential for electrical work and pulling out split pins. Self-locking pliers are adjustable, locking pliers that grip a fastener firmly - and won't let go - when locked into place. Parallel-jaw, adjustable pliers have angled jaws that remain parallel at any degree of opening. They're also referred to as water pump pliers, Channel-lock (the original manufacturer) pliers and arc-joint pliers. Whatever you call them, they're terrific for gripping things with a lot of force.

Slip-joint pliers have two open positions; a figure eight-shaped, elongated slot in one handle slips back-and-forth on a pivot pin on the other handle to change them. Good-quality pliers have jaws made of tempered steel and there's usually a wire-cutter at the base of the jaws. The primary uses of slip-joint pliers are for holding objects, bending and cutting throttle wires and crimping and bending metal parts, not loosening nuts and bolts.

Water pump or 'Channel-lock' pliers have parallel jaws you can open to various widths by engaging different tongues and grooves, or channels, near the pivot pin. Since the tool expands to fit many size objects, it has countless uses for engine and equipment maintenance. Channel-lock pliers come in various sizes. The medium size is adequate for general work; small and large sizes are nice to have as your budget permits. You'll use all three sizes frequently.

Self-locking pliers (of which 'Mole' is a well-known brand name) come in various sizes; the medium size with curved jaws is best for all-around work. However, buy a large and small one if possible, since they're often used in pairs. Although this tool falls somewhere

2.25 If you're persistent and careful, most fasteners can be removed with self-locking pliers

between an adjustable spanner, a pair of pliers and a portable vice, it can be invaluable for loosening and tightening fasteners - it's the only type of pliers that should be used for this purpose.

The jaw opening is set by turning a knurled knob at the end of one handle. The jaws are placed over the head of the fastener and the handles are squeezed together, locking the tool onto the fastener **(see illustration)**. The design of the tool allows extreme pressure to be applied at the jaws and a variety of jaw designs enable the tool to grip firmly even on damaged heads **(see illustration)**. Self-locking pliers are great for removing fasteners that've been rounded off by badly-fitting spanners.

As the name suggests, needle-nose pliers have long, thin jaws designed for reaching into holes and other restricted areas. Most needle-nose, or long-nose, pliers also have wire cutters at the base of the jaws.

Look for these qualities when buying pliers: Smooth operating handles and jaws, jaws that match up and grip evenly when the handles are closed, a nice finish and the word 'forged' somewhere on the tool.

Screwdrivers

Screwdrivers **(see illustration)** come in a wide variety of sizes and price ranges. But don't buy screwdriver sets for five pounds at discount tool stores. Even if they look exactly like more expensive brands, the metal tips and shafts are made with inferior alloys and aren't properly heat treated. They usually bend the first time you apply some serious torque.

A screwdriver consists of a steel blade or shank with a drive tip formed at one end. The most common tips are standard (also called straight slot and flat-blade) and

2.26 Screwdrivers come in a myriad of lengths, sizes and styles

Phillips. The other end has a handle attached to it. Traditionally, handles were made from wood and secured to the shank, which had raised tangs to prevent it from turning in the handle. Most screwdrivers now come with plastic handles, which are generally more durable than wood.

The design and size of handles and blades vary considerably. Some handles are specially shaped to fit the human hand and provide a better grip. The shank may be either round or square and some have a hex-shaped bolster under the handle to accept a spanner to provide more leverage when trying to turn a stubborn screw. The shank diameter, tip size and overall length vary too.

If access is restricted, a number of special screwdrivers are designed to fit into confined spaces. The 'stubby' screwdriver has a specially shortened handle and blade. There are also offset screwdrivers and special screwdriver bits that attach to a ratchet or extension.

The important thing to remember when buying screwdrivers is that they really do come in sizes designed to fit different size fasteners. The slot in any screw has definite dimensions - length, width and depth. Like a bolt head or a nut, the screw slot must be driven by a tool that uses all of the available bearing surface and doesn't slip. Don't use a big wide blade on a small screw and don't try to turn a large screw slot with a tiny, narrow blade. The same principles apply to Allen heads, Phillips heads, Torx heads, etc. Don't even think of using a slotted screwdriver on one of these heads! And don't use your screwdrivers as levers, chisels or punches! This kind of abuse turns them into very bad screwdrivers; it's also dangerous.

Standard screwdrivers

These are used to remove and refit conventional slotted screws and are available in a wide range of sizes denoting the width of the tip and the length of the shank (for example: a 3/8 x 10-inch screwdriver is 3/8-inch wide at the tip and the shank is 10-inches long). You should have a variety of screwdrivers so screws of various sizes can be dealt with without damaging them. The blade end must be the same width and thickness as the screw slot to work properly, without slipping. When selecting standard screwdrivers, choose good-quality tools, preferably with chrome moly, forged steel shanks. The tip of the shank should be ground to a parallel, flat profile (hollow ground) and not to a taper or wedge shape, which will tend to twist out of the slot when pressure is applied **(see illustration)**.

All screwdrivers wear in use, but standard types can be reground to shape a number of times. When reshaping a tip, start by grinding the very end flat at

Misuse of a screwdriver – the blade shown is both too narrow and too thin and will probably slip or break off

The left-hand example shows a snug-fitting tip. The right-hand drawing shows a damaged tip which will twist out of the slot when pressure is applied

2.27 Standard screwdrivers - wrong size (left), correct fit in screw slot (centre) and worn tip (right)

right angles to the shank. Make sure the tip fits snugly in the slot of a screw of the appropriate size and keep the sides of the tip parallel. Remove only a small amount of metal at a time to avoid overheating the tip and destroying the temper of the steel.

Phillips screwdrivers

Phillips screws are sometimes fitted during initial assembly with air tools and are next to impossible to remove later without ruining the heads, particularly if the wrong size screwdriver is used. And don't use other types of cross-head screwdrivers (Torx, Posi-drive, etc.) on Phillips screws - they won't work.

The only way to ensure the screwdrivers you buy will fit properly, is to take a couple of screws with you to make sure the fit between the screwdriver and fastener is snug. If the fit is good, you should be able to angle the blade down almost vertically without the screw slipping off the tip. Use only screwdrivers that fit exactly - anything else is guaranteed to chew out the screw head instantly.

The idea behind all cross-head screw designs is to make the screw and screwdriver blade self-aligning. Provided you aim the blade at the centre of the screw head, it'll engage correctly, unlike conventional slotted screws, which need careful alignment. This makes the screws suitable for machine refitting on an assembly line (which explains why they're sometimes so tight and difficult to remove). The drawback with these screws is that the driving tangs on the screwdriver tip are very small and must fit very precisely in the screw head. If this isn't the case, the huge loads imposed on small flats of the screw slot simply tear the metal away, at which point the screw ceases to be removable by normal methods. The problem is made worse by the normally soft material chosen for screws.

To deal with these screws on a regular basis, you'll need high-quality screwdrivers with various size tips so you'll be sure to have the right one when you need it. Phillips screwdrivers are sized by the tip number and length of the shank (for example: a number 2 x 6-inch Phillips screwdriver has a number 2 tip - to fit screws of only that size recess - and the shank is 6-inches long). Tip sizes 1, 2 and 3 should be adequate for engine repair work **(see illustration)**. If the tips get worn or damaged, buy new screwdrivers so the tools don't destroy the screws they're used on **(see illustration)**.

HINTS & TIPS

- Here's a tip that may come in handy when using Phillips screwdrivers - if the screw is extremely tight and the tip tends to back out of the recess rather than turn the screw, apply a small amount of valve lapping (grinding) compound to the screwdriver tip so it will grip the screw better.

2.28 The tip size on a Phillips screwdriver is indicated by a number from 1 to 4, with 1 the smallest (left - No. 1: centre - No. 2; right - No. 3)

2.29 New (left) and worn (right) Phillips screwdriver tips

Hammers

Using a hammer should always be the last resort. When nothing else will do the job, a medium-size ball peen hammer, a heavy rubber mallet and a heavy soft-brass hammer **(see illustration)** are often the only tools to loosen or refit a part.

A ball-peen hammer has a head with a conventional cylindrical face at one end and a rounded ball end at the other and is a general-purpose tool found in almost any type of workshop. It has a shorter neck than a claw hammer and the face is tempered for striking punches and chisels. A fairly large hammer is preferable to a small one. Although it's possible to find small ones, you won't need them very often and it's much easier to control the blows from a heavier head. As a rule, a single 12 or 16-ounce hammer will work for most jobs, though occasionally larger or smaller ones may be useful.

A soft-face hammer is used where a steel hammer could cause damage to the component or other tools being used. A steel hammer head might crack an aluminium part, but a rubber or plastic hammer can be used with more confidence. Soft-face hammers are available with interchangeable heads (usually one made of rubber and another made of relatively hard plastic). When the heads are worn out, new ones can be fitted. If finances are really limited, you can get by without a soft-face hammer by placing a small hardwood block between the component and a steel hammer head to prevent damage.

Hammers should be used with common sense; the head should strike the desired object squarely and with the right amount of force. For many jobs, little effort is needed - simply allow the weight of the head to do the work, using the length of the swing to control the amount of force applied. With practice, a hammer can be used with surprising finesse, but it'll take a while to achieve. Initial mistakes include striking the object at an angle, in which case the hammer head may glance off to one side, or hitting the edge of the object. Either one can result in damage to the part or to your thumb, if it gets in the way, so be careful. Hold the hammer handle near the end, not near the head, and grip it firmly but not too tightly.

Check the condition of your hammers on a regular basis. The danger of a loose head coming off is self-evident, but check the head for chips and cracks too. If damage is noted, buy a new hammer - the head may chip in use and the resulting fragments can be extremely dangerous. Of course, eye protection is essential whenever a hammer is used.

Punches and chisels

Punches and chisels **(see illustration)** are used along with a hammer for various purposes in the workshop. Drift punches are often simply a length of round steel bar used to drive a component or fastener out of a bore. A typical use would be for removing or refitting a bearing or bush. A drift of the same diameter as the bearing outer race is placed against the bearing and tapped with a hammer to knock it in or out of the bore. Most manufacturers offer special drifts for the various bearings in a particular engine. While they're useful to a busy dealer service department, they are prohibitively expensive for the do-it-your-selfer who may only need to use them once. In such cases, it's better to

2.30 A ball-peen hammer, soft-face hammer and rubber mallet (left-to-right) will be needed for various tasks (any steel hammer can be used in place of the ball peen hammer)

2.31 Cold chisels, centre-punches, pin punches and line-up punches (left-to-right) will be needed sooner or later for many jobs

2.32 A typical general purpose cold chisel (A) - note the angle of the cutting edge (B), which should be checked and resharpened on a regular basis; the mushroomed head (C) is dangerous and should be filed to restore it to its original shape

improvise. For bearing removal and refitting, it's usually possible to use a socket of the appropriate diameter to tap the bearing in or out; an unorthodox use for a socket, but it works.

Smaller diameter drift punches can be purchased or fabricated from steel bar stock. In some cases, you'll need to drive out items like caliper retaining pins. Here, it's essential to avoid damaging the pin or caliper, so the drift must be made from a soft material. Brass or copper is the usual choice for such jobs; the drift may be damaged in use, but the pin and surrounding components will be protected.

Punches are available in various shapes and sizes and a set of assorted types will be very useful. One of the most basic is the centre punch, a small cylindrical punch with the end earth to a point. It'll be needed whenever a hole is drilled. The centre of the hole is located first and the punch is used to make a small indentation at the intended point. The indentation acts as a guide for the drill bit so the hole ends up in the right place. Without a punch mark the drill bit will wander and you'll find it impossible to drill with any real accuracy. You can also buy automatic centre punches. They're spring loaded and are pressed against the surface to be marked, without the need to use a hammer.

Pin punches are intended for removing items like roll pins (semi-hard, hollow pins that fit tightly in their holes). Pin punches have other uses, however. You may occasionally have to remove rivets or bolts by cutting off the heads and driving out the shanks with a pin punch.

They're also very handy for aligning holes in components while bolts or screws are inserted.

Of the various sizes and types of metal-cutting chisels available, a simple cold chisel is essential in any mechanic's workshop. One about 6-inches long with a 1/2-inch wide blade should be adequate. The cutting edge is earth to about 80-degrees **(see illustration)**, while the rest of the tip is earth to a shallower angle away from the edge. The primary use of the cold chisel is rough metal cutting - this can be anything from sheet metal work to cutting off the heads of seized or rusted bolts or splitting nuts. A cold chisel is also useful for turning out screws or bolts with messed-up heads.

All of the tools described in this section should be good quality items. They're not particularly expensive, so it's not really worth trying to save money on them. More significantly, there's a risk that with cheap tools, fragments may break off in use - a potentially dangerous situation.

Even with good-quality tools, the heads and working ends will inevitably get worn or damaged, so it's a good idea to maintain all such tools on a regular basis. Using a file or bench grinder, remove all burrs and mushroomed edges from around the head. This is an important task because the build-up of material around the head can fly off when it's struck with a hammer and is potentially dangerous. Make sure the tool retains its original profile at the working end, again, filing or grinding off all burrs. In the case of cold chisels, the cutting edge will usually have to be reground quite often because the material in the tool isn't usually much harder than materials typically being cut. Make sure the edge is reasonably sharp, but don't make the tip angle greater than it was originally; it'll just wear down faster if you do.

The techniques for using these tools vary according to the job to be done and are best learned by experience. The one common denominator is the fact they're all normally struck with a hammer. It follows that eye protection should be worn. Always make sure the working end of the tool is in contact with the part being punched or cut. If it isn't, the tool will bounce off the surface and damage may result.

Hacksaws

A hacksaw **(see illustration)** consists of a handle and frame supporting a flexible steel blade under tension. Blades are available in various lengths and most hacksaws can be adjusted to accommodate the different sizes. The most common blade length is 10 inches.

Most hacksaw frames are adequate. There's little difference between brands. Pick one that's rigid and

2.33 Hacksaws are handy for little cutting jobs like sheet metal and rusted fasteners

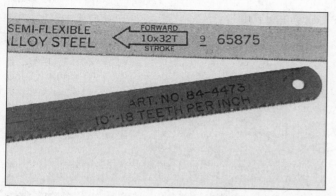

2.34 Hacksaw blades are marked with the number of teeth per inch (TPI) - use a relatively coarse blade for aluminium and thicker items such as bolts or bar stock; use a finer blade for materials like thin sheet stee

When cutting thin materials, check that at least three teeth are in contact with the workpiece at any time. Too coarse a blade will result in a poor cut and may break the blade. If you do not have the correct blade, cut at a shallow angle to the material

The correct cutting angle is important. If it is too shallow (A) the blade will wander. The angle shown at (B) is correct when starting the cut, and may be reduced slightly once under way. In (C) the angle is too steep and the blade will be inclined to jump out of the cut

2.35 Correct procedure for use of a hacksaw

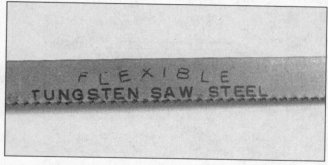

2.36 Good quality hacksaw blades are marked like this

allows easy blade changing and repositioning.

The type of blade to use, indicated by the number of teeth per inch, (TPI) **(see illustration)**, is determined by the material being cut. The rule of thumb is to make sure at least three teeth are in contact with the metal being cut at any one time **(see illustration)**. In practice, this means a fine blade for cutting thin sheet materials, while a coarser blade can be used for faster cutting through thicker items such as bolts or bar stock. When cutting thin materials, angle the saw so the blade cuts at a shallow angle. More teeth are in contact and there's less chance of the blade binding and breaking, or teeth breaking.

When you buy blades, choose a reputable brand. Cheap, unbranded blades may be perfectly acceptable, but you can't tell by looking at them. Poor quality blades will be insufficiently hardened on the teeth edge and will dull quickly. Most reputable brands will be marked 'Flexible High Speed Steel' or a similar term, to indicate the type of material used **(see illustration)**. It is possible to buy 'unbreakable' blades (only the teeth are hardened, leaving the rest of the blade less brittle).

Sometimes, a full-size hacksaw is too big to allow access to a seized nut or bolt. On most saws, you can overcome this problem by turning the blade 90-degrees. Occasionally you may have to position the saw around an obstacle and then refit the blade on the other side of it. Where space is really restricted, you may have to use a handle that clamps onto a saw blade at one end. This allows access when a hacksaw frame would not work at all and has another advantage in that you can make use of broken off hacksaw blades instead of throwing them away. Note that because only one end of the blade is supported, and it's not held under tension, it's difficult to control and less efficient when cutting.

Before using a hacksaw, make sure the blade is suitable for the material being cut and fitted correctly in the frame **(see illustration)**. Whatever it is you're cutting must be securely supported so it can't move around. The saw cuts on the forward stroke, so the teeth must point away from the handle. This might seem

2.37 Correct fitting of a hacksaw blade - the teeth must point away from the handle and butt against the locating lugs

2.38 Get a good assortment of files - they're handy for deburring, marking parts, removing rust, filing the heads off rivets, restoring threads and fabricating small parts

2.39 Files are either single-cut (left) or double-cut (right) - generally speaking, use a single-cut file to produce a very smooth surface; use a double-cut file to remove large amounts of material quickly

obvious, but it's easy to fit the blade backwards by mistake and ruin the teeth on the first few strokes. Make sure the blade is tensioned adequately or it'll distort and chatter in the cut and may break. Wear safety glasses and be careful not to cut yourself on the saw blade or the sharp edge of the cut.

Files

Files **(see illustration)** come in a wide variety of sizes and types for specific jobs, but all of them are used for the same basic function of removing small amounts of metal in a controlled fashion. Files are used by mechanics mainly for deburring, marking parts, removing rust, filing the heads off rivets, restoring threads and fabricating small parts.

File shapes commonly available include flat, half-round, round, square and triangular. Each shape comes in a range of sizes (lengths) and cuts ranging from rough to smooth. The file face is covered with rows of diagonal ridges which form the cutting teeth. They may be aligned in one direction only (single cut) or in two directions to form a diamond-shaped pattern (double-cut) **(see illustration)**. The spacing of the teeth determines the file coarseness, again, ranging from rough to smooth in five basic grades: Rough, coarse, bastard, second-cut and smooth.

You'll want to build up a set of files by purchasing tools of the required shape and cut as they're needed. A good starting point would be flat, half-round, round and triangular files (at least one each - bastard or second-cut types). In addition, you'll have to buy one or more file handles. (Files are usually sold without handles, which are purchased separately and pushed over the tapered tang of the file when in use.) You may need to buy more than one size handle to fit the various files in your tool box, but don't attempt to get by without them. A file tang is fairly sharp and you almost certainly will end up stabbing yourself in the palm of the hand if you use a file without a handle and it catches in the workpiece during use **(see illustration)**. Adjustable handles are also available for use with files of various sizes, eliminating the need for several handles **(see illustration)**.

Exceptions to the need for a handle are fine Swiss pattern files, which have a rounded handle instead of a tang. These small files are usually sold in sets with a number of different shapes. Originally intended for very fine work, they can be very handy for use in inaccessible areas. Swiss files are normally the best choice if piston ring ends require filing to obtain the correct end gap.

The correct procedure for using files is fairly easy to master. As with a hacksaw, the work should be clamped securely in a vice, if needed, to prevent it from moving around while being worked on. Hold the file by the

2.40 Never use a file without a handle - the tang is sharp and could puncture your hand

2.41 Adjustable handles that will work with many different size files are also available

handle, using your free hand at the file end to guide it and keep it flat in relation to the surface being filed. Use smooth cutting strokes and be careful not to rock the file as it passes over the surface. Also, don't slide it diagonally across the surface or the teeth will make grooves in the workpiece. Don't drag a file back across the workpiece at the end of the stroke - lift it slightly and pull it back to prevent damage to the teeth.

Files don't require maintenance in the usual sense, but they should be kept clean and free of metal filings. Steel is a reasonably easy material to work with, but softer metals like aluminium tend to clog the file teeth very quickly, which will result in scratches in the workpiece. This can be avoided by rubbing the file face with chalk before using it. General cleaning is carried out with a file card or a fine wire brush. If kept clean, files will last a long time - when they do eventually dull, they must be renewed; there is no satisfactory way of sharpening a worn file.

Taps and dies

Taps

Tap and die sets **(see illustration)** are available in inch and metric sizes. Taps are used to cut internal threads and clean or restore damaged threads. A tap consists of a fluted shank with a drive square at one end. It's threaded along part of its length - the cutting edges are formed where the flutes intersect the threads **(see illustration)**. Taps are made from hardened steel so they will cut threads in materials softer than what they're made of.

Taps come in three different types: Taper, plug and bottoming. The only real difference is the length of the chamfer on the cutting end of the tap. Taper taps are chamfered for the first 6 or 8 threads, which makes them easy to start but prevents them from cutting threads close to the bottom of a hole. Plug taps are chamfered up about 3 to 5 threads, which makes them a good all around tap because they're relatively easy to start and will cut nearly to the bottom of a hole. Bottoming taps, as the name implies, have a very short chamfer (1-1/2 to 3 threads) and will cut as close to the bottom of a blind hole as practical. However, to do this, the threads should be started with a plug or taper tap.

Although cheap tap and die sets are available, the quality is usually very low and they can actually do more harm than good when used on threaded holes in aluminium parts. The alternative is to buy high-quality

2.42 Tap and die sets are available in inch and metric sizes - taps are used for cutting internal threads and cleaning and restoring damaged threads; dies are used for cutting, cleaning and restoring external threads

taps if and when you need them, even though they aren't cheap, especially if you need to buy two or more thread pitches in a given size. Despite this, it's the best option - you'll probably only need taps on rare occasions, so a full set isn't absolutely necessary.

Taps are normally used by hand (they can be used in machine tools, but primarily for manufacturing purposes). The square drive end of the tap is held in a tap spanner (an adjustable T-handle). For smaller sizes, a T-handled chuck can be used.

The tapping process starts by drilling a hole of the correct diameter. For each tap size, there's a corresponding twist drill that will produce a hole of the correct size. This is important; too large a hole will leave the finished thread with the tops missing, producing a weak and unreliable grip. Conversely, too small a hole will place excessive loads on the hard and brittle shank of the tap, which can break it off in the hole. Removing a broken off tap from a hole is no fun! The correct tap drill size is normally marked on the tap itself or the container it comes in **(see illustration)**. The tap should be used gradually, using a cutting lubricant and backing it out every few turns to clear swarf from the hole.

Dies

Dies are used to cut, clean or restore external threads. Most dies are made from a hex-shaped or cylindrical piece of hardened steel with a threaded hole in the centre. The threaded hole is overlapped by three or four cut-outs, which equate to the flutes on taps and allow metal waste to escape during the threading process. Dies are held in a T-handled holder (called a die stock) **(see illustration)**. Some dies are split at one point, allowing them to be adjusted slightly (opened and closed) for fine control of thread clearances.

Dies aren't needed as often as taps, for the simple reason it's normally easier to fit a new bolt than to salvage one. However, it's often helpful to be able to extend the threads of a bolt or clean up damaged threads with a die. Hex-shaped dies are particularly useful for mechanic's work, since they can be turned with a spanner **(see illustration)** and are usually less expensive than adjustable ones.

The procedure for cutting threads with a die is broadly similar to that described above for taps. When using an adjustable die, the initial cut is made with the die fully

2.43 Taper, plug and bottoming taps (left-to-right)

2.44 If you need to drill and tap a hole, the drill bit size to use for a given bolt (tap) size is marked on the tap

2.45 A die (right) is used for cutting external threads (this one is a split-type/adjustable die) and is held in a tool called a die stock (left)

2.46 Hex-shaped dies are especially handy for mechanic's work because they can be turned with a spanner

opened, the adjustment screw being used to reduce the diameter of successive cuts until the finished size is reached. As with taps, a cutting lubricant should be used, and the die must be backed off every few turns to clear swarf from the cut-outs.

Pullers

You may need a general-purpose puller for some brake work. Pullers can remove seized or corroded parts and push driveshafts from wheel hubs. Universal two- and three-legged pullers are widely available in numerous designs and sizes.

The typical puller consists of a central boss with two or three pivoting arms attached. The outer ends of the arms are hooked jaws which grab the part you want to pull off **(see illustration)**. You can reverse the arms on most pullers to use the puller on internal openings when necessary. The central boss is threaded to accept a puller bolt, which does the work. You can also get hydraulic versions of these tools which are capable of more pressure, but they're expensive.

You can adapt pullers by purchasing, or fabricating, special jaws for specific jobs. If you decide to make your own jaws, keep in mind that the pulling force should be concentrated as close to the centre of the component as possible to avoid damaging it.

Before you use a puller, assemble it and check it to make sure it doesn't snag on anything and the loads on the part to be removed are distributed evenly. If you're dealing with a part held on a shaft by a nut, loosen the nut but don't remove it. Leaving the nut on helps prevent distortion of the shaft end under pressure from the puller bolt and stops the part from flying off the shaft when it comes loose.

Tighten a puller gradually until the assembly is under moderate pressure, then try to jar the component loose by striking the puller bolt a few times with a hammer. If this doesn't work, tighten the bolt a little further and repeat the process. If this approach doesn't work, stop and reconsider. At some point you must make a decision whether to continue applying pressure in this manner. Sometimes, you can apply penetrating oil around the joint and leave it overnight, with the puller in place and tightened securely. By the next day, the taper has separated and the problem has resolved itself.

If nothing else works, try heating the area surrounding the troublesome part with a propane or gas welding torch (we don't, however, recommend messing around with welding equipment if you're not already experienced in its use). Apply the heat to the hub area of the component you wish to remove. Keep the flame moving to avoid uneven heating and the risk of distortion. Keep pressure applied with the puller and make sure that you're able to deal with the resulting hot component and the puller jaws if it does come free. Be very careful to keep the flame away from aluminium parts.

If all reasonable attempts to remove a part fail, don't be afraid to give up. It's cheaper to quit now than to damage components. Either buy or borrow the correct tool, or take the component (or vehicle) to a dealer service department or other garage to have the part removed for you.

Drawbolt extractors

The simple drawbolt extractor is easy to make up and invaluable in every workshop. There are no commercially available tools of this type; you simply

2.47 A two or three-jaw puller will come in handy for many tasks in the workshop and can also be used for working on other types of equipment

2.48 Typical drawbolt uses - in A, the nut is tightened to pull the collar and bush into the large spacer; in B, the spacer is left out and the drawbolt is repositioned to refit the new bush

2.49 A slide hammer with special attachments can be used for removing bearings and bushes from blind holes

Pullers for use in blind bores

Bushes or bearings fitted in 'blind holes' often require special pullers. Some bearings can be removed without a puller if you heat the engine or component evenly in an oven and tap it face down on a clean wooden surface to dislodge the bearing. Wear heavy gloves to protect yourself when handling the heated components. If you need a puller to do the job, get a slide-hammer with interchangeable tips. Slide hammers range from universal two or three-jaw puller arrangements to special bearing pullers. Bearing pullers are hardened steel tubes with a flange around the bottom edge. The tube is split at several places, which allows a wedge to expand the tool once it's in place. The tool fits inside the bearing inner race and is tightened so the flange or lip is locked under the edge of the race.

The slide-hammer consists of a steel shaft with a stop at its upper end. The shaft carries a sliding weight which slides along the shaft until it strikes the stop. This allows the tool holding the bearing to yank it out of the bore **(see illustration)**.

Bench vice

The bench vice **(see illustration)** is an essential tool in a workshop. Buy the best quality vice you can afford. A good vice is expensive, but the quality of its materials and workmanship are worth the extra money. Size is also important - bigger vices are usually more versatile. Make sure the jaws open at least four inches. Get a set of soft jaws to fit the vice as well - you'll need them to grip engine parts that could be damaged by the hardened vice jaws **(see illustration)**.

make a tool to suit a particular application. You can use a drawbolt extractor to pull out stubborn gudgeon pins and to remove bearings and bushes.

To make a drawbolt extractor, you'll need an assortment of threaded rods in various sizes (available at hardware stores), and nuts to fit them. You'll also need assorted washers, spacers and tubing. For things like gudgeon pins, you'll usually need a longer piece of tube.

Some typical drawbolt uses are shown in the accompanying line drawings **(see illustration)**. They also reveal the order of assembly of the various pieces. The same arrangement, minus the tubular spacer section, can usually be used to fit a new bush or gudgeon pin. Using the tool is quite simple. Just make sure you get the bush or pin square to the bore when you fit it. Lubricate the part being pressed into place, where appropriate.

2.50 A bench vice is one of the most useful pieces of equipment you can have - bigger is usually better with vices, so get a vice with jaws that open at least four inches

2.51 Sometimes, the parts you have to jig up in the vice are delicate, or made of soft materials - to avoid damaging them, get a pair of fibreglass or plastic "soft jaws" (A) or fabricate your own with 1/8-inch thick aluminium sheet (B)

Power tools

Really, the only power tool you absolutely need is an electric drill. But if you have an air compressor and electricity, there's a wide range of pneumatic and electric hand tools which can be used with it.

Air compressor

An air compressor **(see illustration)** makes most jobs easier and faster. Drying off parts after cleaning them with solvent, blowing out passages in a block or head, running power tools - the list is endless. Once you buy a compressor, you'll wonder how you ever got along without it. Air tools really speed up tedious procedures

like removing and refitting wheel nuts.

Bench-mounted grinder

A bench grinder **(see illustration)** is also handy. With a wire wheel on one end and a grinding wheel on the other, it's great for cleaning up fasteners, sharpening tools and removing rust. Make sure the grinder is fastened securely to the bench or stand, always wear eye protection when operating it and never grind aluminium parts on the grinding wheel.

Electric drills

Countersinking bolt holes, enlarging oil passages, honing cylinder bores, removing rusted or broken off fasteners, enlarging holes and fabricating small parts - an electric drill **(see illustration)** is indispensable for your workshop. A 3/8-inch chuck (drill bit holder) will handle most jobs. Collect several different wire brushes to use in the drill and make sure you have a complete set of sharp metal drill bits **(see illustration)**. Cordless drills are extremely versatile because they don't force you to work near an outlet. They're also handy to have around for a variety of non-mechanical jobs.

Twist drills

Drilling operations are done with twist drills, either in a hand drill or a drill press. Twist drills (or drill bits, as they're often called) consist of a round shank with spiral flutes formed into the upper two-thirds to clear the waste produced while drilling, keep the drill centred in the hole and finish the sides of the hole.

The lower portion of the shank is left plain and used to hold the drill in the chuck. In this section, we will discuss

2.52 Although it's not absolutely necessary, an air compressor can make many jobs easier and produce better results, especially when air powered tools are available to use with it

2.53 Another indispensable piece of equipment is the bench grinder (with a wire wheel mounted on one arbor) - make sure it's securely bolted down and never use it with the rests or eye shields removed

2.54 Electric drills can be cordless (above) or AC-powered (below)

2.55 Get a set of good quality drill bits for drilling holes and wire brushes of various sizes for cleaning up metal parts - make sure the bits are designed for drilling in metal!

only normal parallel shank drills **(see illustration)**. There is another type of bit with the plain end formed into a special size taper designed to fit directly into a corresponding socket in a heavy-duty drill press. These drills are known as Morse Taper drills and are used primarily in machine shops.

At the cutting end of the drill, two edges are earth to form a conical point. They're generally angled at about 60-degrees from the drill axis, but they can be reground to other angles for specific applications. For general use the standard angle is correct - this is how the drills are supplied.

When buying drills, purchase a good-quality set (sizes 1/16 to 3/8-inch). Make sure the drills are marked 'High Speed steel' or 'HSS'. This indicates they're hard enough to withstand continual use in metal; many cheaper, unmarked drills are suitable only for use in wood or other soft materials. Buying a set ensures the right size bit will be available when it's needed.

Twist drill sizes

Twist drills are available in a vast array of sizes, most of which you'll never need.

Fractional sizes start at 1/64-inch and increase in increments of 1/64-inch. Number drills range in descending order from 80 (0.0135-inch), the smallest, to 1 (0.2280-inch), the largest. Letter sizes start with A (0.234-inch), the smallest, and go through Z (0.413-inch), the largest. Metric drills are marked with the size in millimetres.

This bewildering range of sizes means it's possible to drill an accurate hole of almost any size within reason. In practice, you'll be limited by the size of chuck on your drill (normally 3/8 or 1/2-inch). In addition, very few stores stock the entire range of possible sizes, so you'll have to shop around for the nearest available size to the one you require.

Sharpening twist drills

Like any tool with a cutting edge, twist drills will eventually get dull **(see illustration)**. How often they'll need sharpening depends to some extent on whether they're used correctly. A dull twist drill will soon make itself known. A good indication of the condition of the cutting edges is to watch the waste emerging from the hole being drilled. If the tip is in good condition, two even spirals of waste metal will be produced; if this fails to happen or the tip gets hot, it's safe to assume that sharpening is required.

With smaller size drills - under about 1/8-inch - it's easier and more economical to throw the worn drill away and buy another one. With larger (more expensive) sizes, sharpening is a better bet. When sharpening twist

2.56 A typical drill bit (top), a reduced shank bit (centre), and a tapered shank bit (bottom right)

2.57 Drill bits in the range most commonly used are available in fractional sizes (left) and number sizes (right) so almost any size hole can be drilled

2.58 If a bit gets dull (left), discard it or resharpen it so it looks like the bit on the right

drills, the included angle of the cutting edge must be maintained at the original 120-degrees and the small chisel edge at the tip must be retained. With some practice, sharpening can be done freehand on a bench grinder, but it should be noted that it's very easy to make mistakes. For most home mechanics, a sharpening jig that mounts next to the grinding wheel should be used so the drill is clamped at the correct angle **(see illustration)**.

Drilling equipment

Tools to hold and turn drill bits range from simple, inexpensive hand-operated or electric drills to sophisticated and expensive drill presses. Ideally, all drilling should be done on a drill press with the workpiece clamped solidly in a vice. These machines are expensive and take up a lot of bench or floor space, so they're out of the question for many do-it-yourselfers.

The best tool for the home workshop is an electric drill with a 3/8-inch chuck. Both cordless and AC drills (that run off mains electricity) are available. If you're purchasing one for the first time, look for a well-known, reputable brand name and variable speed as minimum requirements. A 1/4-inch chuck, single-speed drill will work, but it's worth paying a little more for the larger, variable speed type.

Most drills require a key to lock the bit in the chuck. When removing or refitting a bit, make sure the cord is unplugged to avoid accidents. Initially, tighten the chuck by hand, checking to see if the bit is centred correctly. This is especially important when using small drill bits which can get caught between the jaws. Once the chuck is hand tight, use the key to tighten it securely - remember to remove the key afterwards!

2.59 Inexpensive drill bit sharpening jigs designed to be used with a bench grinder are widely available

Drilling and finishing holes
Preparation for drilling

If possible, make sure the part you intend to drill in is securely clamped in a vice. If it's impossible to get the work to a vice, make sure it's stable and secure. Twist drills often dig in during drilling - this can be dangerous, particularly if the work suddenly starts spinning on the end of the drill. Make sure the work supported securely.

Start by locating the centre of the hole you're drilling. Use a centre punch to make an indentation for the drill bit so it won't wander. If you're drilling out a broken-off bolt, be sure to position the punch in the exact centre of the bolt **(see illustration)**.

If you're drilling a large hole (above 1/4-inch), you may want to make a pilot hole first. As the name suggests, it will guide the larger drill bit and minimise drill bit wandering. Before actually drilling a hole, make sure the area immediately behind the bit is clear of anything you don't want drilled.

Drilling

When drilling steel, especially with smaller bits, no lubrication is needed. If a large bit is involved, oil can be used to ensure a clean cut and prevent overheating of the drill tip. When drilling aluminium, which tends to smear around the cutting edges and clog the drill bit flutes, use paraffin as a lubricant.

Wear safety goggles or a face shield and assume a comfortable, stable stance so you can control the pressure on the drill easily. Position the drill tip in the punch mark and make sure, if you're drilling by hand,

the bit is perpendicular to the surface of the workpiece. Start drilling without applying much pressure until you're sure the hole is positioned correctly. If the hole starts off centre, it can be very difficult to correct. You can try angling the bit slightly so the hole centre moves in the opposite direction, but this must be done before the flutes of the bit have entered the hole. It's at the starting point that a variable-speed drill is invaluable; the low speed allows fine adjustments to be made before it's too late. Continue drilling until the desired hole depth is reached or until the drill tip emerges at the other side of the workpiece.

Cutting speed and pressure are important - as a rule, the larger the diameter of the drill bit, the slower the drilling speed should be. With a single-speed drill, there's little that can be done to control it, but two-speed or variable speed drills can be controlled. If the drilling speed is too high, the cutting edges of the bit will tend to overheat and dull. Pressure should be varied during drilling. Start with light pressure until the drill tip has located properly in the work. Gradually increase pressure so the bit cuts evenly. If the tip is sharp and the pressure correct, two distinct spirals of metal will emerge from the bit flutes. If the pressure is too light, the bit won't cut properly, while excessive pressure will overheat the tip.

Decrease pressure as the bit breaks through the workpiece. If this isn't done, the bit may jam in the hole; if you're using a hand-held drill, it could be jerked out of your hands, especially when using larger size bits.

Once a pilot hole has been made, fit the larger bit in the chuck and enlarge the hole. The second bit will follow the pilot hole - there's no need to attempt to guide it (if you do, the bit may break off). It is important,

2.60 Before you drill a hole, use a centre-punch to make an indentation for the drill bit so it won't wander

2.61 Use a large drill bit or a countersink to remove burrs from a hole after drilling or enlarging it

however, to hold the drill at the correct angle.

After the hole has been drilled to the correct size, remove the burrs left around the edges of the hole. This can be done with a small round file, or by chamfering the opening with a larger bit or a countersink **(see illustration)**. Use a drill bit that's several sizes larger than the hole and simply twist it around each opening by hand until any rough edges are removed.

Enlarging and reshaping holes

The biggest practical size for bits used in a hand drill is about 1/2-inch. This is partly determined by the capacity of the chuck (although it's possible to buy larger drills with stepped shanks). The real limit is the difficulty of controlling large bits by hand; drills over 1/2-inch tend to be too much to handle in anything other than a drill press. If you have to make a larger hole, or if a shape other than round is involved, different techniques are required.

If a hole simply must be enlarged slightly, a round file is probably the best tool to use. If the hole must be very large, a hole saw will be needed, but they can only be used in sheet metal.

Large or irregular-shaped holes can also be made in sheet metal and other thin materials by drilling a series of small holes very close together. In this case the desired hole size and shape must be marked with a scribe. The next step depends on the size bit to be used; the idea is to drill a series of almost touching holes just inside the outline of the large hole. Centre punch each location, then drill the small holes. A cold chisel can then be used to knock out the waste material at the centre of the hole, which can then be filed to size. This is a time consuming process, but it's the only practical approach for the home workshop. Success is dependent on accuracy when marking the hole shape and using the centre punch.

High-speed grinders

A good die grinder **(see illustration)** will deburr blocks, radius piston domes and chamfer oil holes ten times as fast as you can do any of these jobs by hand. Used in conjunction with an abrasive disc, it can be used to de-glaze brake discs.

Safety items that should be in every workshop

Fire extinguishers

Buy at least one fire extinguisher **(see illustration)** before doing any maintenance or repair procedures. Make sure it's rated for flammable liquid fires.

2.62 A good die grinder will deburr blocks, radius piston domes, chamfer oil holes and do a lot of other little jobs which would be tedious if done manually

2.63 Buy at least one fire extinguisher before you open shop - make sure it's rated for flammable liquid fires and KNOW HOW TO USE IT!

2.64 Get a pair of heavy work gloves for handling hot or sharp-edged objects and a pair of rubber gloves for washing parts with solvent or brake cleaner

2.65 One of the most important items you'll need in the workshop is a face shield or safety goggles, especially when you're hitting metal parts with a hammer, washing parts, bleeding brakes or grinding something on the bench grinder

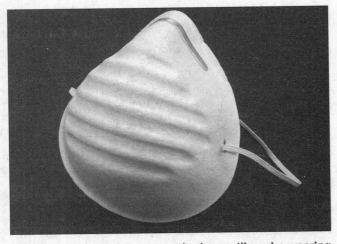

2.66 Don't begin work on your brakes until you're wearing a filtering mask like this

Familiarise yourself with its use when you buy it - don't wait until you need it to figure out how to use it. And be sure to have it checked and recharged at regular intervals. Refer to the safety tips at the end of this chapter for more information about the hazards of fuel and other flammable liquids.

Gloves

If you're handling hot parts or metal parts with sharp edges, wear a pair of industrial work gloves to protect yourself from burns, cuts and splinters **(see illustration)**. Wear a pair of heavy duty rubber gloves (to protect your hands when you wash parts in solvent or brake cleaner.

Safety glasses or goggles

Never work on a bench or high-speed grinder without safety glasses **(see illustration)**. Don't take a chance on getting a metal sliver in your eye. It's also a good idea to wear safety glasses when you're washing parts and while bleeding brakes.

Filtering mask

The linings of most brake pads and shoes contain asbestos, which is extremely hazardous to your health. The dust deposited all over your brakes (and wheels) is made up of a high percentage of asbestos fibres. Be sure to always wear a filtering mask **(see illustration)** when working on or around your brakes - it'll greatly reduce the risk of inhaling asbestos fibres.

Special brake-related tools

Vacuum gauge

The vacuum gauge **(see illustration)** indicates intake manifold vacuum, in inches of mercury (in-Hg). Brake servos depend on a healthy vacuum to operate properly. A hard pedal on a vehicle equipped with a vacuum-actuated brake servo would normally indicate a faulty servo, but before replacing anything it would be a good idea to check the intake manifold vacuum with a gauge like this.

Vacuum/pressure pump

The hand-operated vacuum/pressure pump **(see illustration)** can create a vacuum, or build up pressure, in a circuit to check components that are vacuum or pressure operated, such as brake servos.

2.67 The vacuum gauge indicates intake manifold vacuum, in inches of mercury (in-Hg)

2.69 Many late model vehicles use Torx head fasteners to secure the brake calipers - always use the proper size bit when loosening or tightening these bolts

2.68 The vacuum/pressure pump can create a vacuum in a circuit, or pressurise it, to simulate the actual operating conditions

2.70 A pad spreader like this is used for pushing the caliper piston(s) back into the caliper bore(s) to make room for the new brake pads

Torx Bits

Many owners become surprised, sometimes even frustrated, when they tackle a service or repair procedure and run into a fastener with a little six-pointed, star-shaped recess in its head. These are called Torx head bolts and are becoming increasingly popular with automobile manufacturers, especially for mounting brake calipers **(see illustration)**. It's very important to use the proper Torx bit on these fasteners. Never try to use an Allen key on a Torx fastener - you'll strip the head out and really create a problem!

Brake pad spreader

When replacing brake pads, the caliper piston(s) must be pushed back into the caliper to make room for the

new pads. On some caliper designs (sliding calipers) this can be done before the caliper is removed, using an ordinary C-clamp. On other kinds of calipers (especially multiple-piston calipers) a brake pad spreader is very helpful in accomplishing this task **(see illustration)**. You just unbolt the caliper, slide it off the brake disc, insert this tool between the pads and turn the screw - the piston(s) will be forced to the bottom of the bore(s).

Universal disc brake caliper tool

This kit **(see illustration)** combines two kinds of caliper piston depressors. One serves the same purpose as the tool described above. The other is for use on rear disc brake calipers with threaded handbrake actuators in the caliper pistons. On these

2.71 This universal brake caliper tool works on many different kinds of calipers and greatly facilitates brake pad renewal, especially on rear disc brakes

2.73 This tool will help you cleanly refit dust boots that have a steel case

2.72 This six-in-one rear caliper piston retractor is an economical alternative to the universal disc brake caliper tool (shown in illustration 2.71) - it also simplifies the task of turning the piston on actuator-screw rear calipers

2.74 A seal removal tool like this will facilitate the removal of stubborn seals

Brake caliper dust boot installer

A dust boot installer **(see illustration)** isn't an absolute necessity for overhauling brake calipers, but it eases the dust boot refitting procedure and reduces the chance of damaging the boot or caliper. It's for use only on dust boots with a rigid outer diameter.

Seal removal tool

If you remove your brake discs or drums for machining, and they are integral with the hubs, you'll have to clean and repack the wheel bearings. On some kinds of hubs the seals are difficult to remove, in which case a seal removal tool **(see illustration)** will come in handy.

calipers the pistons can't be pushed into their bores - they have to be rotated back in.

Rear disc brake piston tool

Here's another tool for turning the rear brake caliper pistons back into their bores **(see illustration)**. This one offers six different lug arrangements - one to fit almost any vehicle using this design rear caliper.

2.75 The only way to correctly and safely remove or refit brake shoe retractor springs is to use a spring tool

2.76 Brake spring pliers like this are able to handle just about any spring set-up you're likely to encounter and offer lots of leverage for removing and refitting those really strong springs

2.77 Pliers can be used to remove brake shoe hold-down springs, but if you don't want to fumble around and waste time, do it the right way and use a hold-down spring tool

2.78 If the drum brakes on the vehicle you're working on use hold-down clips instead of springs, use a tool like this

Brake spring tools

If you're replacing drum brake shoes, you'll want to pick up some kind of spring removal/refitting tool **(see illustration)**. They greatly simplify this task, eliminate frustration and can even prevent injury. Many different configurations are available. Be sure to get one that will work on your vehicle.

Brake spring pliers

Another kind of spring removal tool combines three spring tools in one **(see illustration)**. This is probably the most versatile type of brake spring tool available and will work on just about any vehicle with drum brakes.

Hold-down spring tool

This tool, available in different sizes and designs, eases the removal of the brake shoe hold-down springs and cups **(see illustration)**. Just set the tool on the cup, push down and turn 90-degrees and ease up, and the cup and spring are removed.

Hold-down clip tool

Similar to the hold-down spring tool, this device simplifies the removal of brake shoe hold-down clips, used mostly on imported cars and trucks **(see illustration)**.

Brake shoe adjuster tool

These tools are available in a few different shapes to work on many different types of drum brakes, but they're all used for the same thing - to reach through the hole in the backing plate (or drum on some models) and turn the adjuster (or 'star') wheel to expand or retract the brake shoes **(see illustration)**.

Wheel cylinder clip expander

This is a tool not everyone will need - only people who want to easily remove the wheel cylinders on vehicles that use clips to retain the cylinder to the backing plate **(see illustration)**.

2.79 Here's the correct tool to use for adjusting drum brakes (a screwdriver will work, but the way this tool is angled makes turning the star wheel much easier)

2.80 This tool spreads the ears of the wheel cylinder retaining clips on some vehicles

2.81 Hose pinchers are useful for clamping off the hoses to the remote brake fluid reservoir (on vehicles so equipped) when removing the master cylinder

Hose clamps

Hose pinchers, or clamps **(see illustration)**, are very useful tools, provided they are used correctly. Placed over a hose and tightened, they will prevent fluid from flowing through the hose. They're great for using on fluid feed hoses when removing the master cylinder on vehicles that employ remote reservoirs. It reduces the mess resulting from brake fluid running all over the place, and eliminates the need for completely draining the reservoir. **Warning:** *These tools should never be overtightened, and NEVER use them on high-pressure flexible brake lines, such as the ones that connect to the calipers or wheel cylinders.*

Brake cylinder hone

This tool is for use when rebuilding master cylinders or wheel cylinders **(see illustration)**. Lubricated with plenty of brake fluid and run in-and-out the bore at the proper speed, it will get rid of glaze and ridges caused

2.82 You'll need a brake cylinder hone like this if you intend to rebuild cast iron master or wheel cylinders

by the piston cups and provide an optimum sealing surface for the new cups. **Warning:** *Never attempt to hone aluminium cylinders!*

Brake bleed screw spanners

These special spanners **(see illustration)** fit perfectly on bleed valves and are offset so as not to place undue strain on fragile bleed screws.

Vacuum pump brake bleeding kit

When it's time to bleed the brakes and there aren't any

2.83 This long bleed spanner has a six-point ring end - the perfect combination for loosening bleed valves that are rusty and stuck

2.84 This brake bleeding kit will allow you to bleed the brake system by yourself

friends around to pump the brake pedal for you, this device **(see illustration)** will allow you to finish the job. Just hook it up to the bleeder valve (follow the tool manufacturer's instructions), open the bleeder valve and operate the pump. All air will be drawn from the portion of the system you're bleeding.

One-man brake bleeder

This tool **(see illustration)** will also let you complete the brake bleeding procedure by yourself. It's basically a container and hose with a one-way check valve in it. This allows you to open the bleeder valve, pump the pedal to purge the system of air without any air or old fluid being drawn back into the system.

Micrometers

The most accurate way to measure the thickness of a brake disc is with a micrometer. When doing a brake job or just checking your brakes, you'll have to confirm that

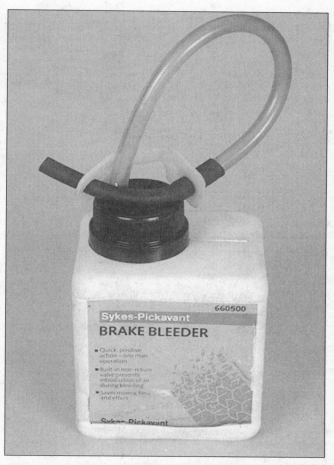

2.85 The one-man brake bleeder helps you achieve the same objective as the vacuum pump bleeder kit, but it's considerably less expensive (the only drawback is that you'll have to get out from underneath the car, hop into the driver's seat, pump the pedal a few times, then get out and tighten the bleeder valve)

2.86 The one-inch micrometer is an essential precision measuring device for determining the thickness of brake discs. If your discs are thicker than one inch, you'll need a one-to-two inch micrometer

2.87 This diagram of a typical one-inch micrometer shows its major components

2.88 Digital micrometers are easier to read than conventional micrometers, are just as accurate and are finally starting to become affordable

2.89 Avoid micrometer "sets" with interchangeable anvils - they're awkward to use when measuring little parts and changing the anvils is a hassle

the discs haven't worn down to their minimum thickness, or that there's enough material left to allow machining. Most discs are less than one-inch in thickness. If this is the case with your vehicle, your tool of choice should be the trusty one-inch outside micrometer **(see illustration)**.

Insist on accuracy to within one ten-thousandths of an inch (0.0001-inch) when you shop for a micrometer. you'll probably never need that kind of precision, but the extra decimal place will help you decide which way to round off a close measurement.

High-quality micrometers have a range of one inch. If you plan to work on a wide variety of vehicles, or if your vehicle is equipped with large, ventilated brake discs, you'll need a one-to-two inch micrometer.

Standard micrometers will work, but a special brake disc micrometer with a pointed anvil is recommended. It will take into account any deep scratches or grooves that a normal micrometer wouldn't be able to measure.

How to read a micrometer

The outside micrometer is without a doubt the most widely used precision measuring tool. It can be used to make a variety of highly accurate measurements without much possibility of error through misreading, a problem associated with other measuring instruments, such as vernier calipers.

Like any slide caliper, the outside micrometer uses the 'double contact' of its spindle and anvil **(see illustration)** touching the object to be measured to determine that object's dimensions. Unlike a caliper, however, the micrometer also features a unique precision screw adjustment which can be read with a great deal more accuracy than calipers.

Why is this screw adjustment so accurate? Because years ago toolmakers discovered that a screw with 40 precision machined threads to the inch will advance one-fortieth (0.025) of an inch with each complete turn. The screw threads on the spindle revolve inside a fixed nut concealed by a sleeve.

On a one-inch micrometer, this sleeve is engraved longitudinally with exactly 40 lines to the inch, to correspond with the number of threads on the spindle. Every fourth line is made longer and is numbered one-tenth inch, two-tenths, etc. The other lines are often staggered to make them easier to read.

The thimble (the barrel which moves up and down the sleeve as it rotates) is divided into 25 divisions around the circumference of its bevelled edge and is numbered from zero to 25. Close the micrometer spindle till it touches the anvil: You should see nothing but the zero line on the sleeve next to the bevelled edge of the thimble. And the zero line of the thimble should be aligned with the horizontal (or axial) line on the sleeve.

2.90 The dial indicator is the only way to measure brake disc runout

2.91 Get an adjustable, flexible fixture like this one, and a magnetic base, to ensure maximum versatility from your dial indicator

Remember: Each full revolution of the spindle from zero to zero advances or retracts the spindle one-fortieth or 0.025-inch. Therefore, if you rotate the thimble from zero on the bevelled edge to the first graduation, you will move the spindle 1/25th of 1/40th, or 1/25th of 25/1000ths, which equals 1/1000th, or 0.001-inch.

Remember: Each numbered graduation on the sleeve represents 0.1-inch, each of the other sleeve graduations represents 0.025-inch and each graduation on the thimble represents 0.001-inch. Remember those three and you're halfway there.

For example: Suppose the 4 line is visible on the sleeve. This represents 0.400-inch. Then suppose there are an additional three lines (the short ones without numbers) showing. These marks are worth 0.025-inch each, or 0.075-inch. Finally, there are also two marks on the bevelled edge of the thimble beyond the zero mark, each good for 0.001-inch, or a total of 0.002-inch. Add it all up and you get 0.400 plus 0.075 plus 0.002, which equals 0.477-inch.

Digital micrometers **(see illustration)** are easier to read than conventional micrometers, are just as accurate and are finally starting to become affordable. If you're uncomfortable reading a conventional micrometer, then get a digital.

Unless you're not going to use them very often, stay away from micrometers with interchangeable anvils **(see illustration)**. In theory, one of these beauties can do the work of five or six single-range micrometers. The trouble is, they're awkward to use when measuring little parts, and changing the anvils is awkward.

Dial indicators

The dial indicator **(see illustration)** is another measuring mainstay. You'll use this tool for measuring brake disc runout (warpage). Make sure the dial indicator you buy is graduated in 0.001-inch increments (or metric equivalent).

Buy a dial indicator set that includes a flexible fixture and a magnetic stand **(see illustration)**. If the model you buy doesn't have a magnetic base, buy one separately. Make sure the magnet is strong. If a weak magnet comes loose and the dial indicator takes a tumble on a concrete floor, you can kiss it good-bye. Also make sure the arm that attaches the dial indicator to the flexible fixture is sturdy and the locking clamps are easy to operate.

Calipers

Vernier calipers **(see illustration)** aren't quite as accurate as a micrometer, but they're handy for quick measurements and they're relatively inexpensive. Most calipers have inside and outside jaws, so you can measure the inside diameter of a hole, or the outside diameter of a part.

Better-quality calipers have a dust shield over the geared rack that turns the dial to prevent small metal particles from jamming the mechanism. Make sure there's no play in the moveable jaw. To check, put a thin piece of metal between the jaws and measure its thickness with the metal close to the rack, then out near the tips of the jaws. Compare your two measurements. If they vary by more than 0.001-inch, the jaw mechanism is deflecting.

2.92 Vernier calipers aren't quite as accurate as micrometers, but they're handy for quick measurements and relatively inexpensive, and because they've got jaws that can measure internal and external dimensions, they're versatile

If your eyes are going bad, or already are bad, vernier calipers can be difficult to read. Dial calipers **(see illustration)** are a better choice. Dial calipers combine the measuring capabilities of vernier calipers with the convenience of dial indicators. Because they're much easier to read quickly than vernier calipers, they're ideal for taking quick measurements when absolute accuracy isn't necessary. Like conventional vernier calipers, they have both inside and outside jaws which allow you to quickly determine the diameter of a hole or a part.

The latest calipers **(see illustration)** have a digital LCD display that indicates both inch and metric dimensions. If you can afford one of these, it's the best type to get.

How to read a vernier caliper

On the lower half of the main beam, each inch is divided into ten numbered increments, or tenths (0.100-inch, 0.200-inch, etc.). Each tenth is divided into four increments of 0.025-inch each. The vernier scale has 25 increments, each representing a thousandth (0.001) of an inch.

First read the number of inches, then read the number of tenths. Add to this 0.025-inch for each additional graduation. Using the English vernier scale, determine which graduation of the vernier lines up exactly with a graduation on the main beam. This vernier graduation is the number of thousandths which are to be added to the previous readings.

2.93 Dial calipers are a lot easier to read than conventional vernier calipers, particularly if your eyesight isn't as good as it used to be!

2.94 The latest calipers have a digital readout that is even easier to read than a dial caliper - another advantage of digital calipers is that they have a small microchip that allows them to convert instantaneously from inch to metric dimensions

For example, let's say:

1) The number of inches is zero, or 0.000-inch;
2) The number of tenths is 4, or 0.400-inch;
3) The number of 0.025's is 2, or 0.050-inch; and
4) The vernier graduation which lines up with a graduation on the main beam is 15, or 0.015-inch.
5) Add them up:

           0.000
           0.400
           0.050
           0.015

6) And you get: 0.465-inch

That's all there is to it!

Storage and care of tools

Good tools are expensive, so treat them well. After you've finished with your tools, wipe off any dirt, grease or metal chips and put them away. Don't leave tools lying around in the work area. General purpose hand tools - screwdrivers, pliers, spanners and sockets - can be hung on a wall panel or stored in a tool box. Store precision measuring instruments, gauges, meters, etc. in a tool box to protect them from dust, dirt, metal chips and humidity.

Fasteners

Fasteners - nuts, bolts, studs and screws - hold parts together. Keep the following things in mind when working with fasteners: All threaded fasteners should be clean and straight, with good threads and unrounded corners on the hex head (where the spanner fits). Make it a habit to renew all damaged nuts and bolts. Almost all fasteners have a locking device of some type, either a lockwasher, locknut, locking tab or thread adhesive.

Don't reuse special locknuts with nylon or fibre inserts. Once they're removed, they lose their locking ability. Fit new locknuts.

Flat washers and lockwashers, when removed from an assembly, should always be refitted exactly as removed. Renew any damaged washers. Never use a lockwasher on any soft metal surface (such as aluminium), thin sheet metal or plastic.

Apply penetrant to rusted nuts and bolts to loosen them up and prevent breakage. Some mechanics use turpentine in a spout-type oil can, which works quite well. After applying the rust penetrant, let it work for a few minutes before trying to loosen the nut or bolt. Badly rusted fasteners may have to be chiselled or sawed off or removed with a special nut breaker, available at tool shops.

If a bolt or stud breaks off in an assembly, it can be drilled and removed with a special tool commonly available for this purpose. Most automotive engineers can perform this task, as well as other repair procedures, such as the repair of threaded holes that have been stripped out.

Fastener sizes

For a number of reasons, car manufacturers are making wider and wider use of metric fasteners. Therefore, it's important to be able to tell the difference between Imperial (sometimes called standard, USS or SAE) and metric hardware, since they cannot be interchanged.

All bolts, whether standard or metric, are sized in accordance with their diameter, thread pitch and length **(see illustration)**. For example, a standard 1/2- 13 x 1 bolt is 1/2 inch in diameter, has 13 threads per inch and is 1 inch long. An M12-1.75x25 metric bolt is 12mm in diameter, has a thread pitch of 1.75 mm (the distance

G Grade marks (bolt strength)
L Length (in inches)
T Thread pitch (number of threads per inch)
D Nominal diameter (in inches)

P Property class (bolt strength)
L Length (in millimetres)
T Thread pitch (distance between threads in millimetres)
D Diameter

2.95a Imperial (SAE and USS) bolt dimensions/grade marks

2.95b Metric bolt dimensions/grade marks

2.96 Bolt strength markings (top - Imperial/ SAE; bottom - metric)

between threads) and is 25 mm long. The two bolts are nearly identical, and easily confused, but they are not interchangeable.

In addition to the differences in diameter, thread pitch and length, metric and standard bolts can also be distinguished by examining the bolt heads. The distance across the flats on a standard bolt head is measured in inches; the same dimension on a metric bolt or nut is sized in millimetres. So don't use an Imperial spanner on a metric bolt, or vice versa.

Most standard bolts also have marks radiating out from the centre of the head **(see illustration)** to denote the grade or strength of the bolt, which is an

indication of the amount of torque that can be applied to it. The greater the number of marks, the greater the strength of the bolt. Grades 0 through 5 are commonly used on automobiles. Metric bolts have a property class (grade) number, rather than a mark, moulded into their heads to indicate bolt strength. In this case, the higher the number, the stronger the bolt. Property class numbers 8.8, 9.8 and 10.9 are commonly used on automobiles.

Strength markings can also be used to distinguish standard hex nuts from metric hex nuts. Many standard nuts have dots stamped into one side, while metric nuts are marked with a number (see illustrations). The greater the number of dots, or the higher the number, the greater the strength of the nut.

Metric studs are also marked on their ends **(see**

2.97a Imperial hex nut strength markings

2.97b Metric nut strength markings

2.98 Metric stud strength markings

illustration) according to property class (grade). Larger studs are numbered (the same as metric bolts), while smaller studs carry a geometric code to denote grade.

It should be noted that many fasteners, especially Grades 0 through 2, have no distinguishing marks on them. When such is the case, the only way to determine whether it's standard or metric is to measure the thread pitch or compare it to a known fastener of the same size.

Standard fasteners are often referred to as SAE, as opposed to metric. However, it should be noted that SAE technically refers to a non-metric fine thread fastener only.

Since fasteners of the same size (both standard and metric) may have different strength ratings, be sure to refit any bolts, studs or nuts removed from your vehicle in their original locations. Also, when replacing a fastener with a new one, make sure that the new one has a strength rating equal to or greater than the original.

Tightening sequences and procedures

Most threaded fasteners should be tightened to a specific torque value (see charts on opposite page). **Warning:** These are general torque specifications for conventional fasteners. Some fasteners used in the brake system (most notably the disc brake caliper bolts or guide pins) are specifically designed for their purposes and would not fall into the categories listed below. Torque is the twisting force applied to a threaded component such as a nut or bolt. Overtightening the

fastener can weaken it and cause it to break, while undertightening can cause it to eventually come loose. Bolts, screws and studs, depending on the material they are made of and their thread diameters, have specific torque values. Be sure to follow torque recommendations closely. For fasteners not assigned a specific torque, a general torque value chart is presented here as a guide. These torque values are for dry (unlubricated) fasteners threaded into steel or cast iron (not aluminium). As was previously mentioned, the size and grade of a fastener determine the amount of torque that can safely be applied to it. The figures listed here are approximate for Grade 2 and Grade 3 fasteners. Higher grades can tolerate higher torque values.

If fasteners are laid out in a pattern - such as cylinder head bolts, sump bolts, differential cover bolts, etc. - loosen and tighten them in sequence to avoid warping the component. Where it matters, we'll show you this sequence. If a specific pattern isn't that important, the following rule-of thumb guide will prevent warping.

First, fit the bolts or nuts finger-tight. Then tighten them one full turn each, in a criss-cross or diagonal pattern. Then return to the first one and, following the same pattern, tighten them all one-half turn. Finally, tighten each of them one-quarter turn at a time until each fastener has been tightened to the proper torque. To loosen and remove the fasteners, reverse this procedure.

How to remove broken fasteners

Sooner or later, you're going to break off a bolt inside its threaded hole. There are several ways to remove it. Before you buy an expensive extractor set, try some of the following cheaper methods first.

First, regardless of which of the following methods you use, be sure to use penetrating oil. Penetrating oil is a special light oil with excellent penetrating power for freeing dirty and rusty fasteners. But it also works well on tightly torqued broken fasteners.

If enough of the fastener protrudes from its hole and if it isn't torqued down too tightly, you can often remove it with self-locking pliers. If that doesn't work, or if the fastener doesn't provide sufficient purchase for pliers, try filing it down to take a spanner, or cut a slot in it to accept a screwdriver **(see illustration)**. If you still can't get it off - and you know how to weld - try welding a flat piece of steel, or a nut, to the top of the broken fastener. If the fastener is broken off flush with - or below - the top of its hole, try tapping it out with a small, sharp punch. If that doesn't work, try drilling out the broken fastener with a bit only slightly smaller than the inside diameter of the hole. For example, if the hole is 1/2-inch in diameter, use a 15/32-inch drill bit. This leaves a shell

Metric thread sizes	Ft-lbs	Nm
M-6	6 to 9	9 to 12
M-8	14 to 21	19 to 28
M-10	28 to 40	38 to 54
M-12	50 to 71	68 to 96
M-14	80 to 140	108 to 190

Pipe thread sizes		
1/8	5 to 8	7 to 10
1/4	12 to 18	17 to 24
3/8	22 to 33	30 to 44
1/2	25 to 35	34 to 47

Non-metric thread sizes		
1/4 – 20	6 to 9	9 to 12
5/16 – 18	12 to 18	17 to 24
5/16 – 24	14 to 20	19 to 27
3/8 – 16	22 to 32	30 to 43
3/8 – 24	27 to 38	37 to 51
7/16 – 14	40 to 55	54 to 74
7/16 – 20	40 to 60	54 to 81
1/2 – 13	55 to 80	75 to 108

A File it flat or slot it
B Weld on a nut
C Use a punch to unscrew it
D Use a stud extractor
E Use a tap to remove the shell

2.99 There are several ways to remove a broken fastener

which you can pick out with a sharp chisel.

If none of the above techniques work, you'll have to resort to some form of screw or stud extractor **(see illustration)**. These are sold in sets which can remove anything from 1/4-inch to 1-inch bolts or studs. Most extractors are fluted and tapered high-grade steel. To use a screw extractor, drill a hole slightly smaller than the OD of the extractor you're going to use. (Extractor sets include the manufacturer's recommendations for what size drill bit to use with each extractor size.) Then screw in the extractor **(see illustration)**. Extractors are reverse-threaded, so the action of screwing it in anti-clockwise will turn the broken fastener out of the hole.

A word to the wise: Even though a stud extractor will usually save your bacon, it can cause even more grief if you're careless or sloppy. Drilling the hole for the extractor off-centre, or using too small, or too big, a bit for the size of the fastener you're removing will only make things worse. So be careful!

How to repair broken threads

Warning: Never attempt to repair the threads of the caliper mounting bolt holes, torque plate mounting bolt holes, stripped-out holes in two-piece calipers, wheel cylinder mounting bolt holes or any other critical brake system component. Instead, renew the part.

Sometimes, the internal threads of a nut or bolt hole can become stripped, usually from overtightening. Stripping threads is an all-too common occurrence, especially when working with aluminium parts, because aluminium is so soft that it easily strips out. Overtightened spark plugs are another common cause of stripped threads.

Usually, external or internal threads are only partially stripped. After they've been cleaned up with a tap or die, they'll still work. Sometimes, however, threads are badly damaged. When this happens, you've got three

2.100 Typical assortment of stud extractors

2.101 When screwing in the stud extractor, make sure it's centred properly

Standard Screw Fits In . . .

Heli-coil Insert In . . .

Heli-coil
Tapped Hole

0287H

2.102 To fit a Heli-Coil, drill out the hole, tap it with the special included tap and screw in the Heli-Coil

choices:
1) Drill and tap the hole to the next suitable oversize and refit a larger diameter bolt, screw or stud.
2) Drill and tap the hole to accept a threaded plug, then drill and tap the plug to the original screw size. You can also buy a plug already threaded to the original size. Then you simply drill a hole to the specified size, then run the threaded plug into the hole with a bolt and jam nut. Once the plug is fully seated, remove the jam nut and bolt.
3) The third method uses a patented thread repair kit like Heli-Coil. These are designed to repair damaged threads in spark plug holes, straight-through holes and blind holes. They are available as kits which can handle a variety of sizes and thread patterns. Drill the hole, then tap it with the special included tap. Fit the Heli-Coil **(see illustration)** and the hole is back to its original diameter and thread pitch.

Regardless of which method you use, be sure to proceed calmly and carefully. A little impatience or carelessness during one of these relatively simple procedures can ruin your whole day's work and cost you a bundle if you wreck an expensive head or block.

Component disassembly

Disassemble components carefully to help ensure that the parts go back together properly. Note the sequence in which parts are removed. Make note of special characteristics or marks on parts that can be refitted more than one way, such as a grooved thrust washer on a shaft. it's a good idea to lay the disassembled parts out on a clean surface in the order in which you removed them. It may also be helpful to make sketches or take instant photos of components before removal.

When you remove fasteners from a component, keep track of their locations. Thread a bolt back into a part, or put the washers and nut back on a stud, to prevent mix-ups later. If that isn't practical, put fasteners in a fishing tackle box or a series of small boxes. A cupcake or muffin tin, or an egg crate, is ideal for this purpose - each cavity can hold the bolts and nuts from a particular area (i.e. sump bolts, valve cover bolts, engine mount bolts, etc.). A pan of this type is helpful when working on assemblies with very small parts, such as the carburettor or valve train. Mark each cavity with paint or tape to identify the contents.

When you unplug the connector(s) between two wire harnesses, or even two wires, it's a good idea to identify the two halves with numbered pieces of masking tape - or a pair of matching pieces of coloured electrical tape - so they can be easily reconnected.

Gasket sealing surfaces

Gaskets seal the mating surfaces between two parts to prevent lubricants, fluids, vacuum or pressure from leaking out between them. Gaskets are often coated with a liquid or paste-type gasket sealing compound before assembly. Age, heat and pressure can cause the two parts to stick together so tightly that they're difficult to separate. Often, you can loosen the assembly by striking it with a soft-face hammer near the mating surfaces. You can use a regular hammer if you place a block of wood between the hammer and the part, but don't hammer on cast or delicate parts that can be easily damaged. When a part refuses to come off, look for a fastener that you forgot to remove.

Don't use a screwdriver or crowbar to prise apart an assembly. It can easily damage the gasket sealing surfaces of the parts, which must be smooth to seal properly. If prising is absolutely necessary, use an old broom handle or a section of hard wood dowel.

Once the parts are separated, carefully scrape off the old gasket and clean the gasket surface. You can also remove some gaskets with a wire brush. If some gasket material refused to come off, soak it with rust penetrant or treat it with a special chemical to soften it, then scrape it off. You can fashion a scraper from a piece of copper tubing by flattening and sharpening one end. Copper is usually softer than the surface being scraped, which reduces the likelihood of gouging the part. The mating surfaces must be clean and smooth when you're done. If the gasket surface is gouged, use a gasket sealer thick enough to fill the scratches when you reassemble the components. For most applications, use a non-drying (or semi-drying) gasket sealer.

Hose removal tips

• **Warning:** *If the vehicle is equipped with air conditioning, do not disconnect any of the A/C hoses without first having the system depressurised by a dealer service department or a service station.* The same precautions that apply to gasket removal also apply to hoses. Avoid scratching or gouging the surface against which the hose mates, or the connection may leak. Take, for example, radiator hoses. Because of various chemical reactions, the rubber in radiator hoses can bond itself to the metal spigot over which the hose fits. To remove a hose, first loosen the hose clamps that secure it to the spigot. Then, with slip-joint pliers, grab the hose at the clamp and rotate it around the spigot. Work it back and forth until it is completely free, then pull it off. Silicone or other lubricants will ease removal if they can be applied between the hose and the outside of the spigot. Apply the same lubricant to the inside of the hose and the outside of the spigot to simplify refitting. Some tool manufacturers make hose removal tools - they look like bent ice picks - which can be inserted between the spigot and the radiator hose to break the seal between rubber and metal.

As a last resort - or if you're planning to renew the hose anyway - slit the rubber with a knife and peel the hose from the spigot. Make sure you don't damage the metal connection.

If a hose clamp is broken or damaged, don't reuse it. Wire-type clamps usually weaken with age, so it's a good idea to renew them with screw-type clamps whenever a hose is removed.

Automotive chemicals and lubricants

Cleaners

A wide variety of automotive chemicals and lubricants - ranging from cleaning solvents and degreasers to lubricants and protective sprays for rubber, plastic and vinyl - is available.

Brake system cleaner

Brake system cleaner removes grease and brake fluid from brake parts like disc brake rotors, where a spotless surfaces is essential. It leaves no residue and often eliminates brake squeal caused by brake dust or other contaminants. Because it leaves no residue, brake cleaner is often used for cleaning other parts as well.

Carburettor and choke cleaner

Carburettor and choke cleaner is a strong solvent for gum, varnish and carbon. Most carburettor cleaners leave a dry-type lubricant film which will not harden or gum up. So don't use carb cleaner on electrical components.

Degreasers

Degreasers are heavy-duty solvents used to remove grease from the outside of the engine and from chassis components. They're usually sprayed or brushed on. Depending on the type, they're rinsed off either with water or solvent. **Warning:** *Never wash brake system components with petroleum-based solvents.*

Demoisturants

Demoisturants remove water and moisture from electrical components such as alternators, voltage regulators, electrical connectors and fuse blocks. They are non-conductive, non-corrosive and non-flammable.

Electrical cleaner

Electrical cleaner removes oxidation, corrosion and carbon deposits from electrical contacts, restoring full current flow. It can also be used to clean spark plugs, carburettor jets, voltage regulators and other parts where an oil-free surface is necessary.

Lubricants

Assembly lube

Assembly lube is a special extreme pressure lubricant, used to lubricate high-load parts (such as main and big-end bearings and cam lobes) for initial start-up of a new engine. The assembly lube lubricates the parts without being squeezed out or washed away until the engine oiling system begins to function.

Graphite lubricants

Graphite lubricants are used where oils cannot be used due to contamination problems, such as in locks. The dry graphite will lubricate metal parts while remaining uncontaminated by dirt, water, oil or acids. It is electrically conductive and will not foul electrical contacts in locks such as the ignition switch.

Heat-sink grease

Heat-sink grease is a special electrically non-conductive grease that is used for mounting electronic ignition modules where it is essential that heat is transferred away from the module.

Penetrating lubricants

Penetrating lubricants loosen and lubricate seized, rusted and corroded fasteners and prevent future rusting or freezing.

Motor oil

Motor oil is the lubricant formulated for use in engines. It normally contains a wide variety of additives to prevent corrosion and reduce foaming and wear. Motor oil comes in various weights (viscosity ratings). The recommended weight of the oil depends on the season, temperature and the demands on the engine. Light oil is used in cold climates and under light load conditions. Heavy oil is used in hot climates and where high loads are encountered. Multigrade oils are designed to have characteristics of both light and heavy oils and are available in a number of weights from 5W-20 to 20W-50. Some home mechanics use motor oil as an assembly lube, but we don't recommend it, because motor oil has a relatively thin viscosity, which means it will slide off the parts long before the engine is fired up.

Silicone lubricants

Silicone lubricants are used to protect rubber, plastic, vinyl and nylon parts.

Wheel bearing grease

Wheel bearing grease is a heavy grease that can withstand high loads and friction, and is used in wheel bearings, balljoints, track rod ends and universal joints. It's also sticky enough to hold parts like the collets for the valve spring retainers in place on the valve stem when you're refitting the springs.

White grease

White grease is a heavy grease for metal-to-metal applications where water is present. It stays soft under both low and high temperatures (usually from -100 to +190-degrees F), and won't wash off or dilute when exposed to water. Another good 'glue' for holding parts in place during assembly.

Sealants

Anaerobic sealant

Anaerobic sealant is much like RTV in that it can be used either to seal gaskets or to form gaskets by itself. It remains flexible, is solvent resistant and fills surface imperfections. The difference between an anaerobic sealant and an RTV-type sealant is in the curing. RTV cures when exposed to air, while an anaerobic sealant cures only in the absence of air. This means that an anaerobic sealant cures only after the assembly of parts, sealing them together.

RTV sealant

RTV sealant is one of the most widely used gasket compounds. Made from silicone, RTV is air curing, it seals, bonds, waterproofs, fills surface irregularities, remains flexible, doesn't shrink, is relatively easy to remove, and is used as a supplementary sealer with almost all low and medium temperature gaskets.

Thread and pipe sealant

Thread and pipe sealant is used for sealing hydraulic and pneumatic fittings and vacuum lines. It is usually made from a Teflon compound, and comes in a spray, a paint-on liquid and as a wrap-around tape.

Chemicals

Anaerobic locking compounds

Anaerobic locking compounds are used to keep fasteners from vibrating or working loose and cure only after refitting, in the absence of air. Medium strength locking compound is used for small nuts, bolts and screws that may be removed later. High-strength locking compound is for large nuts, bolts and studs which aren't removed on a regular basis.

Anti-seize compound

Anti-seize compound prevents seizing, galling, cold welding, rust and corrosion in fasteners. High-temperature anti-seize, usually made with copper and graphite lubricants, is used for exhaust system and exhaust manifold bolts.

Fuel additives

Fuel additives perform several functions, depending on their chemical makeup. They usually contain solvents that help dissolve gum and varnish that build up on carburettor, fuel injection and intake parts. They also serve to break down carbon deposits that form on the inside surfaces of the combustion chambers. Some additives contain upper cylinder lubricants for valves and piston rings, and others contain chemicals to remove condensation from the fuel tank.

Oil additives

Oil additives range from viscosity index improvers to chemical treatments that claim to reduce internal engine friction. It should be noted that most oil manufacturers caution against using additives with their oils.

Safety first

Working on your car can be dangerous. This page shows just some of the potential risks and hazards, with the aim of creating a safety-conscious attitude.

General hazards

■ *Scalding*

☐ Don't remove the radiator or expansion tank cap while the engine is hot.
Engine oil, automatic transmission fluid or power steering fluid may also be dangerously hot if the engine has recently been running.

■ *Burning*

☐ Beware of burns from the exhaust system and from any part of the engine. Brake discs and drums can also be extremely hot immediately after use.

■ *Crushing*

☐ When working under or near a raised vehicle, always supplement the jack with axle stands, or use drive-on ramps.
Never venture under a car which is only supported by a jack.

☐ Take care if loosening or tightening high-torque nuts when the vehicle is on stands. Initial loosening and final tightening should be done with the wheels on the ground.

■ *Fire*

☐ Fuel is highly flammable; fuel vapour is explosive.
Don't let fuel spill onto a hot engine. Do not smoke or allow naked lights (including pilot lights) anywhere near a vehicle being worked on. Also beware of creating sparks (electrically or by use of tools).
☐ Fuel vapour is heavier than air, so don't work on the fuel system with the vehicle over an inspection pit.
☐ Another cause of fire is an electrical overload or short-circuit. Take care when repairing or modifying the vehicle wiring.
☐ Keep a fire extinguisher handy, of a type suitable for use on fuel and electrical fires.

■ *Electric shock*

☐ Ignition HT voltage can be dangerous, especially to people with heart problems or a pacemaker. Don't work on or near the ignition system with the engine running or the ignition switched on.

☐ Mains voltage is also dangerous. Make sure that any mains-operated equipment is correctly earthed. Mains power points should be protected by a residual current device (RCD) circuit breaker.

■ *Fume or gas intoxication*

☐ Exhaust fumes are poisonous; they often contain carbon monoxide, which is rapidly fatal if inhaled. Never run the engine in a confined space such as a garage with the doors shut.
☐ Fuel vapour is also poisonous, as are the vapours from some cleaning solvents and paint thinners.

■ *Poisonous or irritant substances*

☐ Avoid skin contact with battery acid and with any fuel, fluid or lubricant, especially antifreeze, brake hydraulic fluid and Diesel fuel. Don't syphon them by mouth. If such a substance is swallowed or gets into the eyes, seek medical advice.
☐ Prolonged contact with used engine oil can cause skin cancer. Wear gloves or use a barrier cream if necessary. Change out of oil-soaked clothes and do not keep oily rags in your pocket.
☐ Air conditioning refrigerant forms a poisonous gas if exposed to a naked flame (including a cigarette). It can also cause skin burns on contact.

■ *Asbestos*

☐ Asbestos dust can cause cancer if inhaled or swallowed. Asbestos may be found in gaskets and in brake and clutch linings. When dealing with such components it is safest to assume that they do contain asbestos.

Special hazards

■ *Hydrofluoric acid*

☐ This extremely corrosive acid is formed when certain types of synthetic rubber, found in some O-rings, oil seals, fuel hoses etc, are exposed to temperatures above 400ºC. The rubber changes into a charred or sticky substance containing the acid. *Once formed, the acid remains dangerous for years. If it gets onto the skin, it may be necessary to amputate the limb concerned.*

☐ When dealing with a vehicle which has suffered a fire, or with components salvaged from such a vehicle, wear protective gloves and discard them after use.

■ *The battery*

☐ Batteries contain sulphuric acid, which attacks clothing, eyes and skin. Take care when topping-up or carrying the battery.
☐ The hydrogen gas given off by the battery is highly explosive. Never cause a spark or allow a naked light nearby. Be careful when connecting and disconnecting battery chargers or jump leads.

■ *Air bags*

☐ Air bags can cause injury if they go off accidentally. Take care when removing the steering wheel and/or facia. Special storage instructions may apply.

■ *Diesel injection equipment*

☐ Diesel injection pumps supply fuel at very high pressure. Take care when working on the fuel injectors and fuel pipes.
Never expose the hands, face or any other part of the body to injector spray; the fuel can penetrate the skin with potentially fatal results.

A few tips

■ *Do...*

... use eye protection when using power tools, and when working under the vehicle.
... wear gloves or use barrier cream to protect your hands when necessary.
... get someone to check periodically that all is well when working alone on the vehicle.
... keep loose clothing and long hair well out of the way of moving mechanical parts.
... remove rings, wristwatch etc, before working on the vehicle – especially the electrical system.
... ensure that any lifting or jacking equipment has a safe working load rating adequate for the job.

■ *Don't...*

... attempt to lift a heavy component which may be beyond your capability – get assistance.
... rush to finish a job, or take unverified short cuts.

... use ill-fitting tools which may slip and cause injury.
... leave tools or parts lying around where someone can trip over them. Mop up oil and fuel spills at once.
... allow children or pets to play in or near a vehicle being worked on.

Chapter 3
Troubleshooting

This Chapter provides an easy reference guide to the more common problems which may occur in just about any kind of automotive brake system. In the following table, the bold headings contain the various problems that may be encountered. **Note:** *Although the problems included here do apply to the wheel brakes and, to an extent, the hydraulic system of ABS-equipped vehicles, malfunctions that pertain solely to the anti-lock portion of such systems aren't dealt with here. For a description of Anti-lock Brake Systems (ABS) and general troubleshooting procedures, refer to Chapter 10.*

Remember that successful troubleshooting is not a mysterious "black art" practised only by professional mechanics. It's simply the result of a bit of knowledge combined with an intelligent, systematic approach to the problem. Always work by a process of elimination, starting with the simplest solution and working through to the most complex. If necessary, refer to Chapter 1 and remind yourself of the basic braking system principles.

If you keep a close eye on the condition of your brakes and perform routine inspections as described in Chapter 4, you might not ever need the following troubleshooting information. Brakes work hard, though, probably harder than any other system in your car. They're subjected to lots of abuse. Unexpected problems do occur, and a straightforward, logical analysis of the disorder will save you time and unnecessary expense.

Before assuming that a brake problem exists, make sure the tyres are in good condition and properly inflated. Also, the steering and suspension must be in proper alignment and the vehicle must not be loaded with weight in an unequal manner.

If, after using this troubleshooting guide, you are still unable to resolve the problem, seek advice from a professional mechanic. If necessary, have the vehicle towed to a garage. Don't drive a vehicle with defective brakes.

Warning: *The dust created by the brake system may contain asbestos, which is harmful to your health. Never blow it out with compressed air and don't inhale any of it. An approved filtering mask should be worn when working on the brakes. Do not, under any circumstances, use petroleum-based solvents to clean brake parts. Use brake system cleaner only!*

Symptom and cause(s) | Remedy

Vehicle pulls to one side under braking

Symptom and cause(s)	Remedy
Normal effect of road camber.	Recheck on flat surface. If brakes no longer pull, no problem.
Tyre pressures incorrect.	Check and adjust tyre pressures.
Worn, defective, damaged or contaminated front brake pads or rear brake shoes on one side.	Renew as necessary and correct cause of contamination.
Seized or partially seized front brake caliper or rear wheel cylinder piston.	Overhaul or renew caliper or wheel cylinder.
A mixture of brake pad/shoe lining materials fitted between sides.	Fit new pads or shoes of correct type.
Front brake caliper mounting bolts loose.	Tighten bolts; use thread locking compound if necessary.
Rear brake backplate mounting bolts loose.	Tighten bolts; use thread locking compound if necessary.
Worn or damaged steering or suspension components.	Repair or renew as necessary.

Noise (grinding or high-pitched squeal) when brakes applied

Symptom and cause(s)	Remedy
Anti-squeal shims missing from brake pads, or incorrectly fitted.	Fit anti-squeal shims correctly.
Normal characteristic of some asbestos-free linings.	Apply anti-seize/anti-squeal compound to backs of pads. If no improvement, try a different brand of linings.
Brake pad or shoe friction lining material worn down to metal backing.	Renew pads or shoes.
Moisture in brake drums (often after standing overnight in damp weather).	Noise will disappear once brakes have been used a few times.
Excessive corrosion of brake disc or drum. (May be apparent after the vehicle has been standing for some time.)	Reface or renew disc or drum.
Brake linings contaminated with oil or hydraulic fluid.	Renew linings and repair source of contamination.
Foreign object (stone chipping etc) trapped between brake disc and shield.	Remove foreign object.

Excessive brake pedal travel

Symptom and cause(s)	Remedy
Hydraulic fluid level low.	Top up and check for leaks.
Air in hydraulic system.	Bleed system and check for leaks.
Leak in one hydraulic circuit.	Repair leak. Top up and bleed hydraulic system.
Warped brake disc.	Renew disc.
Drum brakes in need of adjustment.	Adjust.
Inoperative rear brake self-adjusting mechanism.	Repair or renew self-adjusting mechanism.

Symptom and cause(s)   Remedy

Excessive brake pedal travel (continued)

Symptom and cause(s)	Remedy
Brake linings extremely worn.	Renew linings.
Faulty master cylinder.	Repair or renew master cylinder.
Brake fluid overheated and vaporised (water in fluid).	Renew brake fluid.

Brake pedal feels spongy when depressed

Symptom and cause(s)	Remedy
Air in hydraulic system.	Bleed system and check for leaks.
Deteriorated flexible rubber brake hoses.	Renew rubber hoses.
Master cylinder mounting nuts loose.	Tighten nuts.
Faulty master cylinder.	Repair or renew master cylinder.

Excessive brake pedal effort required to stop vehicle

Symptom and cause(s)	Remedy
Disconnected, damaged or insecure brake servo vacuum hose.	Reconnect or renew hose.
Faulty servo non-return valve.	Renew valve.
Faulty vacuum servo unit.	Renew servo unit.
Vacuum pump drivebelt broken (if applicable - Diesel engines).	Renew drivebelt.
Faulty vacuum pump (Diesel engines).	Renew pump.
New linings not yet run in.	Run in linings.
Primary or secondary hydraulic circuit failure.	Repair circuit and bleed hydraulic system.
Seized brake caliper or wheel cylinder piston(s).	Repair or renew caliper or wheel cylinder.
Brake pads or brake shoes incorrectly fitted.	Inspect and refit correctly.
Incorrect grade of brake pads or brake shoes fitted.	Fit correct grade of linings.
Water in brake drums (eg after driving through flood water).	Apply brakes repeatedly to boil off water.
Brake pads or brake shoe linings contaminated.	Renew pads or shoes and repair source of leak.

Judder felt through brake pedal or steering wheel when braking

Symptom and cause(s)	Remedy
Normal feature of ABS operation.	No fault.
Wheel nuts loose.	Tighten wheel nuts.
Excessive run-out or distortion of front discs or rear drums.	Renew discs or drums.
Cracked disc or drum.	Renew disc or drum.
Brake pad or brake shoe linings worn.	Renew linings.
Brake caliper or rear brake backplate mounting bolts loose.	Tighten mounting bolts; use thread locking compound if necessary.
Wear in suspension or steering components or mountings.	Repair or renew as necessary.

Symptom and cause(s)   Remedy

Brakes binding

Symptom and cause(s)	Remedy
Seized brake caliper or wheel cylinder piston(s).	Repair or renew caliper or wheel cylinder.
Incorrectly adjusted handbrake mechanism.	Adjust correctly.
Drum brakes incorrectly adjusted.	Adjust correctly.
Faulty self-adjusting mechanism.	Repair or renew self-adjusting mechanism.
Servo pushrod incorrectly adjusted.	Adjust pushrod correctly.
Faulty master cylinder.	Repair or renew master cylinder.

Brakes grab or wheels lock

Pads or shoes contaminated.	Renew pads or shoes and repair source of contamination.
Brake shoe lining loose or damaged.	Renew brake shoes.

Rear wheels locking under normal braking

Rear brake shoe linings contaminated.	Renew brake shoes and repair source of contamination.
Faulty brake pressure regulator.	Renew brake pressure regulator valve.

Handbrake ineffective

Handbrake linkage needs adjustment.	Adjust.
Handbrake linkage seized.	Repair or renew linkage.
Rear brake self-adjusting mechanism faulty.	Repair or renew self-adjusting mechanism.
Handbrake shoes or pads worn out (systems with separate handbrake linings).	Renew shoes or pads.
Rear brake shoe linings contaminated.	Renew brake shoes and repair source of contamination.

Handbrake will not release

Handbrake linkage needs adjustment.	Adjust.
Handbrake linkage seized.	Repair or renew linkage.
Rear brake self-adjusting mechanism faulty.	Repair or renew self-adjusting mechanism.

One brake light does not work

Bulb blown.	Renew bulb.
Poor contact in bulb holder.	Clean contacts.

No brake lights work

Brake light switch wrongly adjusted or faulty.	Adjust or renew switch.
Fuse blown.	Renew fuse. If it blows again, check for short-circuits.

Brake lights will not go out

Brake light switch wrongly adjusted or faulty.	Adjust or renew switch.

Chapter 4
Maintenance

Introduction

The key objective of this Chapter is to establish a preventive maintenance program to minimise the chances of brake trouble or system failure. This is done by maintaining a constant awareness of the condition of the entire braking system and by correcting defects or replacing worn-out parts before they become serious problems. The majority of the operations outlined in this Chapter are nothing more than inspections of the various components that make up the brake system.

Secondly, this preventive maintenance program should cause most, if not all, maintenance and repairs to take place by intent, hopefully eliminating all "unscheduled maintenance." By doing so, all brake system repairs that may become necessary can be performed when and where you choose. Not only will it save you money by catching worn-out brake pads and shoes before they cause serious damage, it'll also save you money by avoiding body shop repair bills, tow truck, ambulance and hospital fees, lawsuits, etc!

The following brake maintenance schedule is very simple, as are the checking procedures that go with it. The maintenance intervals are based on normal operating conditions for a normal passenger vehicle or light truck. If a particular vehicle is subjected to more severe usage, the intervals should be shortened and the inspection procedures performed more often. Vehicles that tow trailers, carry heavy loads, are driven in a lot of stop-and-go traffic or in mountainous regions are going to wear out parts and need service more often than vehicles that enjoy mostly traffic-free highway trips. Mileage isn't always a factor - the important thing is to perform the inspections routinely. If your vehicle is operated under severe conditions, it would be a good idea to at least perform the disc and/or drum brake inspections twice as frequently as outlined below, until you develop a feel for the rate at which your vehicle wears down the brake linings.

The maintenance schedule is basically an outline for the actual inspection and maintenance procedures. The individual procedures are then described in detail. Some of the items on the schedule may be listed at a shorter interval than recommended by some manufacturers, and some of the items listed may not even appear on the maintenance schedules of some manufacturers, but that's OK - it's better to be safe than sorry.

If you're experiencing a specific problem with the brake system, refer to Chapter 3, Troubleshooting, for the proper course of action to take.

Maintenance schedule

Every 250 miles or weekly, whichever comes first

Check the tyres and tyre pressures
Check the wheel nut tightness
Check the brake fluid level and condition
Check the brake pedal "feel" and travel (master cylinder check)
Check the brake servo, if equipped
Check the operation of the brake lights and the brake warning light

Every 6000 miles or 6 months, or whichever comes first

Check the front brakes
Check the brake hoses and lines

Every 12,000 miles or 12 months, whichever comes first

All items listed above, plus:
Check the rear brakes
Check and, if necessary, adjust the handbrake
Check the brake pedal pivot bush and bracket

Every 30,000 miles or 2 years, whichever comes first

All items listed above, plus:
Renew the brake fluid (this is an item for which many manufacturers don't even specify a maintenance interval. However, renewing the brake fluid on a regular basis will prevent contamination in the hydraulic system and all the problems associated with it)
Check the master cylinder for leakage past the primary piston seals

Every 80,000 miles, or 5 years, whichever comes first

Rebuild or renew the master cylinder, calipers and

wheel cylinders (here's another item that most manufacturers don't specifically recommend, but it can prevent a myriad of problems. Master and wheel cylinder cups and caliper pistons and seals don't last forever, so to overhaul or renew them before they pose a problem makes sense. It's up to you).

Inspection and maintenance procedures

Preliminary checks

Tyres and tyre pressures

The first step in a brake system inspection should be of the tyre condition and pressures. If the tyres aren't inflated properly, or if they're in bad shape, there's no way the vehicle is going to stop in a straight line.

Check to see how much tread is left on the tyres. Tread wear can be monitored with a simple, inexpensive device known as a tread depth indicator **(see illustration)**.

Note any abnormal tread wear. Tread pattern irregularities such as cupping, flat spots and more wear on one side than the other are indications of front end alignment and/or balance problems. If any of these conditions are noted, take the vehicle to a tyre specialist or service station to correct the problem.

Look closely for cuts, punctures and embedded nails or tacks. Sometimes a tyre will hold air pressure for a short time or leak down very slowly after a nail has embedded itself in the tread. If a slow leak persists, check the valve stem core to make sure it's tight **(see illustration)**. Examine the tread for an object that may have embedded itself in the tyre. If a puncture is suspected, it can be easily verified by spraying a solution of soapy water onto the puncture area **(see illustration)**. The soapy solution will bubble if there's a leak. Unless the puncture is unusually large, a tyre specialist can usually repair the tyre.

Carefully inspect the inner sidewall of each tyre for evidence of brake fluid leakage. If you see any, inspect the brake hoses, calipers and/or wheel cylinders immediately.

Correct air pressure adds miles to the lifespan of the tyres, improves mileage and enhances overall ride quality. Tyre pressure cannot be accurately estimated by looking at a tyre, especially if it's a radial. A tyre pressure gauge is essential. Keep an accurate gauge in the vehicle. The pressure gauges attached to the nozzles of air lines at garages are often inaccurate.

Always check tyre pressure when the tyres are cold. Cold, in this case, means the vehicle has not been driven over a mile in the three hours preceding a tyre pressure check. A pressure rise of four to eight pounds

4.1 Use a tyre tread depth indicator to monitor tyre wear - they are available at motor factors and service stations and cost very little

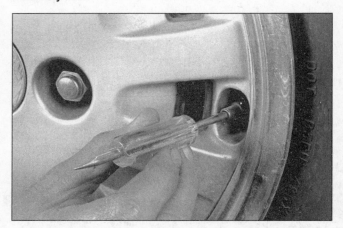

4.2 If a tyre loses air on a steady basis, check the valve core first to make sure it's snug (special tools for doing this are not expensive and are commonly available at motor factors)

4.3 If the valve core is tight, raise the corner of the vehicle with the low tyre and spray a soapy water solution onto the tread as the tyre is turned slowly - leaks will cause small bubbles to appear

4.4 To extend the life of the tyres, check the air pressure at least once a week with an accurate gauge (don't forget the spare!)

is not uncommon once the tyres are warm.

Unscrew the valve cap protruding from the wheel or hubcap and push the gauge firmly onto the valve stem **(see illustration)**. Note the reading on the gauge and compare the figure to the recommended tyre pressure shown on the placard on the driver's side door pillar or in the owner's handbook. Be sure to refit the valve cap to keep dirt and moisture out of the valve stem mechanism. Check all four tyres and, if necessary, add enough air to bring them up to the recommended pressure.

Wheel nut (or bolt) tightness

Loose wheel nuts (or bolts) present a very hazardous situation. Not only is the wheel in danger of falling off, but the brakes won't operate correctly and the vehicle won't come to a straight stop. It will pull to one side or the other, the pedal will pulsate, and there's a good chance the vehicle will go out of control.

If the vehicle that you're working on is equipped with

hubcaps, remove them. Using a wheel nut spanner or a socket and a long extension bar, check the tightness of all of the wheel nuts or bolts. None of them should be able to be tightened more than 1/8-turn. All vehicles have an actual torque specification for their wheel nuts or bolts, but the important thing here is that none are loose.

If you find any wheel nuts that are loose, be sure to check the wheel studs for damage, and the holes in the wheel for elongation. If any of the studs are damaged, renew them (don't attempt to clean up the threads with a die or thread file). The same goes for lug bolts. If any of the holes in the wheel are elongated, renew the wheel.

Brake fluid

The brake master cylinder is mounted in the upper right of the engine compartment, near the bulkhead, on most vehicles. On some models it's located on the passenger side of the engine compartment. On rear-engined vehicles, it's located in the luggage compartment (or inboard of the wing well, with a remote reservoir in the luggage compartment).

The fluid inside can be checked after removing the cover or cap **(see illustrations)**. Before removing the cover, be sure to wipe the top of the reservoir with a clean rag to prevent contamination of the brake system.

When adding fluid, pour it carefully into the reservoir to avoid spilling it on surrounding painted surfaces. Vehicles with translucent plastic reservoirs usually have maximum and minimum level marks - it isn't necessary to remove the cover or cap to check the fluid level **(see illustration)**. Be sure to keep the fluid level within this range. On models with integral reservoirs, add fluid until the level is within 1/4-inch from the top **(see illustration)**.

Most vehicles on the road use DOT 3 approved brake fluid, but it would be a good idea to check your owner's

4.5 On vehicles with this type of reservoir cover, prise the clip off the cover with a screwdriver

4.6 This master cylinder has two caps - each one must be removed to check the fluid level of both hydraulic circuits

handbook - some models (notably many Citroëns) use a type of mineral oil instead of brake fluid. Mixing the brake fluid with the mineral oil in one of these systems would destroy all of the rubber components in the hydraulic system and cause brake failure. **Warning:** *Brake fluid can harm your eyes and damage painted surfaces, so use extreme caution when handling or pouring it. Do not use brake fluid that has been standing open or is more than one year old. Brake fluid absorbs moisture from the air. Excess moisture can cause a dangerous loss of brake performance, because the moisture in the fluid can boil. If you get any fluid in your eyes, immediately flush your eyes with water and seek medical attention.*

At this time, the fluid and master cylinder can be inspected for contamination. The system should be drained and refilled if deposits, dirt particles or water droplets are seen in the fluid.

After filling the reservoir to the proper level, make sure the cover or cap is on tightly to prevent fluid leakage. Make sure the rubber diaphragm, if equipped, is in good condition.

If, upon checking the master cylinder fluid level, you discover one or both reservoirs empty or nearly empty, fill the reservoirs with brake fluid, bleed the system and check the entire hydraulic system for leaks (including behind the master cylinder).

Brake servo (vacuum-operated)

Begin the servo check by depressing the brake pedal

HINTS & TIPS

- The brake fluid level in the master cylinder will drop slightly as the pads at the front wheels wear down during normal operation. If the master cylinder requires repeated additions to keep it at the proper level, it's an indication of leakage in the brake system, which should be corrected immediately. Check all brake lines and connections as described later in this Chapter.

---

several times with the engine off to deplete any vacuum.

Now, depress the pedal and start the engine. If the pedal goes down slightly, operation is normal **(see illustration)**. Release the brake pedal and let the engine run for a couple of minutes.

Turn off the engine and depress the brake pedal several times slowly. If the pedal goes down farther the first time but gradually rises after the second or third depression, the servo is airtight **(see illustration)**.

Start the engine and depress the brake pedal, then stop the engine with the pedal still depressed. If there is

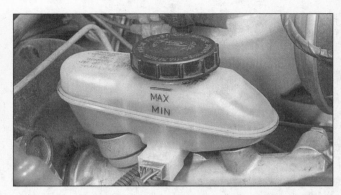

4.7   The brake fluid level in master cylinders with translucent plastic reservoirs is easily checked - the fluid level should be kept near the MAX mark

4.8 On master cylinders with integral, cast iron reservoirs, the brake fluid level should be kept at approximately 1/4-inch from the top

4.9 Push down on the brake pedal then start the engine - the brake pedal should go down slightly, indicating normal booster operation

4.10 With the engine turned off, the pedal should build up with each pump if the booster is functioning properly

no change in the reserve distance (the distance between the pedal and the floor) after holding the pedal for about 30-seconds, the servo is airtight.

If the pedal feels "hard" when the engine is running, the servo isn't operating properly. Refer to Chapter 9 for more servo checking procedures.

Brake pedal freeplay, "feel," and travel (master cylinder check)

Using your hand, push down on the pedal and note how far the pedal travels until resistance is felt **(see illustration)**. This is the pedal freeplay. It's important to have approximately 1/16 to 1/8-inch of freeplay, because this allows the pistons in the master cylinder to return to their at-rest positions when the brake pedal is released, ensuring that the compensating ports are uncovered and can equalise the pressure in the areas in front of the pistons.

Too much freeplay will result in a brake pedal that is too close to the floor under hard braking (it may even hit the floor). Generally, freeplay greater than one inch can be considered too much.

Pedal freeplay on some vehicles is adjusted at the master cylinder pushrod that protrudes from the servo. On other vehicles it's adjusted at the pushrod between the brake pedal and the servo.

If the vehicle is equipped with power brakes, start the engine. Slowly depress the brake pedal a few times. How does it feel? Is it firm or "spongy"? If it feels spongy or springy, chances are there's air in the hydraulic system, in which case it will be necessary to bleed the entire system (see Chapter 9). In addition, the entire system should be inspected for a fluid leak.

Now, with the engine still running, push the pedal down with a considerable amount of force. The pedal should come to a stop at some point and stay there. If the pedal slowly creeps towards the floor, check the entire hydraulic system for a fluid leak. If the pedal meets no resistance until it's a couple of inches from the floor, there's a strong possibility that there's a problem with one of the hydraulic circuits. If there is no evidence of an external fluid leak, the seals in the master cylinder are bad, in which case it must be rebuilt or renewed. See Chapter 9 for master cylinder removal and refitting, as well as the overhaul procedure.

HINTS & TIPS

- Air leaks can also develop in hydraulic systems without the presence of a fluid leak. When this happens, defective wheel cylinder cups are usually the culprit, although old caliper piston seals can cause the same problem.

4.11 There must be at least 1/16 to 1/8-inch freeplay in the brake pedal - if not, the master cylinder pistons won't be able to return all the way, which could result in a low pedal (because the pressure chambers in front of the pistons wouldn't fill up completely)

4.12 With your foot firmly pushing on the brake pedal, measure the distance between the bottom of the pedal and the floor (you may need the help of an assistant) - there should be at least two inches of reserve travel left

With the pedal firmly depressed, measure the distance between the pedal and the floor - this is the reserve distance **(see illustration)**. This specification varies from vehicle to vehicle, but generally there should be at least two inches to spare. Any less than this and you run the risk of the pedal contacting the floor before the brakes are fully utilised.

Inadequate reserve distance can be caused by worn-out brake linings or by a problem in the hydraulic circuit.

Brake warning light

The brake warning light on the instrument panel rarely fails, but it is a very important component of the brake system. Although in service it will usually come on only when you're in the midst of a braking problem, it can warn you of some problems before they become catastrophic.

On some models the brake warning light doubles as the "handbrake on" warning light. Refer to the owner's handbook for your vehicle for details of brake warning light operation, including checking procedures if appropriate.

Some vehicles have float-operated switches in their master cylinder reservoirs. If the fluid level drops below a certain level, the switch will complete the circuit and turn the warning light on. If your vehicle is like this, make sure the fluid is at the proper level.

Another type of warning light is operated by a switch which senses a pressure difference in the brake hydraulic circuits. If this type of light comes on, it indicates that there may be air or a leak in one half of the hydraulic system. Check the entire system for leaks.

If the light doesn't come on when it should, check the fuses. If they're all OK, check the bulb. If there's still a problem, it must be in the switch or in the wiring.

Brake lights

Have an assistant stand behind the vehicle while you depress the brake pedal. All of the brake lights should come on (on some vehicles the ignition key must be turned to the On position). If any bulbs are burned out, renew them.

If none of the lights come on, refer to Chapter 8 for further diagnosis.

Front brakes

Since your front brakes do most of the work, you should inspect them twice as often as the rear. Before removing the wheels, however, the wheel bearings should be checked for proper adjustment. Loose wheel bearings can cause a host of problems, such as inconsistent pedal travel, brake chatter, pedal pulsation, and the vehicle pulling to one side or the other when the brakes are applied. For this inspection, refer to the section titled "Wheel bearing, check, repack and adjustment." Take note, however, that not all wheel bearings are adjustable - some are sealed units which will require renewal if the bearings are sloppy. This includes the front hub bearings on front-wheel drive vehicles.

Drum brakes

If your vehicle is equipped with front drum brakes, refer to the section referenced in the previous paragraph ("Wheel bearing check, repack and adjustment") to remove the hub nut, then slide the drum off. If it won't come off, the shoes have probably begun to wear ridges into the drum and will have to be retracted. For this procedure and the remainder of the drum brake inspection, refer to the Drum brakes inspection procedure, under Rear brakes, since the procedure is the same as for rear drum brakes. When the inspection is complete, refit the drum and wheel bearings and adjust the bearings as described in the aforementioned sidebar. **Note:** *Be sure to clean, inspect and repack the bearings if they appear*

somewhat dry, dirty, or if it has been more than 20,000 miles since the last time they were packed. Also, adjust the brake shoes as described in the section entitled Drum brake adjustment.

While the wheels are off, be sure to check the brake hoses as described later in this Chapter.

Wheel bearing check, repack and adjustment

Note: *The wheel bearing repack and adjustment portions of this procedure do not apply to vehicles with sealed bearings or to the front axle of front-wheel drive or four-wheel drive vehicles, nor to the rear axle on vehicles with heavy-duty (full-floating) rear axles. If your vehicle falls into any of these categories, consult a shop manual or the appropriate Haynes Owners Workshop Manual.*

• In most cases the front wheel bearings will not need servicing until the brake pads are changed. However, the bearings should be checked whenever the front of the vehicle is raised for any reason. Several items, including a torque wrench and special grease, are required for this procedure **(see illustration)**.

Check

• Block the wheels at the opposite end of the vehicle being inspected, raise the appropriate end of the vehicle and support it securely on axle stands placed under the frame rails, subframe or the seam below the sills where the body is mated with the floorpan (monocoque vehicles only). Spin each wheel and check for noise, rolling resistance and freeplay.

• Grasp the top of each tyre with one hand and the bottom with the other. Move the wheel in-and-out on the spindle. If there's any noticeable movement, the bearings should be checked and then repacked with grease or renewed if necessary. **Note:** *In the case of vehicles with sealed bearing assemblies, the bearings aren't adjustable. Some sealed bearings are integral with the wheel hub, requiring renewal of the entire hub. Others have the sealed bearing assembly pressed into the hub, which will require the services of an automotive engineering works or other repair facility equipped with a hydraulic press and the necessary adapters to remove the old unit and press the new one in.*

Repack

Warning: *The dust created by the brake system may contain asbestos, which is harmful to your health. Never blow it out with compressed air and don't inhale any of it. An approved filtering mask should be worn when*

4.13 Tools and materials needed for front wheel bearing maintenance

1 **Hammer** - A common hammer will do just fine
2 **Grease** - High-temperature grease that is formulated specially for front wheel bearings should be used
3 **Wood block** - If you have a scrap piece of 2x4, it can be used to drive the new seal into the hub
4 **Needle-nose pliers** - Used to straighten and remove the split pin in the spindle
5 **Torque wrench** - This is very important in this procedure; if the bearing is too tight, the wheel won't turn freely - if it's too loose, the wheel will "wobble" on the spindle. Either way, it could mean extensive damage
6 **Screwdriver** - Used to remove the seal from the hub (a long screwdriver is preferred)
7 **Socket/extension bar** - Needed to loosen the nut on the spindle if it's extremely tight
8 **Brush** - Together with some clean solvent, this will be used to remove old grease from the hub and spindle

working on the brakes. Do not, under any circumstances, use petroleum-based solvents to clean brake parts. Use brake system cleaner only!

Note: *This procedure applies to adjustable wheel bearing assemblies on the front wheels of rear-wheel drive vehicles and the rear wheels of front-wheel drive vehicles.*

• Remove the wheel. You'll probably have to lower the vehicle to break the wheel nuts (or bolts) loose. After that, raise the vehicle and support it on axle stands once again. **Note:** *If you're simply adjusting the wheel bearings (not cleaning and repacking them), skip to Step 21.*

• If the wheel you're working on is equipped with a disc brake, remove the brake caliper (see Chapter 5) and hang it out of the way on a piece of wire. A wood block can be slid between the brake pads to keep them separated, if necessary.

• Prise the dust cap out of the hub using a screwdriver or hammer and chisel **(see illustration)**.

• Straighten the bent ends of the split pin, then pull the split pin out of the nut lock **(see illustration)**. Discard the split pin and use a new one during reassembly.

• Remove the nut lock, nut and washer from the end of the spindle **(see illustration)**.

• Pull the hub/disc or drum assembly out slightly, then push it back into its original position. This should force the outer bearing off the spindle enough so it can be removed.

• Pull the hub/disc or drum assembly off the spindle. If you're working on a drum brake and the drum won't pull off, the brake shoes will have to be retracted. Refer to the shoe retraction procedure described in the Drum brakes subheading under the Rear brakes section.

• Use a screwdriver to prise the seal out of the rear of the hub **(see illustration)**. As this is done, note how the seal is refitted.

• Remove the inner wheel bearing from the hub.

4.14 Dislodge the dust cap by working around the outer circumference with a hammer and chisel

4.15 Remove the split pin and discard it - use a new one when the hub nut is reinstalled

4.16 Exploded view of a typical hub and wheel bearing assembly

4.17 Use a large screwdriver to prise the grease seal out of the rear of the hub

4.18 Work grease into the bearing rollers by pressing it against the palm of your hand

• Use solvent to remove all traces of the old grease from the bearings, hub and spindle. A small brush may prove helpful; however make sure no bristles from the brush embed themselves inside the bearing rollers. Allow the parts to air dry.

• Carefully inspect the bearings for cracks, heat discolouration, worn rollers, etc. Check the bearing races inside the hub for wear and damage. If the bearing races are defective, the hubs should be taken to a machine shop with the facilities to remove the old races and press new ones in. Note that the bearings and races come as matched sets and old bearings should never be fitted on new races.

• Use high-temperature wheel bearing grease to pack the bearings. Work the grease completely into the bearings, forcing it between the rollers, cone and cage from the back side **(see illustration)**.

• Apply a thin coat of grease to the spindle at the outer bearing seat, inner bearing seat, shoulder and seal seat.

• Put a small quantity of grease inboard of each bearing race inside the hub. Using your finger, form a dam at these points to provide extra grease availability and to keep thinned grease from flowing out of the bearing.

• Place the grease-packed inner bearing into the rear of the hub and put a little more grease outboard of the bearing.

• Place a new seal over the inner bearing and tap the seal evenly into place with a hammer and blunt punch until it's flush with the hub.

• Carefully place the hub assembly onto the spindle and push the grease-packed outer bearing into position.

Adjustment

Note: *This is a general procedure which applies to most adjustable wheel bearing assemblies on the front wheels of rear-wheel drive vehicles and the rear wheels of front-wheel drive vehicles.*

• Refit the washer and spindle nut. Tighten the nut only slightly (no more than 12 lbf ft).

• Spin the hub in a forward direction while tightening the spindle nut to approximately 20 lbf ft to seat the bearings and remove any grease or burrs which could cause excessive bearing play later.

• Loosen the spindle nut 1/4-turn, then using your hand (not a spanner of any kind), tighten the nut until it's snug. Refit the nut lock and a new split pin through the hole in the spindle and the slots in the nut lock. If the nut lock slots don't line up, remove the nut lock and turn it slightly until they do. Ideally, when the wheel bearings are properly adjusted there should be no play in the bearings, but no preload either. You should be able to push the washer under the lock nut back and forth with a screwdriver (without prising), but you shouldn't be able to feel any slop in the bearing. **Note:** *If you do feel some play in the bearing, tighten the hub nut a little more than hand-tight, but don't exceed 10 or 15 inch-pounds of preload. If there's still play, the wheel bearings may be excessively worn.*

• Bend the ends of the split pin until they're flat against the nut. Cut off any extra length which could interfere with the dust cap.

• Refit the dust cap, tapping it into place with a hammer.

• On models with disc brakes, place the brake caliper near the disc and carefully remove the wood spacer. Refit the caliper (see Chapter 5).

• Refit the wheel on the hub and tighten the wheel nuts.

• Grasp the top and bottom of the tyre and check the bearings in the manner described earlier in Steps 2 and 3.

• Lower the vehicle.

Disc brakes

Warning: *The dust created by the brake system may contain asbestos, which is harmful to your health. Never blow it out with compressed air and don't inhale any of it. An approved filtering mask should be worn when working on the brakes. Do not, under any circumstances, use petroleum-based solvents to clean brake parts. Use brake system cleaner only!*

Disc brakes are used on the front wheels of most vehicles. Extensive disc damage can occur if the pads are not renewed when needed.

Loosen the wheel nuts, raise the front of the vehicle and support it securely on axle stands placed under the frame rails, subframe or the seam below the sills where the body is mated with the floorpan (monocoque constructed vehicles only), if not already done. Block the wheels at the opposite end of the vehicle to prevent it from rolling. The disc brake calipers, which contain the pads, are visible with the wheels removed. There is an outer pad and an inner pad in each caliper. All pads should be inspected.

Before inspecting the brakes, position a drain pan under the brake assembly, clean the entire brake with brake system cleaner and allow it to dry.

Most calipers have a "window" or opening to inspect the pads. Check the thickness of the pad lining by looking into the caliper at each end and down through the inspection window at the top of the housing **(see illustrations)**. If the pad material has worn to the manufacturer's minimum recommended thickness, the pads should be renewed. Ideally, the pads should be changed before they become that thin. Some pads are equipped with metal wear sensors, consisting of a small, bent piece of metal which is attached to the backing plate of one of the brake pads. When the pad wears

4.19 Look through the caliper inspection window to inspect the brake pads (arrow)

4.20 The pad lining which rubs against the disc (arrow) can also be inspected by looking at each end of the caliper

4.21 The brake wear indicator (arrow) will contact the disc and make a squealing noise when the pad is worn out

down to its specified limit, the metal sensor rubs against the disc and makes a squealing sound **(see illustration)**. If your vehicle is equipped with such sensors, and the tips of the sensors are nearing the disc surface, you might as well go ahead and renew the brake pads.

If you're unsure about the exact thickness of the remaining lining material, remove the pads for further inspection or renewal (see Chapter 5).

Make sure the caliper mounting bolts, guide pins or retaining plates (depending on caliper design) are secure. Also check the tightness of the caliper mounting (or anchor) plate fasteners, if equipped.

Check around the area of the caliper piston bore(s) for wetness, which would indicate a leaking piston seal. On fixed calipers, check around the transfer tube fittings (if equipped) or at the seam where the caliper halves mate. If the caliper is leaking, refer to Chapter 9 and rebuild or renew the calipers.

If the brake pedal has been pulsating, the discs are probably warped. Refer to Chapter 5 and measure the disc runout with a dial indicator.

Before refitting the wheels, check for leakage and/or damage (cracks, splitting, etc.) around the brake hoses and connections, as described later in this Chapter.

Check the condition of the disc as described in Chapter 5.

Brake hoses and lines

About every six months, with the vehicle raised and supported securely on axle stands, the rubber hoses which connect the steel brake lines with the front and rear brake assemblies should be inspected for cracks, chafing of the outer cover, leaks, blisters and other damage **(see illustration)**. These are important and vulnerable parts of the brake system and inspection should be complete. A light and mirror will be helpful for a thorough check. If a hose exhibits any of the above conditions, renew it.

Internally split brake hoses

Some of the trickiest brake problems to diagnose are caused by internally split brake hoses. This malady can restrict pressure from reaching a brake, or it can act like a one-way valve and cause the brake to lock up **(see illustration)**. This is not a common problem, and mostly affects older vehicles with neglected brake systems. It can also be caused by clamping a brake hose shut with locking pliers - something that should never be done.

If you're faced with a brake that won't release, which may be characterised by the vehicle pulling to one side or an overheated brake, open the bleed valve on that

4.22 Here are some samples of common brake hose defects

SOFTENING   CRACKING

SWOLLEN   LEAKAGE

PRESSURE TO BRAKE
BLOCKED - OFF

PRESSURE TRAPPED
IN BRAKE, PREVENTING
IT FROM RELEASING

2112-4-4.23 HAYNES

4.23 An internally split hose can be very difficult to diagnose

particular caliper or wheel cylinder. If the disc or drum now turns, suspect an internally split hose. Renew the hose and bleed the system (see Chapter 9).

Conversely, if one brake (or both rear brakes on models with a solid rear axle) will not apply but the rest do, there are two possibilities - a "seized" caliper (or wheel cylinder), or an internally split hose that refuses to pass fluid. Attach a bleeder hose to the bleeder screw on the brake that won't apply. Have an assistant depress the brake pedal while you crack open the bleeder screw. If fluid flows out the bleeder hose, the brake hose is OK - the caliper or wheel cylinder is malfunctioning. If no fluid flows out of the bleeder hose, follow the brake hose to where it meets the metal brake line. Disconnect the line and have your helper push the brake pedal - if fluid squirts from the line, the problem is an internally split brake hose. Renew the hose and bleed the system.

The metal brake lines should also be inspected. While they aren't subjected to the same punishment that the brake hoses are, they're still fair game to objects thrown up from the tyres, and to vibration. Make sure all of the metal clips securing the lines are in place. Check the lines for twists, dents, crimping and kinks **(see illustration)**. Make sure none of the lines travel too close to any hot or moving parts. If you find a damaged section of line, it should be renewed with a genuine factory renewal part, or equivalent, with the lines pre-bent and the fittings already in place. Never attempt to repair a brake line with rubber hose, and never use

TWISTED

DENTED

CRIMPED

BENT

4.24 Typical metal brake line defects

substandard materials to fabricate a line. Brake lines are made of high-quality seamless, double-thickness steel tubing. They are coated (usually with a copper-lead alloy) to prevent corrosion.

Rear brakes

If you're working on a front-wheel drive vehicle, it's a good idea to check the rear wheel bearing adjustment before proceeding with the brake check. See the section entitled "Wheel bearing check, repack and adjustment" for this procedure.

Disc brakes

If your vehicle is fortunate enough to be equipped with rear disc brakes, refer to the disc brake inspection procedure under the Front brakes subheading. The procedures are identical.

Drum brakes

Warning: *The dust created by the brake system may contain asbestos, which is harmful to your health. Never blow it out with compressed air and don't inhale any of it. An approved filtering mask should be worn when working on the brakes. Do not, under any circumstances, use petroleum-based solvents to clean brake parts. Use brake system cleaner only!*

Loosen the wheel nuts or bolts, raise the vehicle and support it securely on axle stands placed under the frame rails, subframe, the seam below the sills where the body is mated with the floorpan (monocoque constructed vehicles only) or under the rear axle housing (vehicles with solid rear axles only), if not already done. Block the wheels at the opposite end of the vehicle to prevent it from rolling. Release the handbrake.

Some vehicles are equipped with a rubber plug in the brake backing plate (or in the drum on some models) near the edge of the drum. When removed, the brake shoe lining is visible through the hole **(see illustration)**. This is sufficient for a quick check of the brake shoes, but for a thorough check, the drums must be removed.

Remove the brake drum. If you're working on the rear brakes of a front-wheel drive vehicle, or on a vehicle with front drum brakes, and the drum is integral with the hub, refer to the section entitled "Wheel bearing check, repack and adjustment" for the removal procedure. If the hubs on your vehicle are sealed, but retained by a lock nut, remove the nut and discard it (a new one should be used upon reassembly). If the drum is not integral with the hub, remove it by pulling it off the axle and brake assembly. **Note:** *Some brake drums are*

4.25 Some vehicles are equipped with holes in the backing plates (or in the brake drums) that allow you to view the brake lining thickness

4.27 Push the self-adjusting lever aside and turn the star wheel

4.26 Use a hammer and chisel to remove the plug from the brake backing plate or brake drum

4.28 Here's a cutaway view of the retracting procedure. The screwdriver is pushing the adjuster lever off the star wheel, while the adjusting tool (if you don't have one, another screwdriver can be used) turns the star wheel to reduce the length of the adjuster screw. This allows the shoes to move away from the drum, providing clearance for drum removal.

retained to the axle flange by two or three small screws. If this proves difficult, make sure the handbrake is released, then squirt penetrating oil around the centre hub area and around the wheel studs. Allow the oil to soak in and try to pull the drum off again.

If the drum still cannot be pulled off, the brake shoes will have to be retracted. This is done by first removing the small rubber plug from the backing plate or brake drum. On some vehicles there is a lanced cut-out in the backing plate or drum instead of a plug. If this is the case, knock the lanced portion out with a hammer and chisel **(see illustration)** (you'll retrieve it after the drum has been removed). **Note:** *Rubber plugs are available from a dealer service department or car accessory shop - be sure to fit one in the hole when you're done.*

With the plug removed, insert a thin screwdriver and lift or push the adjusting lever off the star wheel, then use an adjusting tool or screwdriver to back off the star wheel several turns **(see illustrations)**. This will move the brake shoes away from the drum. If the drum still won't pull off, tap around its inner circumference with a soft-face hammer.

With the drum removed, do not touch any brake dust (see the Warning at the beginning of this Section). Position a drain pan under the brake assembly, clean the entire brake with brake system cleaner and allow it to dry.

Observe the thickness of the lining material on both brake shoes. If the material has worn away to within 1/16-inch of the recessed rivets or metal backing, the shoes should be renewed **(see illustrations)**. The shoes should also be renewed if they're cracked, glazed (shiny surface) or contaminated with brake fluid, grease or gear oil.

Make sure that all the brake assembly springs are connected and in good condition.

Check the brake components for any signs of fluid leakage. If the brake linings are wet, identify the source of the fluid. If it's gear oil, the rear axle seal is leaking

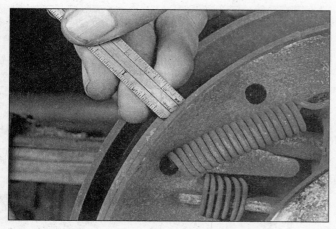

4.29 The lining thickness of a brake shoe with bonded lining is measured from the outer surface of the lining to the metal shoe - be sure to check both ends and in the centre

4.30 A tyre tread depth gauge works well for measuring the thickness of the remaining material on brake shoes with riveted linings

4.31 Carefully peel the wheel cylinder boot back and check for leaking fluid - any leakage indicates the cylinder must be replaced or rebuilt

and must be renewed. Carefully prise back the rubber dust boots on the wheel cylinders located between the brake shoes **(see illustration)**. Any leakage is an indication that the wheel cylinders should be overhauled immediately (see Chapter 9). Check the brake hoses and connections for signs of leakage.

Clean the inside of the drum with brake system cleaner. Again, be careful not to breathe the dangerous asbestos dust.

Check the inside of the drum for cracks, score marks, deep scratches and hard spots, which will appear as small discolourations. If these imperfections cannot be removed with fine emery cloth, the drum must be taken to a machine shop equipped to resurface the drums.

If, after the inspection process all parts are in good working condition, refit the brake drum. If it was necessary to retract the brake shoes to get the drum off, adjust the brake shoes (see the sidebar on drum brake adjustment). If your vehicle has sealed hubs retained by a locknut, tighten the nut securely (preferably you should consult a Haynes Owners Workshop Manual that covers your particular vehicle).

Refit the wheels and lower the vehicle.

Drum brake adjustment

Most drum brakes are equipped with self-adjusters but some (mainly on older vehicles) are not, and will need periodic adjustment to compensate for wear. Even the brake shoes on self-adjusting drum brakes have to be adjusted when they are first fitted. This is because the self-adjusters maintain a specified clearance between the brake shoe lining and the drum, but won't compensate for a large gap (not until after many applications of the footbrake or handbrake, depending on design). Brakes that are out of adjustment will result a low pedal condition and can also cause the vehicle to pull to one side or the other when the brakes are applied.

Loosen the wheel nuts or bolts, raise the vehicle and support it securely on axle stands placed under the frame rails, subframe, the seam below the sills where the body is mated with the floorpan (monocoque constructed vehicles only) or under the rear axle housing (vehicles with solid rear axles only), if not already done. Block the wheels at the opposite end of the vehicle to prevent it from rolling. Release the handbrake if you're adjusting rear drum brakes.

Remove the adjustment hole plug(s) in the brake backing plate or drum, if applicable. Rotate the wheel and make sure that the handbrake isn't causing any brake drag. If there is any drag, back off the handbrake adjusting nut. Using a screwdriver or brake adjusting tool used in the correct location, turn the adjuster star

4.32 On some older vehicles, the adjuster is slotted and can be turned with a screwdriver - this turns an eccentric which spreads the shoes apart (or conversely, allows them to retract)

4.33 Other older vehicles also use eccentric adjusters, but the adjuster screw is a square-drive affair protruding from the backing plate

wheel or the adjuster screw until the drum is locked in place **(see illustrations)**. Some brakes (leading/leading shoe brakes [see Chapter 1]) have two adjusters. If you are working on one of these kinds of brakes, adjust the shoes one at a time.

Now, back-off the star wheel or adjuster screw eight to ten notches, or just to the point where the drum rotates freely without the brake shoes dragging (if the shoes are allowed to drag they may get too hot and expand, causing the drum to bind). To accomplish this it will be necessary to disengage the adjusting lever from the star wheel by inserting a thin screwdriver through the hole in the backing plate or drum, pushing or pulling the lever off the star wheel **(see illustration)**. **Note:** *Leading/leading shoe brakes don't have adjuster levers - simply turn the star wheel in the other direction to back-off the shoes.*

4.34 Here's the most common kind of adjuster set-up. Insert a screwdriver through the hole in the backing plate (or brake drum) and turn the adjuster star wheel until the brake shoes drag on the drum . . .

4.35 . . . then, using another screwdriver or an adjusting tool, push (or pull) the lever off the adjuster wheel and back it off 8 to 10 clicks

If necessary, adjust the handbrake as described later in this Chapter.

Refit the wheels and lower the vehicle.

Handbrake

The handbrake or parking brake is lever, pullrod or pedal operated and, on most vehicles, is self-adjusting through the automatic adjusters in the rear brake drums (a very few manufacturers place the handbrake on the front wheels). However, supplementary adjustment may be needed in the event of cable stretch, wear in the linkage or after fitting of new components.

Check

Check the entire length of each handbrake cable for wear, fraying, rust, kinks, etc. Apply multi-purpose grease to all friction areas and to the adjuster screw(s)

Many vehicles have a specification as to how many clicks the handbrake lever or pedal is supposed to ratchet, but the most obvious method to check the adjustment of the handbrake is to park the vehicle on a hill or on a steep driveway, apply the handbrake and place the transmission in Neutral (be sure to stay in the car during this check). The lever or pedal should ratchet anywhere between five and eight clicks or so. If the vehicle rolls, the handbrake should be adjusted.

Adjustment

If your handbrake is lever-actuated, look through the slot in the centre console or peel back the boot and look for the end(s) of the handbrake cable(s) and the adjusting nut(s). If your vehicle has this set-up, apply the handbrake two clicks and tighten the nut until the handbrake lever travel is within reason **(see illustration)**. It may be necessary to remove the centre console for access to the nut(s). If there are two cables, tighten each nut equally. If the handbrake is pullrod-actuated, look up under the dash for a turnbuckle-type adjuster **(see illustration)**. On other models, the equaliser (the point where the front cable meets the rear cables) is located under the centre console, which will require removal of the console **(see illustration)**. Raise the rear of the vehicle, support it securely on axle stands and release the handbrake. Turn the wheels to confirm that the brakes are not dragging.

On many cars and vans the adjuster is located under the vehicle. Raise the rear of the vehicle (or the front on vehicles with the handbrake on the front wheels) until the wheels are clear of the earth, support it securely on axle stands and block the front wheels. Release the handbrake pedal or lever.

Locate the handbrake equaliser. Hold the rod from turning with locking pliers, then loosen the locknut, if equipped, and tighten the adjuster nut **(see illustrations)** until a slight drag is felt when the rear wheels are turned. **Note:** *If the threads appear rusty, apply penetrating oil before attempting adjustment.*

Loosen the adjuster nut until there's no longer any drag when the rear wheels are turned, then loosen the cable adjusting nut an additional two turns.

Tighten the locknut, then apply and release the handbrake several times. Confirm that the brakes do not drag. Lower the vehicle to the earth.

Handbrake shoe adjustment (vehicles with rear disc brakes containing a drum style handbrake)

This kind of handbrake set-up is almost identical to a full-size service drum brake assembly, only smaller, and its actuation is not hydraulic, but mechanical. It even has an adjuster screw with a star wheel. To adjust the shoes on this kind of handbrake (which will almost never need adjustment, unless you occasionally forget to release the handbrake before driving) refer to the sidebar entitled "Drum brake adjustment."

4.36a On some vehicles, the handbrake cable is adjusted at the lever

4.36b On some vehicles with pullrod-actuated handbrakes, the adjuster is located up under the dash

4.37 The handbrake equaliser on this vehicle is located underneath the centre console - once the console has been removed, the handbrake can be adjusted by tightening this nut (arrow) at the equaliser

Brake pedal and bracket

Rarely do problems develop in this area, but when they do they have the potential to be very serious. Therefore, it's a good idea to crawl under the dash periodically and inspect the pedal pivot and the support bracket.

Working under the dash, grasp the pedal and wiggle it from side-to-side. If there's any slop in the pedal

Chapter 4

bushes, the bushes should be renewed **(see illustration)** (see Chapter 8).

Also, be sure to check the pedal for distortion and fatigue.

Brake fluid renewal

As stated in the maintenance schedule, many manufacturers don't actually specify an interval for replacing the brake fluid, but it's a great preventive maintenance step. Dirty, contaminated, moisture-laden fluid will deteriorate brake system components and, besides leaks, can cause dangerous problems like boiling fluid and loss of braking pressure.

To renew the fluid in your hydraulic system, simply bleed the brakes at each wheel until clean, clear brake fluid flows out. If performed at the interval specified, this method is sufficient.

Master cylinder seal check

Unbolt the master cylinder (without disconnecting the lines), pull it forward off the servo or bulkhead and

4.38 In this arrangement, the handbrake cable is located at the rear of the vehicle, where the left and right cables meet - to adjust, hold the threaded rod with a pair of pliers and turn the adjusting nut

4.39 On this type of handbrake cable equaliser, simply hold the threaded rod stationary and turn the nut to adjust the cable

check for leakage. You won't find this item on any manufacturer's maintenance schedule, but leaks can develop in the master cylinder and fluid can escape past the secondary cup or O-ring of the primary piston. This can go unnoticed for a long time. The dropping fluid level may at first be mistaken for normal brake pad wear, when in actuality it is leaking into the power servo (which will damage the servo) or onto the floor in the driver's footwell (which will damage the driver's shoes).

Rebuild or renew the master cylinder if you find leakage (see Chapter 9).

Rebuild or renew the hydraulic cylinders (master cylinder, calipers and/or wheel cylinders)

This is another maintenance item that isn't recommended by all manufacturers. You might even think it sounds like a waste of money and time. But, it's a sure way to know that your hydraulic components are in top shape. Brake pads and shoes are easy to check, and you can gauge how they are wearing just by looking at them. You can't see inside of a master cylinder or caliper, though, so you really don't know what kind of shape they're in. Refer to Chapter 9 for the rebuilding or renewal procedures.

1	Retaining clip	6	Brake pedal	11	Actuator lever
2	Bush	7	Actuator	12	Spacer
3	Pinch bolt	8	Bolt	13	Retaining clip
4	Washer	9	Pushrod		
5	Nut	10	Washer		

4.40 Typical brake pedal mounting details

Chapter 5
Disc brakes

Introduction

This Chapter is divided into two sections: Brake pad renewal and Brake disc inspection, removal and refitting.

The first section is subdivided into three parts and depicts the brake pad renewal procedures for fixed calipers, sliding calipers and floating calipers, in that order. If you aren't sure which kind of caliper you're about to work on, refer to Chapter 1 and read the information on caliper design under the Disc brakes subheading.

If you're renewing rear brake pads, refer to the appropriate sub-section, depending on caliper design, and follow the procedure outlined there. However, if you're working on a vehicle that has rear calipers with integral handbrake mechanisms, don't attempt to push the piston into its bore with a C-clamp - refer to the section entitled "Rear brake pad renewal - calipers with integral handbrake mechanisms."

The second section deals with inspection, removal and refitting of the brake disc.

Information on brake caliper overhaul can be found in Chapter 9.

Brake pad renewal

Warning: *Disc brake pads must be renewed on both front or rear wheels at the same time - never renew the pads on only one wheel. Also, the dust created by the brake system may contain asbestos, which is harmful to your health. Never blow it out with compressed air and don't inhale any of it. An approved filtering mask should be worn when working on the brakes. Do not, under any circumstances, use petroleum-based solvents to clean brake parts. Use brake system cleaner only!*

Note 1: *When servicing the brakes, use only high-quality, nationally recognised brand-name pads.*

Note 2: *This procedure also applies to the rear disc brakes on vehicles equipped with a separate handbrake mechanism (not built into the caliper). If you're working on a vehicle that has rear calipers with integral handbrake mechanisms, don't attempt to push the piston into its bore with a C-clamp - refer to the section entitled "Rear brake pad renewal - calipers with integral handbrake mechanisms."*

The brake pad renewal procedures are covered through a sequence of illustrations, laid out in order from removing the old pads to fitting the new ones. The captions presented with the illustrations will walk you through the entire procedure, one step at a time. Work only on one brake assembly at a time, using the assembled brake for reference, if necessary.

Regardless of the type of brake you're working on, there are a few preliminary steps to be taken before yanking the old pads out. First, park the vehicle on a level surface, open the bonnet and locate the master cylinder - it's usually mounted on the bulkhead or the brake servo on the driver's side of the bulkhead (but on some vehicles it's on the other side of the engine compartment). Cover all painted areas around the master cylinder (wing included), remove the reservoir cover or cap(s) and remove about half of the fluid from the reservoir. It is necessary to do this so the reservoir doesn't overflow when the caliper piston(s) is pushed back into its bore to make room for the new pads. This can be accomplished with a suction pump, a siphoning kit or an old poultry baster or hydrometer. **Warning:** *Brake fluid is poisonous - don't start the siphoning action by mouth. If you use a poultry baster, never again use that baster for cooking!* Discard the fluid.

If you haven't already done so, this is a good time to put on your filtering mask, latex gloves and eye protection. Your hands aren't too dirty yet, and brake dust tends to get all over the wheels and inside of the wheel covers, so put them on before removing the wheels.

Next, remove the wheel covers (if fitted) from the front wheels and loosen the wheel nuts about one-half turn. Raise the vehicle and support it securely on axle stands. Remove the wheels, but remember to only work on one brake at a time.

Before touching or disassembling anything, clean the caliper, pads and disc with brake system cleaner and allow it to dry **(see illustration)**. Don't ever use compressed air or a brush to remove the brake dust.

Now, refer to the appropriate procedure under Fixed caliper brake pad renewal, Sliding caliper brake pad renewal or Floating caliper brake pad renewal. Be sure to stay in order and read the captions that accompany each illustration. Before fitting the new pads, inspect the brake discs as outlined later in this Chapter. If machining is necessary, remove the discs and have them resurfaced by an automotive machine shop (if they are still thick enough to undergo machining). **Note:** *Professionals recommend resurfacing the brake discs whenever replacing the brake pads, as this will produce*

5.1 Before removing anything, clean the caliper and pads with brake cleaner and allow it to dry. Position a drain pan under the brake to catch the residue. DO NOT USE COMPRESSED AIR TO BLOW THE DUST FROM THE PARTS!

a smooth, flat surface that will eliminate brake pedal pulsations and other undesirable symptoms related to questionable discs. At the very least, if you elect not to have the discs resurfaced, deglaze them with sandpaper or emery cloth, using a swirling motion to ensure a non-directional finish. Be careful not to get grease on the brake disc or brake pads.

After you have successfully fitted the pads on one side of the vehicle, repeat the procedure on the other brake.

There are also a couple of things you must do before you can call the job complete. As soon as you have lowered the vehicle and tightened the wheel nuts securely, check the brake fluid level in the master cylinder reservoir. If necessary, add some to bring it to the desired level (see Chapter 4). Refit the reservoir cover or cap, but don't close the bonnet yet.

Before starting the engine, depress the brake pedal a few times to bring the pads into contact with the disc. The pedal will go to the floor for the first couple of pumps, but will build up after that. If this is not done, you'll probably crash into something on the other side of the street after you back out of your driveway!

Now that you have a solid brake pedal, recheck the fluid level. It may have gone down some as the piston(s) in the caliper were forced outward, shoving the pads up against the discs.

Lastly, before committing the vehicle to normal service, road test it in an isolated area, if possible. For the first few hundred miles or so, try to avoid hard braking to allow the new pads to bed in.

Fixed caliper

Warning: *The dust created by the brake system may contain asbestos, which is harmful to your health. Never blow it out with compressed air and don't inhale any of it. An approved filtering mask should be worn when working on the brakes. Do not, under any circumstances, use petroleum-based solvents to clean brake parts. Use brake system cleaner only!*

Tools required (these will suffice for most applications, however, the calipers on your vehicle may differ slightly):

Jack and axle stands
Wheel nut (or bolt) spanner
Filtering mask
Safety glasses or goggles
Latex gloves
Hammer
Pin punch
Needle-nose pliers
Crowbar or large screwdriver (two in the case of three- or four-piston calipers)

Materials required

Brake pads
Brake system cleaner
Brake anti-squeal compound
High-temperature brake grease
Brake fluid
Split pins (if applicable)

1 Retaining pins
2 Spring clip or split
   pin
3 Dust cover
4 Bleeder screw
5 Caliper body
6 Piston (inner)
7 Piston seal
8 Dust boot
9 Pad assembly
10 Anti-rattle spring
11 Dust boot
12 Piston seal
13 Piston (outer)

5.2 Exploded view of a typical fixed brake caliper assembly

Remove the old brake pads

5.3 If equipped, prise off the cover from the caliper, noting how it's fitted

5.4 Some vehicles are equipped with electric wear sensors that plug unto the pads. When the pads wear down to the sensors, the probes on the sensors earth out on the brake disc, completing the circuit and turning on a light on the instrument panel. To remove these sensors, pull them out of their mounting slots with a pair of pliers. Note: If the pads have worn down to the sensors, be sure to renew the sensors.

5.5 The brake pads on most fixed calipers are held in the caliper with one or two retaining pins. The retaining pins are usually secured by split pins, spring-steel clips or the ends of the anti-rattle springs. If your retaining pin has a split pin like this one, remove the split pin and discard it (a new split pin must be used when refitting). If spring steel clips or the ends of the anti-rattle springs secure the retaining pins, pull them out with a pair of pliers

5.6 On some vehicles, the pads aren't secured by retaining pins, but are trapped in the caliper with two hold-down clips. To remove the clips, unscrew the bolts (arrows)

5.7 This caliper has retaining pins secured by spring steel clips. It also is equipped with anti-rattle springs - be careful not to let the springs fly out as you remove the retaining pins.

5.8 Use a hammer and a small punch to knock the retaining pin(s) out of the caliper. Note: Some retaining pins, like the pins on this Mercedes, don't have retaining clips or split pins. Instead, the retaining pins are fitted with spring-steel collars around their heads that fit tightly into the holes in the caliper frame (if they don't fit tightly, renew them).

A Pad retaining pin
B Spring clip
C Anti-squeal shim
    (note the
    directional arrow)
D Anti-rattle spring
E Brake pad

5.9 Typical brake pad arrangement on a fixed caliper

5.10 After removing the pad retaining pin(s), pull out one of the old brake pads (not both). You may need to use a pair of pliers to free the pad.

Preparation for fitting

5.11 To make room for the new, thicker pad, push the caliper piston straight back into its bore as far as possible. A crowbar or large screwdriver will work. If the caliper half has two pistons in it, you'll need two crowbars. Caution: Be careful not to cock the piston sideways at all - damage to the caliper bore or the piston seal could result. Before fitting the new pad, check for fluid leakage around the caliper piston. If any is found, rebuild or renew the calipers (see Chapter 9).

5.12 Prepare the new brake pads for fitting by applying an anti-squeal compound to the backing plate (1) and a light film of high-temperature brake grease to the edges of the pads where they ride in the caliper (2). Both of these items can be purchased at your local car accessory shop. Allow a few minutes for the compound to "set up" before fitting the pads. Note: Be sure to clean the caliper in the area where the brake pads make contact. Warning: Do not touch the pad friction material - if you get any grease on the pad, remove it immediately with brake system cleaner.

Fit the new pads

5.13 Insert the new pad into the caliper, along with the anti-squeal shim, if one was present when you took the old pad out. Note: Many anti-squeal shims are directional - they have an arrow stamped in them that must point in the same direction as the forward rotation of the brake disc. Remember, don't get any grease on the pad lining. After fitting the pad, repeat Steps 5.10 to 5.13 on the other pad.

5.14 Refit the retaining pins and anti-rattle springs (if equipped), or the hold-down springs. On this design, the rather stiff anti-rattle spring must be held down as the retaining pin is inserted.

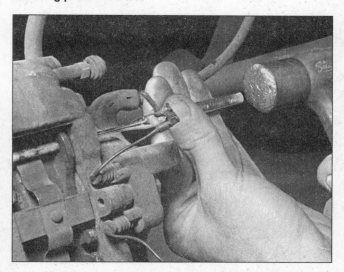

5.15 Continue to drive the pins fully in. On models that use clips to secure the retaining pins, they can simply be pushed in, but on pins with spring-steel collars like this Mercedes, you'll have to knock them in until they're seated. Install the retaining pin clip(s) or cotter pin(s). If equipped with pad wear sensors, insert the probes of the sensors into the holes in the pad material, then seat the sensor in the cutout in the pad backing plate.

All models

Repeat the entire procedure to renew the pads on the other wheel. Don't forget to pump the pedal a few times to bring the pads into contact with the disc. Be sure to then check the brake fluid level.

Sliding caliper

Warning: *The dust created by the brake system may contain asbestos, which is harmful to your health. Never blow it out with compressed air and don't inhale any of it. An approved filtering mask should be worn when working on the brakes. Do not, under any circumstances, use petroleum-based solvents to clean brake parts. Use brake system cleaner only!*

Tools required (these will suffice for most applications, however, the calipers on your vehicle may differ slightly):

Jack and axle stands
Wheel nut (or bolt) spanner
Filtering mask
Safety glasses or goggles
Latex gloves
Large C-clamp
Needle-nose pliers
Length of wire (a straightened-out coat-hanger will work)
Spanner, socket, Allen key or hammer and punch, depending on caliper design (to remove caliper bolts or pins)

Materials required

Brake system cleaner
Brake pads
Retaining clips, anti-rattle springs, caliper pins or keys (depending on caliper design), if damaged
Brake anti-squeal compound
High-temperature brake grease (slide rail grease)
Thread locking compound (non-hardening) (for calipers that are secured by bolts)
Brake fluid

Remove the caliper

5.16 On most calipers, a C-clamp can be used to depress the piston into its bore; this aids removal of the caliper and fitting of the new pads. If the design of the caliper doesn't permit this, the piston(s) can be depressed after the caliper has been removed. DO NOT attempt this on rear calipers with integral handbrake mechanisms.

5.17 On calipers held in place with a retainer clip and anti-rattle spring, unscrew the bolt and remove the clip and spring from each end of the caliper. Inspect the clip and anti-rattle spring for cracks or distortion. If any are found, renew all the anti-rattle springs and clips.

5.18 If your caliper is retained by pins that are driven into the slot between the caliper and the caliper mounting (sometimes called the caliper bracket), squeeze the end of the lower caliper pin with a pair of pliers and knock the pin into the groove as far as possible . . .

5.19 . . . then use a hammer and punch to drive the pin out completely. Proceed to remove the upper pin in the same manner. Check the pins for rust or other damage. If they were very easy to remove or appear damaged, renew them.

5.20 If the caliper on your vehicle is secured by a key, remove the key retaining bolt (some use Allen head bolts, others use conventional hex-head bolts) . . .

5.21 . . . then drive the caliper key out with a hammer and punch (be careful not to lose the caliper support spring). Check the key and support spring for damage and wear, replacing them if necessary.

5.22 Another retention method, although somewhat less common, uses guide plates that wedge the caliper into the mounting. To remove the caliper, pull out the retaining pin from the guide plate . . .

5.23 . . . then tap out the guide plate with a punch and hammer. Check the retaining pins and guide plates for wear. Renew as necessary.

5.24 After the retention devices have been removed, lift the caliper up and off the brake disc. Take care not to kink or pull on the brake hose

5.25 If the caliper isn't going to be removed for service, suspend it with a length of wire - DON'T let it hang by the brake hose. Now would be a good time to check around the caliper piston for leakage. Carefully prise up the dust boot, where it meets the piston - if any brake fluid or rust is found, rebuild or renew the calipers (see Chapter 9).

Remove the brake pads

5.26 On some calipers, the outer pad is secured to the caliper by a spring clip. To remove the pad, push it towards the piston to dislodge the torque buttons (arrow), then slide the pad out of the caliper.

5.27 Some outer pads are held in the caliper frame by "ears" on the pad backing plate. Most of the time these can simply be snapped out of the caliper, but if the pad sticks, knock it out of the caliper with a hammer.

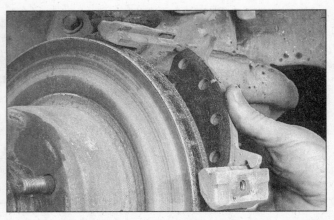

5.28 Remove the inner brake pad from the caliper adapter. On some set-ups the pad will slide right out of the adapter . . .

5.29 . . . but on models with an anti-rattle clip on the pad, it could be a tight fit. Prise the pad out of the adapter with a screwdriver, if necessary.

5.30 On some designs, both pads ride in the caliper mounting. Take note of any springs and shims that may be present, remove them, then prise the pads out of the mounting

Preparation for fitting

5.31a Apply a coat of anti-squeal compound to the backing plates of the new pads. if necessary, allow the compound to dry for a few minutes before fitting the pads (follow the directions on the bottle or tube).

5.31b If applicable, fit a new anti-rattle clip (or clips) onto the pad. Most sliding caliper designs use these clips on only one end of the inner pad (usually at the bottom)

5.32 Some brake pads are marked for left and right sides of the vehicle - be sure they are fitted in the correct positions

5.33 Push the caliper piston(s) completely into the caliper bore(s) to ensure plenty of room for the new pads. Use a wood block and a C-clamp, but don't use excessive force. DO NOT attempt this on rear calipers with integral handbrake mechanisms.

5.34 You can also use the old inner pad if a wood block won't fit, as shown on this twin-piston sliding caliper.

5.35 Clean the grooves on the ends of the caliper where it slides into the adapter (mounting). Also clean the grooves or rails on the adapter, then apply a light film of high-temperature brake grease to the sliding surface of the caliper . . .

5.36 ... or to the sliding surfaces of the mounting

Fit the new pads

5.37 If the outer pads on your vehicle are secured to the caliper with a spring clip like this, push the pad into position on the caliper frame, making sure the torque buttons seat fully into the cut-outs (arrows).

5.38 If the outer pad on your vehicle has bent "ears" like this, set the pad into the caliper frame and check the fit by moving it back and forth, as indicated by the arrows. They should fit tightly - if there's any slop ...

5.39 ... set the pad against a wood block and tap the ear with a hammer, then re-check the fit (this might take a couple of tries to get right).

5.40 When you fit the new inner brake pad on a design like this, make sure the "ears" (arrows) at either end of the pad backing plate are properly seated into the machined surfaces of the caliper adapter.

5.41 On models that have an anti-rattle clip (or clips on the pad(s), set the lower end of the pad into the groove or notch in the caliper mounting, compress the clip and slide the upper end of the pad into position. If both pads on your vehicle ride in the caliper mounting, see illustration 5.30.

5.42 Refit the caliper over the brake pads and disc. On calipers retained by pins, set the pins in their grooves and drive them into place . . .

5:43 . . . making sure they are driven in completely. Make sure the pin tabs on each side of the spindle flank (caliper mounting) are exposed.

5.44 If the caliper is secured by a caliper key, insert a screwdriver between the spindle flank (adapter or mounting) and the caliper to create a gap for the key . . .

5.45 . . . then insert the caliper support key and spring clip into the slot. Drive the key and spring into place, then refit the bolt, tightening it securely.

5.46 If your caliper is retained by an anti-rattle spring and retainer clip, refit them (with the anti-rattle spring on top of the retainer clip, like this). Apply a drop of non-hardening thread locking compound and tighten the bolts.

5.47 If your caliper is secured by guide plates, slide the plates into the gaps between the caliper and the caliper mounting, then refit the retaining pins

All models

Repeat the entire procedure to renew the pads on the other wheel. Don't forget to pump the pedal a few times to bring the pads into contact with the disc. Be sure to then check the brake fluid level.

Floating caliper

Warning: *The dust created by the brake system may contain asbestos, which is harmful to your health. Never blow it out with compressed air and don't inhale any of it. An approved filtering mask should be worn when working on the brakes. Do not, under any circumstances, use petroleum-based solvents to clean brake parts. Use brake system cleaner only!*

Note: *If the brake pads on your vehicle are held in the caliper by retaining pins, refer to the Fixed caliper brake pad renewal procedure.*

Tools required (these will suffice for most applications, however, the calipers on your vehicle may differ slightly):

Jack and axle stands
Wheel nut (or bolt) spanner
Filtering mask
Safety glasses or goggles
Latex gloves
Large C-clamp
Needle-nose pliers
Length of wire (a straightened-out coat-hanger will work)
Spanner, socket, Allen key or Torx key, depending on caliper design (to remove caliper bolts or pins)

Materials required

Brake system cleaner
Brake pads
Caliper bushes and mounting bolts or guide pins (if worn or damaged)
Brake anti-squeal compound
High-temperature brake grease (slide rail grease)
Brake fluid

Remove the caliper

5.48 If equipped, remove the anti-rattle spring - this kind can simply be prised off.

5.49 To remove this kind of anti-rattle spring, depress the ends and pull the spring out.

5.50 Use a large C-clamp to compress the piston(s) into the caliper. DO NOT attempt this on rear calipers with integral handbrake mechanisms.

5.51 On some calipers, all you have to do is remove the lower bolt, or guide pin (arrow) . . .

5.52 . . . and swing the caliper up for access to the brake pads . . .

5.53 . . . then insert a bolt or punch into the hole in the caliper mounting (also referred to as the adapter or torque plate) to keep the caliper from falling. If there is no provision for supporting the caliper like this, use a piece of wire and attach it between the caliper and a suspension component

5.54 On some calipers both bolts (guide pins) must be removed (arrows). Some models use Allen or Torx-head bolts - always use the proper tool to avoid damaging the bolts.

5.55 Don't ever allow the caliper to hang by the brake hose - hang it from the coil spring or other suspension member with a piece of wire.

Remove the brake pads - caliper adapter-mounted pads

5.56 Remove the anti-squeal shims from the pads, if present. Note how they are positioned - some models have only one shim per pad, but some may have two.

5.59 Remove the inner brake pad

5.57 Remove the anti-rattle springs (if fitted) from the brake pads. Renew these springs if they are damaged.

5.60 On some designs, the brake pads are retained by an anti-rattle spring which traverses the width of the caliper adapter. To remove the pads, prise down the lower anti-rattle clip and remove the outer brake pad . . .

5.58 Remove the outer brake pad from the caliper adapter.

5.61 . . . then pull the anti-rattle clips away from the pad with your index fingers and force the inner brake pad out with your thumbs

Remove the brake pads - caliper-mounted pads

5.62 Remove the inner pad by snapping it out of the piston

5.65 Most other outer pads are held to the caliper frame with a spring clip. Push the pad away from the caliper frame and slide it off the caliper (it may be necessary to prise it off with a screwdriver)

Preparation for fitting

5.63 On some calipers, the outer pad is fastened by tabs that fit through holes in the caliper and are bent over. Remove the pad by bending the tabs straight out with a pair of pliers . . .

5.66 Carefully peel back the edge of the piston boot and check for corrosion and leaking fluid. If any is present, rebuild or renew the calipers (see Chapter 9).

5.64 . . . then dislodge it from the caliper with a hammer

5.67 Check the anti-rattle clips, if present, for cracks and distortion. Fit new ones if necessary

5.68 Apply anti-squeal compound to the back sides of both new brake pads. Allow the compound to "set up" for a few minutes before fitting them (follow the instructions on the product).

5.69 If applicable, remove the pad retainer spring from the old inner pad and snap it into the new pad, in the direction shown (arrow).

5.70 If the old pads were equipped with anti-rattle springs like this, prise them off and transfer them to the new pads. If they are worn or bent, fit new ones.

5.71 Some brake pads are marked for left and right sides of the vehicle - be sure they are fitted in the correct positions.

5.72 Inspect the caliper bolts and bushes (A) for damage and the contact surfaces (B) for corrosion. Clean the contact surfaces with brake system cleaner and sandpaper if they are dirty.

5.73 If the piston isn't completely bottomed in the caliper, use a C-clamp and the old inner pad to bottom the piston in the caliper bore. DO NOT attempt this on rear calipers with integral handbrake mechanisms.

5.74 Apply a light coat of high-temperature brake grease (caliper slide rail grease) to the upper steering knuckle (or caliper adapter)-to-caliper contact surface

5.75 Also lubricate the lower contact surface with the same grease

5.76 Wipe off the caliper mounting bolts (guide pins) and apply a thin coat of silicone grease (or high-temperature brake grease) to their sliding surfaces

Fit the new brake pads - caliper adapter-mounted pads

5.77 Fit the new brake pads in the caliper adapter - make sure their upper and lower notches are properly engaged with the projections on the adapter.

5.78 On pads that have "ears," make sure the ears engage properly with the flats on the caliper adapter

5.79 On models equipped with this type of anti-rattle clip, position the clips on the anchor plate and fit the inner brake pad . . .

5.80 . . . place the lower end of the outer pad on the anchor plate and push it down against the anti-rattle clip, then lift up on the upper anti-rattle clip and swing the top of the pad into position

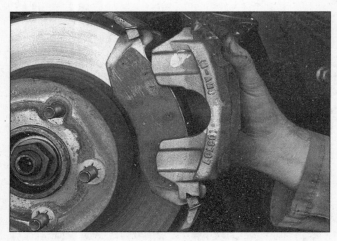

5.81 Refit the caliper (on this design the notch in the lower edge of the caliper must be engaged with the anchor plate) and tighten the mounting bolts (guide pins). Note: It's a good idea to put a drop of thread-locking compound (the non-hardening type) on the threads of the mounting bolts before refitting them. Refit the anti-rattle spring, if applicable. Make sure the brake hose doesn't get twisted when refitting the caliper.

Fit the new pads - caliper-mounted pads

5.82 Fit the inner pad by pushing the clip straight into the piston

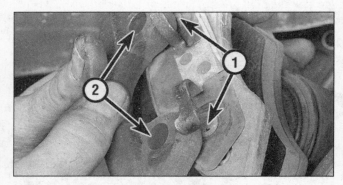

5.83 To fit the new outer pad into the caliper, slide the pad into the caliper, making sure if applicable that the locating lugs on the pad (1) seat into the mounting holes in the caliper frame (2). If your pad has bent "ears" that fit over the top of the caliper frame, see illustrations 5.38 and 5.39.

5.84 Refit the caliper/brake pad assembly over the disc and onto the caliper adapter (mounting). If the outer pad on your vehicle is equipped with an anti-rattle spring (1) like this one, position the anti-rattle spring under the upper arm of the mounting with the notches in the upper edge of both pads (2) resting on the upper arm of the mounting. Then, rotate the caliper down until the notches in the opposite end of the pads seat against the lower arm of the mounting. Make sure the brake hose doesn't get twisted when refitting the caliper.

5.85 Apply silicone grease (or high-temperature brake grease) to the caliper pins (mounting bolts) and to the inside the insulators. Insert the pins through the caliper housing and into the caliper mounting. Note: It's a good idea to put a drop of thread locking compound (the non-hardening type) to the threads of the mounting bolts before refitting them. Start the threads by hand, then tighten the pins.

5.86 On models where the outer pad is positioned by bendable "ears" that protrude through holes in the caliper frame, insert a large screwdriver between the outer pad flange and the brake disc to seat the pad, then bend the tabs over with a hammer.

All models

Repeat the entire procedure to renew the pads on the other wheel. Don't forget to pump the pedal a few times to bring the pads into contact with the disc. Be sure to then check the brake fluid level.

Rear brake pad renewal - calipers with integral handbrake mechanisms.

Warning: *The dust created by the brake system may contain asbestos, which is harmful to your health. Never blow it out with compressed air and don't inhale any of it. An approved filtering mask should be worn when working on the brakes. Do not, under any circumstances, use petroleum-based solvents to clean brake parts. Use brake system cleaner only!*

To renew the rear brake pads on vehicles that have handbrake mechanisms built into the rear calipers, follow the procedure under the appropriate heading (fixed, sliding or floating caliper brake pad renewal) to remove the caliper and extract the brake pads. The only differences you'll encounter when replacing the pads on a caliper with an integral handbrake mechanism are these:

a) Sometimes it's necessary to unclip the brake hose and/or the handbrake cable from a bracket to allow caliper removal. In almost all cases, though, the brake hose can remain attached to the caliper.

b) DO NOT attempt to push the piston into the caliper bore by using a C-clamp, as shown in illustrations 5.16, 5.33, 5.50 and 5.73. To make room for the new pads, the caliper piston will have to be bottomed in its bore, but on most models you can't do it by pushing the piston in. The piston will have to be turned in, like a big screw **(see illustrations)**.

c) On some calipers, the piston can be pushed into the bore, but only after removing the handbrake lever from the back of the caliper **(see illustrations)**.

d) After the job has been completed, operate the handbrake until satisfactory handbrake pedal or lever travel is obtained.

5.87 To make room for the new brake pads on rear calipers with integral handbrake mechanisms, engage the tips of a pair of needle-nose pliers with the slots or cut-outs in the piston face, then rotate the piston clockwise until it stops. Be careful not to distort the dust boot - if it sticks to the piston, insert a small, blunt screwdriver between the piston and the boot, then gently drag the screwdriver around the piston to break the bond.

5.88 If you need a little more leverage than a pair of needle-nose pliers provides, use a pin spanner. Special tools are also available to turn the piston in, but in most cases the methods shown here work just fine.

5.89 Before fitting the new pads, adjust the position of the piston so the cut-outs are aligned like this. Most inner brake pads on these calipers are equipped with a pair of pegs or a D-shaped projection that fits into the cut-outs or slot. Make sure the projections on the pads engage properly with the slot or cut-outs.

1 Nut
2 Lever
3 Return spring
4 Bracket bolt
5 Lever seal (sealing ridge faces caliper)
6 Handbrake cable

5.90 If the rear caliper on your vehicle doesn't lend itself to rotating the piston, remove the handbrake lever from the back of the caliper . . .

5.91 . . . then, using two pairs of adjustable pliers, squeeze the inner pad and the outer part of the caliper frame together to bottom the piston

5.92 When fitting the new inner pad, position the tangs of the pad retainer as shown, then clip the pad into the retainer - make sure the tab on the retainer fits into the "D" notch in the piston face. After refitting the caliper, refit the handbrake seal (if removed) and lever.

Brake disc inspection, removal and refitting

Warning: *The dust created by the brake system may contain asbestos, which is harmful to your health. Never blow it out with compressed air and don't inhale any of it. An approved filtering mask should be worn when working on the brakes. Do not, under any circumstances, use petroleum-based solvents to clean brake parts. Use brake system cleaner only!*

Inspection

If you haven't already done so, loosen the wheel nuts, raise the front of the vehicle and support it securely on axle stands. Apply the handbrake. Remove the wheels.

If the brake disc on your vehicle is not integral with the wheel hub, refit the wheel nuts and tighten them securely. This clamps the disc tightly against the hub and will allow for an accurate runout check. If you tighten the wheel nuts but there's still a gap between the nut and the hub, fit washers between the nuts and the hub.

Turn the brake disc - if it is difficult to turn, depress the piston(s) in the caliper with a C-clamp **(see illustration 5.16 or 5.50)** (sliding and floating calipers) or, in the case of fixed calipers, prise the brake pads away from the disc a little.

Visually inspect the disc surface for score marks and other damage **(see illustration)**. Light scratches and

5.93 The brake pads on this vehicle were obviously neglected, as they wore down to the rivets and cut deep grooves into the disc - wear this severe means the disc must be renewed

5.94 To check disc runout, mount a dial indicator as shown and rotate the disc

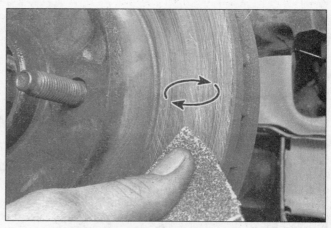

5.95 Using a swirling motion, remove the glaze from the disc with sandpaper or emery cloth

5.96 The minimum wear dimension is stamped or cast into the centre of the disc, or . . .

5.97 . . . on the disc "hat" area, or . . .

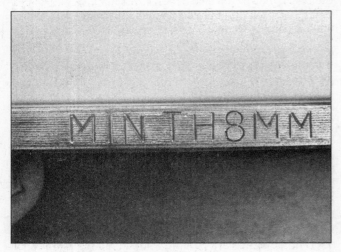

5.98 . . . on the edge of the disc

5.99 Use a micrometer to measure disc thickness

shallow grooves are normal after use and won't affect brake operation. Deep grooves - over 0.015-inch deep - require disc removal and refinishing by an automotive machine shop. Be sure to check both sides of the disc.

To check disc runout, place a dial indicator at a point about 1/2-inch from the outer edge of the disc **(see illustration)**. Set the indicator to zero and turn the disc. Generally, the indicator reading should not exceed 0.004-inch. If it does, the disc should be refinished by an automotive machine shop. Some manufacturers allow for more runout than 0.004-inch, but runout is not desirable - the less the better. Some manufacturers regard a runout of 0.004-inch to be excessive. **Note:** *Professionals recommend resurfacing the brake discs, when replacing the brake pads, regardless of the dial indicator reading (to produce a smooth, flat surface that will eliminate brake pedal pulsations and other undesirable symptoms related to questionable discs). At the very least, if you elect not to have the discs resurfaced, deglaze them with sandpaper or emery cloth* **(see illustration)**.

The disc must not be machined to a thickness less than the specified minimum thickness. The minimum (or discard) thickness is sometimes cast into the disc (see illustrations). The disc thickness can be checked with a micrometer **(see illustration)**. Measure the thickness in several places around the disc. You shouldn't wind up with readings that are more than 0.0005-inch different. If you do, the disc parallelism is out of the range that most manufacturers specify as acceptable.

Removal

Remove the brake caliper. On sliding and floating calipers, follow the caliper removal steps described in the Brake pad renewal procedure. Then, on models with

5.100 To remove the caliper adapter (mounting), remove these two bolts (arrows)

5.102 Some vehicles have brake discs that are bolted to the hubs

5.101 On vehicles with fixed calipers, remove the two caliper-to-steering knuckle or rear knuckle bolts (arrows)

5.103 On the front brakes of many and four-wheel drive vehicles the discs are also bolted to the hubs, but the entire assembly must be removed because the disc fits against the backside of the hub

adapter plates that would interfere with removal of the disc, remove the adapter plate. To do this, remove the two adapter plate-to-steering knuckle (or rear knuckle) bolts **(see illustration)**. On vehicles with fixed calipers, remove the two bolts that retain the caliper to the steering knuckle (or rear knuckle) **(see illustration)**.

On some vehicles, the disc is an integral part of the hub. To remove the disc on these models, refer to the Chapter 4 section entitled "Wheel bearing check, repack and adjustment" for the hub/disc removal procedure. **Note:** *If the disc is to be taken to a machine shop for resurfacing, clean out all the old grease from the hub before the machine work is done. Then, when you get it back, clean the hub out again to ensure no*

metal chips remain.

Some vehicles have a similar arrangement, where the disc seems to be an integral part of the hub, but is actually detachable. On rear-wheel drive models the disc is removed like any other integral disc/hub assembly, but the disc can be unbolted and separated from the hub **(see illustration)**. Many smaller front-wheel drive and four-wheel drive vehicles use a set-up like this, too, but the disc/hub assembly has to be pulled off the front driveshaft and pressed (usually) from the steering knuckle **(see illustration)**.

On other vehicles the brake disc slips over the hub and wheel studs and can simply be pulled off (of course, you'll have to remove the wheel nuts if you refitted them). An exception to this rule are the vehicles

5.104 If the disc retaining screws are stuck, use an impact screwdriver to loosen them

5.105 If the disc sticks to the hub, thread two bolts into the holes in the disc and tighten them to force the disc off the hub

which use screws to retain the disc to the hub. Sometimes these screws become rusted and will have to be soaked with penetrating oil and removed with an impact screwdriver **(see illustration)**. It's also a good idea to apply penetrating oil around the area where the disc meets the hub.

Even if you use penetrating oil, the disc might still refuse to come off. Check to see if the disc has two or three threaded holes in the area where the wheel seats. If it does, thread bolts of the correct size and thread pitch into the holes and tighten them to force the disc off

---

HINTS & TIPS

- Before separating the disc from the hub, mark the relationship of the disc to one of the wheel studs. If the wheels were dynamically balanced on the vehicle, returning the disc to the original position will retain the balance.

---

the hub **(see illustration)**. If you're removing a rear brake disc with a drum-type handbrake inside the centre of the disc, and the disc won't come off, remove the plug from the handbrake adjusting access hole. Engage the notches in the adjusting star wheel with a suitable tool (such as a screwdriver) and retract the handbrake shoes. Now pull the disc off the hub.

Refitting

Refitting is the reverse of removal. If you're refitting a disc with an integral hub, repack the wheel bearings, refit the disc and adjust the bearings as described in the Chapter 4 section "Wheel bearing check, repack and adjustment."

Refit the caliper adapter (if applicable), and tighten the bolts. Refit the caliper, also tightening the bolts.

If your vehicle is equipped with a drum-type handbrake inside of the hub of the disc, be sure to adjust the handbrake shoes (see Chapter 7).

Chapter 6
Drum brakes

Introduction

This Chapter is divided into two sections: Brake drum removal, inspection and refitting and Brake shoe renewal.

The first section deals with removal of the brake drum for access to the brake shoes, adjuster(s), handbrake mechanism and wheel cylinder, and inspection and refitting of the brake drum.

The second section is subdivided into two parts and depicts the brake shoe renewal procedures for the two most typical drum brake designs: Duo-servo and leading/trailing-type drum brakes.

If you aren't sure which kind of brake you're about to work on, refer to Chapter 1 and look at the information under the Drum brakes subheading.

Information on wheel cylinder overhaul or renewal can be found in Chapter 9.

Brake drum removal, inspection and refitting

Warning: *The dust created by the brake system may contain asbestos, which is harmful to your health. Never blow it out with compressed air and don't inhale any of it. An approved filtering mask should be worn when working on the brakes. Do not, under any circumstances, use petroleum-based solvents to clean brake parts. Use brake system cleaner only!*

Removal

Loosen the wheel nuts, raise the vehicle and support it securely on axle stands. Block the wheels at the opposite end of the vehicle so it can't roll. If a rear brake drum is to be removed, release the handbrake. Remove the wheel(s).

If you're removing a drum that is integral with the hub assembly (one that can't be separated from the hub), refer to the Chapter 4 section entitled "Wheel bearing check, repack and adjustment" for the drum removal procedure.

If you're removing a brake drum that simply slips off an axle or hub flange, apply penetrating oil around the area where the drum meets the hub or axle flange, and also around the wheel studs. Allow the penetrant a few minutes to seep in.

Check the drum for the presence of screws that secure the drum to the hub or axle flange. If present, remove them. It may be necessary to use an impact screwdriver to break the screws loose **(see illustration 5.104 in Chapter 5)**.

Mark the relationship of the brake drum to one of the wheel studs or to the hub **(see illustration)**. This will preserve the balance if the wheels have been dynamically balanced on the vehicle. Try to pull the drum off. If it sticks, the brake shoes will have to be retracted. Refer to Chapter 4 and follow the procedure described under the Drum brakes portion of the Rear

6.1 **Mark the relationship of the drum to the hub (or one of the wheel studs) so the balance will be retained**

6.2 **If the brake drum refuses to slide off the hub, screw two bolts of the proper size and thread pitch into the threaded holes and tighten them evenly, a little at a time. The drum will be pushed off by the bolts**

6.3 The maximum drum diameter is cast or stamped into the brake drums. You'll usually find this dimension on the inside of the drum, but some manufacturers cast it into the outside of the drum.

6.4 Remove the glaze from the drum surface with sandpaper or emery cloth.

6.5 Measuring the diameter of the brake drum with a large vernier caliper.

brakes section.

If the drum is stuck to the hub or axle flange, look for two or three threaded holes in the drum that look like they have no apparent purpose. If your drum is equipped with such holes, fit two (or three) bolts of the correct size and thread pitch into the threaded holes in the drum. Tighten the bolts, a little at a time, until the drum is forced off **(see illustration)**.

Inspection

Check the drum for cracks, score marks, deep scratches and hard spots, which will appear as small discoloured areas. If the hard spots cannot be removed with sandpaper or emery cloth, or if any of the other conditions listed above exist, the drum must be taken to an automotive engineering works to have it turned. **Note:** *Professionals recommend resurfacing the drums whenever a brake job is done. Resurfacing will eliminate the possibility of out-of-round or tapered drums. If the drums are worn so much that they can't be resurfaced without exceeding the maximum allowable diameter (sometimes stamped into the drum)* **(see illustration)**, *then new ones will be required. At the very least, if you elect not to have the drums resurfaced, remove the glazing from the surface with emery cloth or sandpaper using a swirling motion* **(see illustration)**.

If you have a brake drum micrometer or a vernier caliper that's large enough, measure the inside diameter of the drum at four different locations around the drum (45-degree intervals) **(see illustration)**. Write down each measurement. Generally, a drum that is 0.010-inch out-of-round needs to be machined. Some manufacturers would consider 0.010-inch out-of-round too much.

Also, check the diameter of the brake drum at the innermost portion of the friction surface and at the outermost portion of the friction surface. Subtract one measurement from the other to calculate drum taper. If the drum exhibits a taper of 0.005-inch or more, it should be resurfaced.

Note: *If the drum is to be taken to an engineering works for resurfacing, clean out all of the old grease from the hub (if applicable) before the machine work is done. Then, when you get it back, clean the hub out again to ensure no metal chips remain.*

Refitting

Before refitting the brake drum, make sure the friction surface is perfectly clean. If it isn't, or if in doubt, wash the drum thoroughly with brake system cleaner. Also confirm that the brake shoes are clean and all of the components of the drum brake assembly are in order.

If you're refitting a drum that slips over the wheel studs, do just that. Make sure the match marks you applied to the drum and wheel stud are aligned. If you're refitting a brake drum that's integral with the wheel hub, clean and repack the wheel bearings as described in the Chapter 4 section entitled "Wheel bearing check, repack and adjustment." Refit the hub/drum assembly and adjust the wheel bearings as described in Chapter 4.

Regardless of the type of drum you've just refitted, adjust the drum brakes. This is also covered the Chapter 4 section entitled "Drum brake adjustment."

Brake shoe renewal

Warning: *Drum brake shoes must be renewed on both wheels at the same time - never renew the shoes on only one wheel. Also, the dust created by the brake system may contain asbestos, which is harmful to your health. Never blow it out with compressed air and don't inhale any of it. An approved filtering mask should be worn when working on the brakes. Do not, under any circumstances, use petroleum-based solvents to clean brake parts. Use brake system cleaner only!*

Note: *Whenever the brake shoes are renewed it is advisable to also renew the retracting and hold-down springs. Due to the continuous heating/cooling cycle the springs are subjected to, they lose their tension over a period of time and may allow the shoes to drag on the drum and wear at a much faster rate than normal. When renewing the rear brake shoes, use only high-quality, nationally recognised brand-name parts.*

Note: *Professionals recommend resurfacing the drums whenever a brake job is done. Resurfacing will eliminate the possibility of out-of-round or tapered drums. If the drums are worn so much that they can't be resurfaced without exceeding the maximum allowable diameter (sometimes stamped into the drum)* **(see illustration 6.3),** *new ones will be required. At the very least, if you elect not to have the drums resurfaced, remove the glazing from the surface with sandpaper or emery cloth using a swirling motion.*

Regardless of the type of brake you're working on, there are a few preliminary steps to be taken before disassembling the brake. First, park the vehicle on a level surface, open the bonnet and locate the master cylinder - it's usually mounted on the bulkhead or the brake servo on the driver's side of the bulkhead (but on some vehicles it's on the other side of the engine compartment). Cover all painted areas around the master cylinder (wing included), remove the reservoir cover or cap(s) and remove about one-quarter of the fluid from the reservoir. It is necessary to do this so the reservoir doesn't overflow when the wheel cylinder

6.6 Before beginning work, wash away all traces of brake dust with brake system cleaner - DO NOT use compressed air or a brush.

pistons are pushed back into their bores to make room for the new linings. This can be accomplished with a suction pump, a siphoning kit or an old poultry baster or hydrometer. **Warning:** *Brake fluid is poisonous - don't start the siphoning action by mouth. If you use a poultry baster, never again use that baster for cooking!* Discard the fluid.

If you haven't already done so, this is a good time to put on your filtering mask, latex gloves and eye protection. Your hands aren't too dirty yet, and brake dust tends to get all over the wheels and inside the wheel covers, so put them on before removing the wheels.

Next, remove the wheel trim (if applicable) from the wheels and loosen the wheel nuts about one-half turn. Raise the vehicle and support it securely on axle stands. Remove the wheels, but remember to only work on one brake at a time. You can use the other side as a model if you aren't sure about something. Another good idea is to make sketches or take instant photos of the areas you think you might have trouble with. The handbrake actuator and the adjuster mechanism are good examples of areas to concentrate on. Always note the orientation of the adjuster screw star wheel and all of the various springs.

Remove the brake drum by following the procedure under the heading Brake drum removal, inspection and refitting.

Before touching or disassembling anything, clean the brake assembly with brake system cleaner and allow it to dry **(see illustration).** Don't ever use compressed air or a brush to remove the brake dust.

Now, refer to the appropriate procedure under Duo-servo brake shoe renewal or Leading/trailing brake shoe renewal. Be sure to stay in order and read the captions

FRONT OF VEHICLE

ANCHOR PIN PLATE

RETRACTING SPRING

ANCHOR PIN

BRAKE CYLINDER

SECONDARY SHOE AND LINING

PARKING BRAKE LINK

RETRACTING SPRING

PARKING BRAKE LINK SPRING

CABLE GUIDE

BRAKE SHOE HOLD DOWN SPRING

PRIMARY SHOE AND LINING

SELF-ADJUSTER CABLE

PARKING BRAKE LEVER

PIVOT HOOK

ADJUSTER LEVER SPRING

PIVOT NUT

SOCKET

ADJUSTING LEVER

PARKING BRAKE CABLE

ADJUSTING SCREW

6.7 Rear drum brake components (with cable-actuated self-adjuster mechanism) - left side

that accompany each illustration. Before refitting the brake drum, inspect it as outlined previously in this Chapter. If machining is necessary, remove the drums and have them resurfaced by an automotive engineering works (if they are still thick enough to undergo machining). **Note:** *Professionals recommend resurfacing of brake drums whenever replacing the brake shoes, as this will produce a smooth, flat surface that will eliminate brake pedal pulsations and other undesirable symptoms related to questionable drums. At the very least, if you elect not to have the drums resurfaced, de-glaze them with sandpaper or emery cloth, using a swirling motion to ensure a non-directional finish. Be careful not to get grease on the brake drum or brake shoes.*

After you have successfully fitted the shoes on one side of the vehicle, repeat the procedure on the other brake. Then refer to Chapter 4 and adjust the shoes, referring to the section entitled "Drum brake adjustment."

As soon as you have lowered the vehicle and tightened the wheel nuts securely, check the brake fluid level in the master cylinder reservoir. If necessary, add some to bring it to the desired level (see Chapter 4) Pump the brake pedal a few times, then recheck the fluid level.

Adjust the handbrake (see Chapter 4).

Lastly, before committing the vehicle to normal

service, road test it in an isolated area, if possible. For the first few hundred miles or so, try to avoid hard braking to allow the new shoes to bed in.

Duo-servo brake

Warning: *The dust created by the brake system may contain asbestos, which is harmful to your health. Never blow it out with compressed air and don't inhale any of it. An approved filtering mask should be worn when working on the brakes. Do not, under any circumstances, use petroleum-based solvents to clean brake parts. Use brake system cleaner only!*
Note: *The following procedure depicts the brake shoe renewal sequence for drum brakes with lever-actuated self-adjusters and cable-actuated self adjusters. Follow the photo sequence and read the accompanying caption, but simply ignore the steps which do not apply to the type of brake you are working on. The same goes for front drum brakes - just ignore all of the references to handbrake components.*

Tools required:

Jack and axle stands
Wheel nut (or bolt) spanner
Filtering mask
Safety glasses or goggles
Latex gloves
Brake spring pliers
Brake hold-down spring tool
Brake shoe adjusting tool (or a suitable screwdriver)

Materials required:

Brake shoes
Brake hardware kit
Brake system cleaner
High-temperature brake grease
Brake fluid

1   Hold-down pins
2   Backing plate
3   Handbrake lever
4   Secondary brake shoe
5   Shoe guide (also called "anchor pin plate")
6   Handbrake strut
7   Actuator lever
8   Actuator link
9   Return (or retracting) spring
10 Return (or retracting) spring
11 Hold-down spring
12 Lever pivot
13 Lever return spring
14 Strut spring
15 Adjusting screw assembly (with "star wheel")
16 Adjusting screw spring
17 Primary brake shoe

6.8 Exploded view of a typical rear drum brake (with lever-actuated self-adjuster mechanism) - left side

Remove the old brake shoes

6.9 Pull back on the adjuster lever and turn the star wheel to retract the brake shoes (this will make removal of the return springs easier and, on models with cable-actuated handbrakes, will ease removal of the adjuster cable).

6.10 Remove the shoe return springs - the tool shown here is available at most motor factors and makes this job much easier and safer.

Chapter 6

6.11 On models with cable-actuated adjusters, remove the return spring and cable guide from the secondary shoe . . .

6.14 . . . followed by the anchor pin plate.

6.12 . . . then remove the self adjuster cable and anchor pin plate.

6.15 Also on models with lever-actuated adjusters, prise the actuator lever spring out with a large screwdriver.

6.13 On models with lever-actuated adjusters, pull the bottom of the actuator lever toward the secondary brake shoe, compressing the lever return spring. The actuator link can now be removed from the top of the lever . .

6.16 Slide the handbrake strut out from between the axle flange and the primary shoe.

6.17 Remove the hold-down springs and pins. The hold-down spring tool shown here is available at most motor factors and greatly simplifies this step. To remove the springs, push down on the retainer, turn it 1/4-turn to align the slot in the retainer with the blade on the pin, then release.

6.18 On models with lever-actuated adjusters, remove the actuator lever and pivot - be careful not to let the pivot fall out of the lever.

6.19 Spread the top of the shoes apart and slide the assembly around the axle.

6.20 Unhook the handbrake lever from the secondary shoe, if the design of the brake permits.

6.21 Some handbrake levers simply hook onto the cable and are easily detached. On this design, the lever is usually fastened to the secondary brake shoe with a clip and is not easily separated (it's easier to do it on the workbench).

6.22 Other handbrake levers are fastened with a clip, but don't readily separate from the cable, either. In this case, pull on the cable end with a pair of pliers and swing the cable out of the slot.

6.23 Spread the bottom of the shoes apart and remove the adjusting screw assembly.

Preparation for refitting

6.24 If the handbrake lever is still fastened to the secondary shoe, remove it by prising off the C-clip. Take note of any washers that may be present.

6.25 Here's another kind of clip that is commonly used to retain the handbrake lever. Spread the ends of the clip and prise it off the pin.

6.26 Clean the adjusting screw with brake system cleaner, dry it off and lubricate the threads and end with high-temperature brake grease. The screw portion of the adjuster will need to be threaded in further than before to allow the drum to fit over the new shoes.

6.27 Feel the brake shoe contact points on the backing plate. If they are rough or a ledge has worn into them, file them smooth. Lubricate these contact points with high-temperature grease.

6.28 If the handbrake lever was mounted to a pin on the old shoe, fit a new adjuster lever pin in the new shoe . . .

6.29 . . . then refit the lever and a new C-clip

6.30 If your brake uses this type of clip, fit a new clip over the pin and squeeze the ends together (note the spring washer under the clip)

Fit the new shoes

6.31 Note: On models with cable-actuated adjusters, you may find it easier to fit the shoes on the backing plate, then refit the adjuster screw, adjuster spring and lever. Connect the adjuster spring between the new shoes (with the long portion of the spring pointing to the secondary [rear] shoe on most designs), refit the adjuster screw assembly (with the long part pointing to the primary [front] shoe on most designs), then connect the handbrake cable (if disconnected from the lever).

6.32 Spread the shoes apart and slide them into position on the backing plate.

6.33 Insert the handbrake lever into the opening in the secondary brake shoe. If you separated the handbrake cable from the end of the lever, connect it now if you haven't already done so.

6.34 Refit the hold-down pin through the backing plate in the primary shoe, then refit the spring and retainer. If you're working on a brake with a cable-actuated self-adjuster, refit the hold-down pin, spring and retainer through the secondary shoe also.

6.35 On models with lever-actuated adjusters, insert the lever pivot into the actuator lever, place the lever over the secondary shoe hold-down pin and refit the hold-down spring and retainer.

6.38 On models with lever-actuated adjusters, hook the lower end of the actuator link to the actuator lever, then loop the top end over the anchor pin . . .

6.36 Guide the handbrake strut behind the axle flange and engage the rear end of it in the slot on the handbrake lever. Spread the shoes enough to allow the other end of the strut to seat against the primary shoe.

6.39 . . . and refit the lever return spring over the tab on the actuator lever. Push the bottom of the spring up onto the brake shoe.

6.37 Place the anchor pin plate over the anchor pin

6.40 If you're working an a model with cable-actuated adjusters, place the end of the cable over the anchor pin . . .

6.41 . . . then hook the end of the secondary shoe return spring through the cable guide and into the hole in the shoe. Make sure the cable sits in the guide.

6.44 If you're working on a model with cable-actuated adjusters, hook the adjuster lever spring into the proper hole at the bottom of the primary shoe . . .

6.42 Refit the shoe retractor springs. The tool shown here is actually the handle of the brake spring pliers. This tool makes this step much easier and safer.

6.45 . . . then hook the adjuster lever spring and cable into the adjuster lever. Pull the cable down and to the rear, inserting the hook on the lever into the hole in the secondary shoe.

6.43 Bend the ends of the return springs around the anchor pin, so the end of the spring is parallel with the long part of the spring.

6.46 Wiggle the brake assembly to ensure that the shoes are centred on the backing plate. Make sure the handbrake strut and the wheel cylinder pushrods (if applicable) engage properly with the brake shoes.

6.47 Turn the adjusting screw star wheel to adjust the shoes in or out as necessary. The brake drum should slide over the shoes and turn with a very slight amount of drag.

6.48 Exploded view of a typical leading/trailing drum brake assembly (Toyota)

6.49 Assembled view of the components of a typical leading/trailing drum brake (Ford)

Leading/trailing brake

Warning: *The dust created by the brake system may contain asbestos, which is harmful to your health. Never blow it out with compressed air and don't inhale any of it. An approved filtering mask should be worn when working on the brakes. Do not, under any circumstances, use petroleum-based solvents to clean brake parts. Use brake system cleaner only!*

Note 1: *The following procedure depicts a rear brake shoe renewal sequence for leading/trailing type drum brakes. Follow the photo sequence and read the caption below each illustration, but simply ignore the steps which do not apply to the type of brake you are working on. The same goes for front drum brakes - just ignore all of the references to handbrake components.*

Note 2: *Most leading/trailing drum brakes are similar in design, regardless of manufacturer. The differences lie primarily in the handbrake actuating mechanism. As there are many different handbrake actuator set-ups, it is not possible to cover every variation in a manual of this size. Before disassembling any components, be sure to pay close attention to the way all of the components are situated. Note how the retractor springs are fitted - is there a long, straight portion of the spring passing over the self-adjuster star wheel? If so, make a note. Also note the mounting holes of all springs. It's a good idea to make sketches or even take instant photographs of the brake assembly, especially the handbrake components, before actually removing them. Remember to work only on one brake at a time, referring to the other brake for reference, if necessary. At the beginning of the sequence are a few exploded views of typical leading/trailing drum brake assemblies.*

Tools required:

Jack and axle stands
Wheel nut (or bolt) spanner
Filtering mask
Safety glasses or goggles
Latex gloves
Brake spring pliers
Brake hold-down spring tool
Brake shoe adjusting tool (or a suitable screwdriver)

Materials required:

Brake shoes
Brake hardware kit
Brake system cleaner
High-temperature brake grease
Brake fluid

6.50 Exploded view of a typical leading/trailing drum brake assembly (Honda)

1   Backing plate
2   Adjuster spring
3   Adjuster
4   Handbrake lever
5   Brake shoe
6   Piston
7   Wheel cylinder body
8   Hold-down pin
9   Hold-down spring
10 Anchor spring
11 Shoe retracting spring
12 Clip spring
13 Bleeder screw
14 Wheel cylinder boot

0069-H

6.51 Exploded view of a typical leading/trailing drum brake assembly (Hyundai, Dodge, Mitsubishi)

1 Actuator spring
2 Upper return spring
3 Spring connecting link
4 Adjuster actuator
5 Spring washer
6 Lower return spring
7 Hold-down spring assembly
8 Hold-down pin
9 Leading brake shoe
10 Trailing brake shoe
11 Adjuster socket
12 Spring clip
13 Adjuster nut
14 Adjuster screw
15 Retaining clip
16 Pin
17 Spring washer
18 Handbrake lever
19 Screw and lock washer
20 Boot
21 Piston
22 Piston cup
23 Spring assembly
24 Bleeder screw
25 Wheel cylinder
26 Bleed screw cap
27 Backing plate
28 Access hole plug

6.52 Exploded view of a typical leading/trailing drum brake assembly (General Motors/Vauxhall)

Remove the old brake shoes

6.53 Unhook the return spring (also called retractor spring) from the leading brake shoe. A pair of locking pliers can be used to stretch the spring and pull the end out of the hole in the shoe.

6.54 Remove the shoe hold-down springs. On this type, depress the hold-down spring and turn the retainer 90-degrees, then release it. This special tool makes removal much easier - they're available at most motor factors and aren't very expensive.

6.55 If your brake is equipped with a spring steel type of hold-down clip, push down on the clip and turn the hold-down pin with a pair of pliers. A special tool is also available, which makes this step even quicker and easier (see illustration 2.78 in Chapter 2).

6.56 Some brakes aren't equipped with hold-down springs, but have a "horseshoe" type spring which serves as a hold-down spring and a shoe return spring. If your brake is like this, wedge a flat-bladed screwdriver under the spring and prise it out of the leading brake shoe, then remove the shoe.

6.57 Remove the leading shoe from the backing plate and unhook the anchor spring from the bottom end of the shoe. If the brake you are working on has a lower shoe-to-shoe return spring instead of a spring that passes under the anchor plate, remove it using the technique shown in illustration 6.53, if necessary.

6.58 Remove the hold-down spring from the trailing shoe.

6.59 If the brake you're working on is equipped with a horseshoe spring prise it out of the trailing shoe.

6.60 Pull the trailing shoe (and adjuster assembly, if applicable) away from the backing plate . . .

6.61 . . . then hold the end of the handbrake cable with a pair of pliers and pull it out of the handbrake lever.

6.62 If your brake has a handbrake set-up like this, remove the adjusting lever spring.

6.63 If the brake is equipped with a captive adjuster screw (retained by the return spring), unhook the spring from the shoe and slide the adjuster and spring off.

6.64 Prise the C-clip apart and remove it to separate the handbrake lever and adjuster lever from the rear shoe. Take note of any washers or shims that may be present.

Preparation for refitting

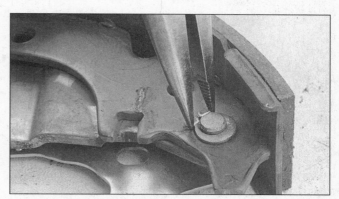

6.65 Assemble the handbrake lever and adjuster lever to the new rear shoe and crimp the C-clip closed with a pair of pliers. Always use a new clip and be sure to refit any shims or washers, if any were present upon separation.

6.66 Clean the adjusting screw with brake system cleaner, dry it off and lubricate the threads and end with high-temperature brake grease. The screw portion of the adjuster will need to be threaded in further than before to allow the drum to fit over the new shoes.

6.67 Feel the brake shoe contact points on the backing plate. If they are rough or a ledge has worn into them, file them smooth. Lubricate these contact points with high-temperature grease.

6.68 If the adjuster screw is a captive type, refit it onto the rear shoe. Make sure the end fits properly into the slot in the shoe and hook the spring into the opening in the shoe.

6.69 Refit the adjuster lever spring, if applicable.

6.70 Hold the trailing shoe assembly up to the backing plate, pull the handbrake cable spring back and hold it there with a pair of pliers, then place the cable into the hooked end of the handbrake lever.

6.71 Place the trailing shoe against the backing plate, being careful not to get any grease on the friction linings. Pass the hold-down pin through its hole in the brake shoe, then refit the hold down spring and retainer.

6.72 If your brake has a quadrant-type adjuster mechanism, refit it now and push the lever in about half-way (arrow).

6.73 Connect the anchor spring (if applicable) to the bottom of each shoe and mount the leading shoe to the backing plate (again, be careful not to get any grease on the lining material). Refit the hold-down spring and retainer.

6.76 Refit the adjuster lever (if it is a detachable one like this) on the handbrake lever pivot pin . . .

6.74 If the brake has a shoe-to-shoe return spring, refit it between the two shoes, making sure the straight portion of the spring is connected to the trailing shoe (it's designed like this so as not to interfere with the handbrake lever).

6.77 . . . then refit the leading shoe hold-down pin, spring and retainer - stretch the return spring, with the straight part of the spring over the adjuster lever, and hook it in the notch on the adjuster lever (arrow).

6.75 If the adjuster assembly on your brake is non-captive (not retained by the return spring), refit it now. Spread the shoes apart and insert each end of the adjuster in the proper slots in the shoes. If the slot in the handbrake lever end of the adjuster is stepped, like this one, make sure the longer part of the slot is positioned over the handbrake lever. Note: Some adjuster screws are marked to indicate which side of the vehicle they go on. If this is the case, be sure to refit the adjuster on the proper side. Also, this mark usually faces up.

6.78 Make sure the shoes are seated properly in the slots in the wheel cylinders and are engaged with the adjuster screw assembly.

6.79 Using a screwdriver, stretch the return spring into its hole in the front shoe.

6.81 Wiggle the assembly to make sure it is seated properly against the backing plate. Refit the brake drum, then adjust the brakes as described in Chapter 4.

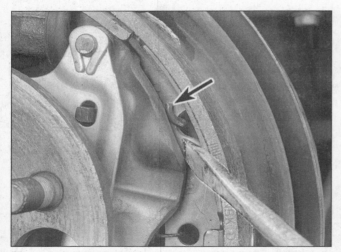

6.80 Prise the handbrake lever forward and check to see that the return spring didn't come unhooked from the trailing shoe.

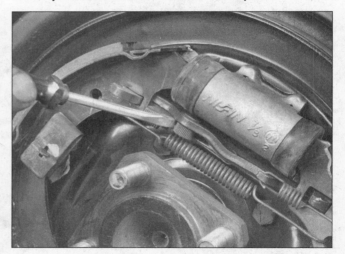

6.82 If your brake has a quadrant-style adjuster mechanism and the brake drum won't go back on after replacing the shoes, it will be necessary to retract the shoes. Put a screwdriver between the two parts of the ratchet and push in - spring pressure will retract the shoes.

Chapter 7
Handbrakes

Introduction

The handbrake is sometimes called the parking brake, because its main use is for preventing the vehicle from moving when it is parked. It is also referred to as the emergency brake, but on most vehicles it would be quite useless in an emergency situation where the regular service brakes have failed, unless there were plenty of straight, unoccupied road ahead.

Almost all car manufacturers place the handbrake at the rear wheels. The most popular exceptions to this rule are Subaru, Saab and (needless to say) Citroën. They place the handbrakes on the front wheels. Some older vehicles had the handbrake mounted on the

transmission extension housing, with a small brake drum on the driveshaft. This arrangement is still used on some Land Rovers.

There are four basic types of handbrake or parking brakes in use today, but regardless of design they share two things in common. One, they are all actuated by a lever, a pedal or a pullrod in the driver's compartment. Two, a cable or set of cables (sometimes one, sometimes two or more) connects the pedal, lever or pullrod with the handbrakes at the wheels.

On models with drum brakes at the rear wheels, the handbrake is simply incorporated into the drum brake assembly. A lever is connected to the top of the secondary, or trailing brake shoe (depending on brake

1	Nut	15	Piston
2	Handbrake lever	16	Circlip
3	Return spring	17	Piston locator
4	Bolt	18	Piston seal
5	Bracket	19	Actuator screw
6	Lever seal	20	Balance spring and retainer
7	Not used	21	Thrust washer
8	Outer brake pad	22	Shaft seal
9	Inner brake pad	23	Cap
10	Pad retainer	24	Bleeder screw
11	Bolt boot	25	Caliper housing
12	Sleeve	26	Wear sensor
13	Piston dust boot	27	Mounting bolt
14	Check valve		

7.1 Exploded view of a typical rear brake caliper with an actuator screw-type handbrake mechanism

7.2 Exploded view of a typical rear brake caliper with an adjuster spindle (pushrod)-type handbrake mechanism

7.3 Typical drum-in-disc type handbrake mechanism

1	Operating lever	4	Adjuster nut
2	Pad carrier assembly	5	Adjuster bolt
3	Pawl assembly	6	Handbrake pad

7.4 Cutaway view of a handbrake mechanism that is attached to a rear caliper and uses separate pads

7.5 Some vehicles use a single handbrake cable to operate both handbrake mechanisms, like on this Jaguar

design) and attached to the handbrake cable at the bottom. A strut (duo-servo type) or strut/adjuster screw (leading/trailing type) is placed between the two brake shoes, near the top. When the lever attached to the brake shoe is pulled by the handbrake cable it pushes (via the handbrake strut) the primary, or leading shoe against the brake drum. This causes the pivot of the lever to bear against the secondary, or trailing brake shoe, forcing it against the brake drum, thereby locking the wheel. See Chapter 6 for more information on the drum brakes.

There are three common kinds of handbrake set-ups on vehicles with disc brakes on the rear wheels (actually, if the handbrakes are situated on the front wheel brakes, only one of these designs is used). The most common type is fitted to floating or sliding calipers and operates the caliper through a large actuator screw that winds into the back of the caliper piston **(see illustration)**. When the handbrake is set, the cable pulls on a lever attached to the actuator screw, causing the screw to turn. The helical thread on the screw tries to turn the piston, but the piston is prevented from turning because it is engaged with the brake pad by one or two lugs that fit into the backing plate of the inner brake pad. This causes the piston to move out, applying the brake pads the same way it does when hydraulic pressure pushes it out. This system works well, but with age the actuator screws tend to seize in the caliper piston, and the seal around the actuator screw is a potential source of brake fluid leakage.

A similar type of handbrake arrangement that is integral with the caliper uses a cam-driven adjuster spindle (or pushrod) to force the piston out from the caliper **(see illustration)**.

Another type of handbrake on vehicles with disc brakes at the rear wheels is like a little drum brake mounted inside the hub, or "hat" portion of the brake disc **(see illustration)**. The brake shoes are anchored to a small backing plate and operate just like the handbrake mechanism on a vehicle with drum brakes. The nice thing about this design is that it is virtually trouble-free, unless you forget to release the handbrake from time to time.

A less common kind of handbrake set-up employs an extra set of small brake pads mounted in a fixture attached to each rear caliper **(see illustration)**. They're like small, mechanically actuated calipers mated to the hydraulic calipers. Automatic adjusters in the handbrake pad carriers compensate for wear. On some vehicles that use this system, a single handbrake cable is connected to an operating lever on each mechanism **(see illustration)**, or to a linkage that operates both mechanisms.

Handbrake adjustment

Refer to Chapter 4, Maintenance, for the handbrake adjustment procedure.

Component renewal

Handbrake lever

On most vehicles you'll have to remove the centre console for access to the handbrake lever bolts. Once this has been done, unscrew the upper handbrake cable nut (the adjusting nut) and pull the cable from the lever **(see illustration)**. Some vehicles have both cables attached to the lever. It may be necessary to remove a trim piece from the lever for access to the adjuster nut.

Remove the nuts or bolts holding the lever to the floorpan **(see illustration)** and detach the lever. On some models it may be necessary to unplug the electrical connector from the handbrake light switch.

Refitting is the reverse of removal, but be sure to adjust the handbrake cable(s) by following the procedure outlined in Chapter 4.

1	Screw	5	Bolts
2	Covers	6	Lever assembly
3	Handbrake switch connector	7	Grip
		8	Release button
4	Adjusting nut	9	Return spring

7.6 Typical handbrake lever details

7.7 On some vehicles, the handbrake lever is mounted to the side of the centre hump

1	Bolt	3	Release rod
2	Pedal assembly	4	Bolt

7.8 Typical parking brake pedal mounting details

7.9 Typical parking brake pedal assembly with a vacuum release diaphragm

1 Pullrod
2 Handbrake light switch
3 Primary cable
4 Intermediate lever
5 Secondary cable

7.10 Typical handbrake pullrod assembly

Parking brake pedal or pullrod

If necessary for access to the pedal, remove the under-dash panel and/or the kick panel trim. Unplug the electrical connector from the warning light switch.

If you're removing a pedal assembly, disconnect the release rod or cable from the pawl lever on the mechanism **(see illustration)**. If equipped with a vacuum-operated release, disconnect the vacuum hose or, if the vacuum release diaphragm is not mounted on the pedal assembly, disconnect the link rod from the assembly **(see illustration)**.

If you're removing a handbrake pullrod, detach the cable from the end of the pullrod **(see illustration)** or remove the clevis pin and detach the rod from the lever **(see illustration)**.

Remove the bolts or nuts and detach the pedal or pullrod assembly. Refitting is the reverse of removal, but be sure to adjust the handbrake as described in Chapter 4.

7.11 Here's another typical pullrod-actuated handbrake mechanism

7.12 Typical two-cable handbrake cable arrangement

1 Adjusting nut
2 Bolt
3 Front cable
4 Spring
5 Cable connector
6 Clip
7 Rear cables
8 Bolts
9 Spring
10 Clip

7.13 Typical three-cable handbrake cable arrangement

7.14 Typical multiple-cable handbrake cable arrangement

7.15 Some handbrake cables are connected to the pedal assembly by a nut. Others, like this one, are attached by a clip (A). To detach the cable casing from the pedal bracket, depress the tangs (B) and slide the casing from the bracket

7.16 Detach the other end of the cable from the frame bracket

7.17 Separate the cables at the equaliser . . .

7.18 . . . or at the cable connector (push the cable toward the centre opening and pull it out)

7.19 On this type of rear cable set-up, prevent the rod from turning by holding it with a pair of locking pliers, then remove the adjusting nut. The rear cables can now be separated at the adjuster

7.20 Unclip the handbrake cable end from the handbrake lever on the trailing shoe, then remove the shoe and lever assembly

7.21 Depress the retention tangs (arrows) to free the cable and casing from the backing plate. A pair of pliers can be used for this. Alternative methods include a close fitting box-end spanner slipped over the retainer, which will compress the tangs, or a small hose clamp tightened over the tangs.

7.22 On some vehicles the handbrake cable casing is attached to the backing plate by a bolt (arrow)

7.23 Typical handbrake cable-to-caliper attachment details

Handbrake cable(s)

Some vehicles are equipped with only one handbrake cable, but chances are that your vehicle has two, maybe even three or four cables to actuate the handbrake mechanisms **(see illustrations)**. These cables are retained by a series of clips or clamps and sometimes also by guide wires and springs, to keep tension on the cables to prevent them from interfering with other parts.

Before renewing a handbrake cable, loosen the adjusting nut(s) to provide some slack. See Chapter 4 for a sampling of handbrake cable adjusters.

Front cable

If the vehicle is equipped with a lever-actuated handbrake, remove the centre console. If the brake is pedal-actuated, remove the kick panel, if it's in the way.

Detach the cable from the lever, pedal or pullrod. In most cases this will involve removing a nut or a clip from the end of the cable **(see illustration)**.

Raise the vehicle and support it securely on axle stands.

Remove any bolts or clips retaining the cable casing, then push the cable and casing through the grommet and out from the floorpan. Some casings are retained by locking tangs which must be depressed to allow them to pass through the bracket **(see illustration)**. If the cable casing does not continue out through the floorpan, however, pull the cable and casing into the interior of the vehicle instead.

Detach the other end of the cable from the equaliser or cable connector (see illustrations). Refitting is the reverse of removal. Make sure the grommet around the cable casing where it passes through the floor is properly seated. Adjust the brake by following the procedure described in Chapter 4.

Rear cable

Loosen the rear wheel nuts, raise the vehicle and support it securely on axle stands. Remove the wheel.

Detach the cable from the connector, equaliser or adjuster **(see illustration)**.

Disconnect the cable casing from any mounting brackets or clips.

If the vehicle has rear drum brakes, remove the brake drum (see Chapter 5) and detach the end of the cable from the handbrake lever **(see illustration)**. In some cases this will require removal of the brake shoes. Depress the tangs on the cable casing retainer and push the cable and casing out through the backing plate **(see illustration)**, or unscrew the bolt retaining the casing to the backing plate **(see illustration)**.

If the vehicle has disc brakes, detach the cable from

7.24 Unhook the handbrake shoe return springs - a special brake spring removal tool makes this much easier and is available at most motor factors (some designs use a shoe-to-shoe spring at the top and the bottom of the shoes, instead of the arrangement shown here).

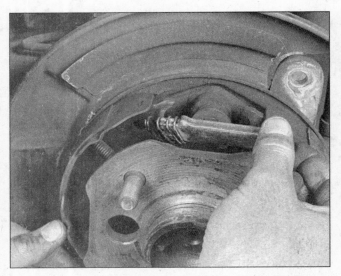

7.25 Turn and lift out the shoe strut and spring, if fitted.

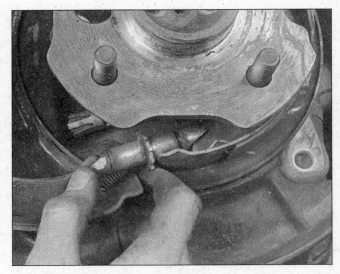

7.27 Pull the front shoe out and remove the adjuster screw

7.26 Remove the shoe hold-down springs. This particular type requires an Allen key. Other styles are like the more conventional hold-down spring retainers as found in a drum brake assembly.

7.28 Twist the shoe and remove the shoe-to-shoe spring

the handbrake lever on the caliper (or from the actuating lever on vehicles with drum-in-disc handbrake assemblies), separate the cable casing from its bracket (it's usually retained by a clip) and remove the cable **(see illustration)**.

Refitting is the reverse of removal. Be sure to adjust the brake as outlined in Chapter 4.

Handbrake shoes (drum-in-disc type handbrake)

Warning: *The dust created by the brake system may contain asbestos, which is harmful to your health. Never blow it out with compressed air and don't inhale any of it. An approved filtering mask should be worn when working on the brakes. Do not, under any circumstances, use petroleum-based solvents to clean brake parts. Use brake system cleaner only!*

Note: *All four handbrake shoes should be renewed at the same time, but only work on one brake assembly at a time, using the other side for reference, if necessary.*

Loosen the rear wheel nuts, raise the vehicle and support it securely on axle stands. Remove the wheels.

Remove the brake disc (see Chapter 5). Before

7.29 Pull the cable out and up to free it from the lever on the rear shoe (some designs don't use a lever attached to the shoe - the shoes are spread apart by an actuator on the backing plate)

7.31 Apply a light coat of high-temperature grease to the handbrake shoe contact areas (shaded areas) on the backing plate

7.30 Use a pair of pliers to crimp the C-clip to the pivot pin

7.32 Clean the adjuster screw and apply high-temperature grease to the indicated areas (arrows)

removing anything else, clean the handbrake assembly with brake system cleaner. Position a drain pan under the brake to catch the fluid and residue.

Remove the handbrake shoe return springs from the anchor pin (see illustration). Some designs don't have an anchor pin, but have two shoe-to-shoe springs instead.

Spread the tops of the shoes apart and remove the shoe strut and spring assembly, if equipped (see illustration). Take note as to how the strut is positioned.

Remove the hold-down springs from the shoes (see illustration). Pull the front shoe from the backing plate and remove the adjuster (see illustration), then detach the shoe-to-shoe spring (see illustration).

If the handbrake is actuated by a lever attached to the rear shoe, detach the cable from the lever (see illustration), then remove the shoe. Using a screwdriver, spread the C-clip on the handbrake lever pivot pin then remove the lever, shim (if equipped) and pin. Transfer the parts to the new rear shoe and crimp the C-clip to the pin using a pair of pliers (see

7.33 When assembled, the tension spring and adjuster screw should be arranged like this

7.34 Be sure to align the access hole with the adjuster cut-out (arrows) when refitting the disc over the parking brake assembly

illustration).

Thoroughly wash the backing plate with brake system cleaner. Feel the shoe contact areas on the backing plate - it they're rough, smooth them out with a file or sandpaper. Apply a thin coat of high-temperature grease to the contact areas **(see illustration)**.

Clean the adjuster screw threads, then apply a film of high-temperature grease to the moving parts of the adjuster **(see illustration)**.

If it was necessary to detach the cable from the handbrake lever on the rear shoe, reattach it now. Mount the rear shoe to the backing plate and refit the hold-down spring.

Connect the shoe-to-shoe spring between the bottom of each shoe, then refit the adjuster **(see illustration)**. Position the front shoe on the backing plate and refit the hold-down spring. Refit the handbrake strut. Make sure you refit it with the spring end facing proper direction. Refit the shoe return springs.

Refit the brake disc. If the disc isn't retained by screws, temporarily refit a couple of wheel nuts to hold the disc in place. **Note:** *If the axle flange has a notch machined into it that corresponds with the adjuster hole in the disc, be sure to refit the disc with the adjuster hole over the notch* **(see illustration)**.

Adjust the handbrake shoes by referring to the Chapter 4 section entitled "Drum brake adjustment."

Refit the brake caliper and wheel. Lower the vehicle and tighten the wheel nuts securely.

Chapter 8
Brake pedals and brake light switches

8.1 Brake pedal mounting details (Ford)

8.2 Brake pedal mounting details (Toyota)

Brake pedal assemblies

There are two basic designs of brake pedal assemblies - ones that are mounted on the floor, and the hanging type. Most operate the master cylinder (via the brake servo, if equipped) through a pushrod, but some

1	Pedal shaft cover	13	Master cylinder support bracket
2	Clutch pedal		
3	Brake pedal	14	Bolt
4	Rubber pad	15	Lockwasher
5	Pivot bush	16	Nut
6	Pedal shaft	17	Clevis pin
7	Bracket	18	Spring washer
8	Lockwasher	19	Plain washer
9	Bolt	20	Split pin
10	Return spring	21	Locknut
11	Lockwasher	22	Pedal limit stop
12	Bolt		

8.3 Brake pedal mounting details (Triumph)

are connected to a pullrod and lever assembly, which in turn actuates the master cylinder. Some vehicles, especially ones that are marketed in countries that have right-hand drive vehicles as well as in countries that have left-hand drive vehicles, have brake pedals attached to a shaft that traverses the bulkhead to actuate the master cylinder, which is mounted on the side opposite the driver.

On some vehicles equipped with a manual transmission, the brake pedal pivots on the same shaft as the clutch pedal.

Brake pedals seldom require attention, but, as stated in Chapter 4, it's a good idea to crawl under the dash occasionally to inspect the pedal bushes and mounting hardware. Refer to the accompanying illustrations for examples of typical brake pedal assemblies **(see illustrations)**.

8.4 Brake pedal mounting details (Jeep)

8.5 Brake pedal mounting details (Hyundai, Dodge, Mitsubishi) - this design uses a cross-shaft to actuate the master cylinder

1 Pedal
2 Return spring
3 Clevis
4 Locknut
5 Pullrod
6 Brake light switch

8.6 Brake pedal mounting details (Saab) - this design uses a pullrod to operate a lever mechanism, which depresses the servo pushrod

1 Pin and clip
2 Return spring
3 Nut
4 Lockwasher
5 Bolt
6 Pedal
7 Seal
8 Clamp screw
9 Lockwasher
10 Brake pedal lever
11 Seal
12 Clutch pedal lever
13 Bush
14 Seal
15 Thrust washer
16 Woodruff key
17 Shaft
18 Brake pedal lever
19 Return spring
20 Seal
21 Bush

8.7 Brake pedal mounting details (VW)

1 Clutch pedal
2 Pedal shaft
3 Bush
4 Locating pin
5 Brake pedal
6 Master cylinder pushrod
7 Pushrod lock plate
8 Not used
9 Bush
10 Mounting tube
11 Accelerator pedal roller
12 Accelerator connecting
   lever
13 Clip
14 Accelerator pedal lever pin
15 Mounting bracket
16 Circlip
17 Stop plate

8.8 Brake pedal mounting details (VW)

8.9 Brake pedal mounting details (Jaguar)

Removal and refitting

Removal and refitting of the brake pedal usually involves nothing more than detaching the return spring, disconnecting the master cylinder (or servo) pushrod from the pedal, removing a nut or clip and withdrawing the pivot shaft. On some vehicles it will be necessary to remove the clutch pedal, if the brake pedal hangs from the clutch pedal shaft.

If it becomes necessary to remove the brake pedal on your vehicle, carefully study the arrangement of the brake pedal and bushes, the mounting of the brake light switch, how the brake pedal is attached, and, if your vehicle is equipped with a manual transmission, how the clutch pedal is mounted. Make a sketch of all the components, both fitted and as you remove them. Lay all the parts out in order after they're removed. Inspect the pivot bushes and shaft for wear, replacing parts as necessary. If any split pins or spring clips were removed, be sure to renew them.

Before refitting the pedal assembly, lubricate the pivot bushes and shaft with multi-purpose grease. Adjust the pedal freeplay and check the pedal reserve distance as outlined in Chapter 4.

Brake light switches
Check

Have an assistant stand behind the vehicle while you depress the brake pedal. All of the brake lights should come on (on some vehicles the ignition switch must be turned to the On position). If any bulbs are burned out, renew them.

If none of the lights come on, check the fuses. If the fuses are OK, check the brake light switch. There are two kinds of brake light switches - mechanically operated and hydraulically operated.

Hydraulically operated switches

Hydraulically operated switches are usually screwed into the end of the master cylinder. When pressure is built up in the system, the switch completes the circuit and sends power to the brake lights. With the ignition key On, use a test light to check for power on one side of the switch. If there's no power on either terminal, trace the circuit for a broken or unplugged wire. If there is power, have an assistant depress the brake pedal while you probe the other side of the switch with the test light. If the test light comes on, the switch is OK. The problem lies somewhere between the switch and the brake lights. If power is not available when the pedal is depressed, the switch is faulty.

Mechanically operated switches

Mechanically operated switches are mounted on the brake pedal arm or on a bracket near the top of the brake pedal. When the pedal is at rest, the switch plunger is depressed by the brake pedal arm, which raises one of the contacts inside the switch and opens the circuit. When the brake pedal is depressed, the spring-loaded plunger extends from the switch body, the contacts inside the switch connect, and the circuit is completed. To test the switch, probe the terminals of the switch with a test light - one of the terminals should be "live" (on some vehicles it may be necessary to turn the ignition key to the On position). Now, probe the other terminal with the test light and depress the brake pedal - the test light should light up. If it doesn't, the switch is defective. If it does, but the brake lights don't come on, the problem lies somewhere between the switch and the brake lights.

Renewal

Hydraulically operated switch

Unplug the wires from the switch. Unscrew the switch and fit the new one, tightening it securely. Bleed the circuit of the brake system from which the switch was removed (see Chapter 9). This can usually be done right at the master cylinder, but if after doing so the brake pedal feels spongy, bleed the circuit at the wheels.

Mechanically operated switch

Disconnect the battery earth lead, then detach the wires from the switch.
a) If the switch is retained by a locknut, unscrew the nut and detach the switch from its bracket **(see illustration)**. If the switch has an adjusting nut on it, measure the distance from the end of the switch to the adjusting nut, then fit the adjusting nut on the new switch in the same location. Fit the switch in its bracket, then fit the locknut. If necessary, loosen the locknut and adjusting nut and adjust the switch in or out to provide proper brake light operation. Make sure the switch allows the pedal to fully return to its at-rest position.
Note: *Some brake light switches regulate the brake pedal height (at-rest position). Each vehicle with this type of set-up has its own pedal height specification, but a general setting can be made while still ensuring that*

8.10 This brake light switch (arrow) is attached to a mounting bracket and is retained by a locknut and an adjusting nut. Some switches like this are threaded into the bracket and only have a locknut (Toyota)

8.11 This type of brake light switch simply pushes into the clip on the mounting bracket. The brake pedal automatically adjusts the position of the switch (General Motors)

the switch isn't prohibiting the pedal from returning far enough, which could prevent the master cylinder pistons from returning fully. Detach the master cylinder (or servo) pushrod from the brake pedal. Adjust the switch so the pushrod mounting hole or pin in the pedal arm is in alignment with the hole in the pushrod clevis (or mounting) hole. Reattach the pushrod to the pedal arm. (This adjustment probably won't be necessary if the dimensions of the new switch are the same as the old one, and the adjusting nut has been fitted in the same position on the new switch as it was on the old one.)

b) Some switches look like they're threaded, but upon closer inspection you notice that the "threads" are serrations. This type of switch is held in its bracket by a plastic bush or a pressed-metal clip **(see illustration)**. To remove it, simply pull it out of the bracket (if it's stubborn, you may have to prise it out). Fit the new switch by pushing it into its mounting hole. Depress the brake pedal, then push the switch in a little more. Release the brake pedal - the pedal will push the switch back into its bracket, adjusting it automatically.

c) If the switch is attached to the brake pedal where the master cylinder (or servo) pushrod is attached, remove the nuts and bolt (or clip) from the pedal and detach the pushrod and switch, carefully noting how the switch and pushrod fit together (see illustration 8.4). Also note the locations of any spacers or bushes. Refit the switch by reversing the removal procedure. Tighten the fasteners securely.

d) Another type of switch simply clips to the brake pedal and to the steering column **(see illustration)**. On one variation of this design, the switch clips to the pedal and the arm of the switch is retained to the steering column with a spring clip or split pin **(see illustration)**. Detach the electrical connector, remove the clip or split pin from the switch arm (if applicable), then unclip the switch from the pedal and steering column. Refit the switch by reversing the removal procedure. Some of these switches have a "set lever" for adjusting the switch. To adjust, depress the pedal and, using a hooked tool, pull on the set lever while listening for a click. Release the pedal.

1 Cruise control connector
2 Brake light switch
3 Wave washer
4 Retaining clip
5 Wire hook (for adjusting the switch)

8.12 This kind of brake light switch clips onto the brake pedal. The actuating arm is attached to the steering column by a retaining clip (General Motors/Vauxhall)

8.13 This brake light switch snaps onto the steering column and the brake pedal and uses no bolts or clips (General Motors/Vauxhall)

Chapter 9
Hydraulic systems and servos

Introduction

This Chapter deals with the removal, refitting, bleeding and, where applicable, the overhaul procedures of the components that make up the brake hydraulic system. Because of their close relationship with the master cylinder, brake servos are also included in this Chapter.

There are a few important things to remember when working on the hydraulic system:

a) Cleanliness cannot be over-emphasised. Before opening any part of the hydraulic system, clean the fittings and surrounding area with brake system cleaner. This will prevent dirt from contaminating the fluid in the lines.

b) Never re-use old brake fluid. It contains moisture which could boil as heat is conducted through the brake linings to the hydraulic components. When brake fluid boils, gas bubbles are produced. Since gas is compressible, a spongy brake pedal or a complete loss of braking pressure can result. Also, old brake fluid might be tainted with contaminants, which can cause problems. Always use new brake fluid from a small, sealed brake fluid container. Since brake fluid is hygroscopic (meaning it is able to absorb moisture), fluid stored in an open container, or even in a sealed large container (if it's been sitting on the shelf for a long time) may contain too much moisture.

c) **Warning:** *Brake fluid can harm your eyes and damage painted surfaces, so take great care when handling or pouring it. If you get any fluid in your eyes, immediately flush your eyes with water and seek medical attention.*

d) Before attempting to overhaul a hydraulic component, check on the availability and cost of parts, as well as the availability and cost of a new or rebuilt unit. Sometimes rebuilt parts are cheaper than an overhaul kit! Also, not all master cylinders, calipers and wheel cylinders are rebuildable.

e) When overhauling a hydraulic component, work in a spotlessly clean environment. A single grain of dirt can potentially ruin the entire job.

f) Never use petroleum-based solvents for cleaning brake system components. Use brake system cleaner - it leaves no residue when it dries. Brake fluid will also clean hydraulic components, but if you're cleaning parts that are very dirty, it takes quite a bit of fluid to remove it all. Methylated spirit can also be used, but it contains water - if this is used, you'll have to wait a little longer to let the parts dry. Brake system cleaner is the best way to go.

g) Don't use compressed air to dry off brake parts. Even filtered compressed air may contain too much moisture. It might even contain traces of oil.

h) Never hone an aluminium (or any non-cast iron) hydraulic cylinder.

i) Whenever any part of the hydraulic circuit is opened, that part of the system must be bled of air (refer to the Brake system bleeding procedure in this Chapter).

Master cylinder

Warning: *This procedure does not apply to master cylinders that are directly attached to, or integral with, an Anti-lock Brake System (ABS) hydraulic control unit. Many ABS units require a special tool to cycle the valves in the ABS modulator or hydraulic control unit to ensure complete system bleeding. Vehicles equipped with such ABS systems should be taken to a dealer service department or other properly equipped garage for any master cylinder work.*

The following procedure depicts the removal, overhaul and refitting procedures for the brake master cylinder. Follow the sequence of illustrations, being careful to read the caption under each one. Also be sure to read any accompanying text.

HINTS & TIPS

- Remember, not all master cylinders are rebuildable. Before beginning work, check with accessory shops or dealer parts departments for parts availability and prices. Rebuilt master cylinders are available on an exchange basis, which makes this job quite easy, and much less time consuming.

Removal

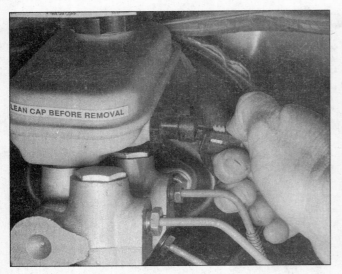

9.1 If fitted, unplug the electrical connector from the fluid level sensor

9.3 Remove the master cylinder mounting nuts - some vehicles have two nuts, some have three and others have four. Remove the master cylinder from the vehicle, being careful not to spill any fluid on the vehicle's paint. Remove the reservoir caps, or cover and gasket, then discard any fluid remaining in the reservoir.

9.2 Place rags under the brake line fittings and prepare caps or plastic bags to cover the ends of the lines once they're disconnected. Caution: Brake fluid will damage paint. Cover all painted surfaces and avoid spilling fluid during this procedure. Loosen the tube nuts at the ends of the brake lines where they enter the master cylinder. To prevent rounding off the flats on these nuts, a split ring spanner, which wraps around the nut, should be used. Pull the brake lines away from the master cylinder slightly and plug the ends to prevent contamination. Also plug the openings in the master cylinder to prevent fluid spillage.

Overhaul

Warning: *It's essential that you obtain the correct rebuild kit for the master cylinder you're servicing. Be sure to state the year, make and model of the vehicle when buying a kit. If you're still unsure, take the master cylinder with you when buying parts. DO NOT try to use the rebuild kit for a cast iron master cylinder in an aluminium unit, or vice versa. And don't open a new parts kit until you've compared the contents to the old parts you're removing from the master cylinder you intend to rebuild. Always verify parts availability before beginning a master cylinder rebuild.*

Note: *When disassembling the master cylinder, lay out all of the components in order. If the overhaul kit contains piston seals rather than entire piston assemblies, renew the seals on one piston at a time. Before disassembling a piston, make a sketch, noting the location of all seals, washers, springs, retainers, etc. Most importantly, pay attention to the direction the seal lips face. Refer to the accompanying illustrations to familiarise yourself with the master cylinder components* **(see illustrations)**.

1 Pressure differential warning switch
2 O-ring
3 Front proportioning valve
4 O-ring
5 Rear proportioning valve
6 O-ring
7 Plug
8 O-ring
9 Pressure differential switch piston assembly
10 Reservoir cover
11 Reservoir diaphragm
12 Reservoir
13 Grommet
14 Circlip
15 Primary piston assembly
16 Secondary seal (of secondary piston)
17 Spring retainer
18 Primary seal (of secondary piston)
19 Secondary piston
20 Spring
21 Cylinder body

9.4 An exploded view of a typical detachable-reservoir master cylinder with built-in proportioning valves and an integral pressure differential warning switch (General Motors/Vauxhall)

9.5 An exploded view of a typical cast iron master cylinder

9.6 Exploded view of a detachable-reservoir master cylinder with built-in proportioning valves (General Motors/Vauxhall)

1 Fluid level sensor
2 Proportioning valve cap
3 O-ring
4 Spring
5 Proportioning valve piston
6 Proportioning valve seal
7 Reservoir cap
8 Diaphragm
9 Roll pin
10 Reservoir
11 O-ring
12 O-ring
13 Circlip
14 Primary piston assembly
15 Secondary seal
16 Spring retainer
17 Primary seal (of secondary piston)
18 Secondary piston
19 Spring
20 Master cylinder body

Remove the reservoir (detachable reservoir models only)

9.7 Some reservoirs are secured by a retaining screw (arrow). Remove the screw and carefully pull the reservoir off the master cylinder body.

9.8 On some master cylinders, the reservoir is attached with a pair of roll pins which can be removed with a hammer and a small punch. Once the pins are removed, pull the reservoir off.

9.9 If the reservoir sticks in the grommets, carefully prise it off.

9.10 Remove the grommets from the master cylinder body.

9.11 Some detachable reservoirs are retained by a large bolt in the centre of the reservoir. Remove the bolt . . .

9.12 . . . then slide the hose clamp back on the hose and detach the hose from the fitting. If the sealing washers on the fitting bolt have been leaking, leave the hose attached and remove the fitting bolt and sealing washers, instead.

Remove the master cylinder pistons

Note: *Mount the master cylinder in a vice, with the jaws of the vice clamping on the cylinder mounting flange. Use padded jaws or a rag to prevent damage to the flange mounting surface.*

9.13 Using a Phillips screwdriver, depress the pistons, then remove the piston stop bolt or screw (be sure to use a new sealing washer on the stop bolt when you're reassembling the master cylinder). Note: Not all master cylinders have a stop bolt or screw.

9.14 On some master cylinders, the piston stop is a screw or pin which is accessed from inside the reservoir.

9.15 Depress the pistons again and remove the circlip or retainer

9.16 Some master cylinders use a stopper cap like this instead of a circlip. Depress the pistons and use a hooked tool to bend the tang up, then remove the stopper cap.

9.17 Remove the primary piston assembly from the master cylinder . . .

9.18 . . . followed by the secondary piston assembly. If the piston is stuck inside the bore, remove the cylinder from the vice and tap it against a wood block. Pull the piston straight out - the bore could be damaged if the piston becomes cocked. Note: Some (although very few) manufacturers call this piston the primary piston, and the one removed in the previous step the secondary piston.

Inspect and prepare the master cylinder

Clean the cylinder bore with brake system cleaner and inspect the bore for scoring and pitting. **Warning:** *DO NOT, under any circumstances, use petroleum-based solvents to clean brake parts.* Light scratches and corrosion on the cylinder bore walls can be usually be removed with crocus cloth or with a hone. However, deep scratches or score marks mean the cylinder must be replaced with a new unit. **Warning:** *Never attempt to hone an aluminium master cylinder.* If the pistons or bore are severely corroded, renew the master cylinder. Always use new piston cups and seals (or piston assemblies) when overhauling a master cylinder.

9.19 If equipped, unscrew the proportioning valves from the master cylinder

9.20 If you have a cast iron unit and you received new tube seats in the overhaul kit, screw a self-tapping screw into each tube seat . . .

9.21 . . . then use a crowbar as a fulcrum and remove the tube seats by levering them out with a pair of needle-nose pliers. The best way to drive the new seats into place is with a spare section of brake line (a flared end) with a tube fitting. Place the flared portion of the line over the seat, slide the tube nut into place and thread it into the outlet. Tighten the fitting to push the seat into place.

Overhaul the pistons

Note 1: *Some master cylinder rebuild kits come with all of the seals for each piston. Others come with the seals for one of the pistons (usually the secondary piston) and an entire new piston assembly. Some kits simply furnish two new piston assemblies. Use all of the parts in the overhaul kit. The following portion of this sequence depicts typical seal renewal procedures for a variety of master cylinders - it may differ slightly from the pistons in your master cylinder. As you disassemble your pistons, BE SURE to note how the components are arranged (make a sketch if necessary). Ignore any steps which don't apply to your pistons.*

Note 2: *A few manufacturers have named the pistons exactly opposite that of most manufacturers - they call the piston nearest the front of the vehicle the primary piston, and the piston nearest the brake servo (or bulkhead) the secondary piston.*

9.22 Begin overhaul of the secondary piston assembly by removing the spring, which can be pulled straight off.

9.23 Remove the piston seal retainer, followed by the seal.

9.24 Remove the seal protector, if fitted, by inserting a thin instrument through one of the holes in the piston.

9.25 Prise the remaining piston seals off the piston

9.26 Lubricate the new seals with clean brake fluid and fit them on the piston, making sure all of the components of the piston are situated in the right place, and the seal lips are facing the proper direction (the two outer seals must face the ends of the pistons. If there are three seals, the one in the centre faces the spring end). When fitting the seals, use your fingers only, or you may damage them.

9.27 Some secondary pistons only have two seals - the seal lips must face the ends of the pistons.

9.28 The seals on the primary piston are removed in the same manner as the seals on the secondary piston were (see illustrations 9.22 to 9.25). When fitting the primary seal on the end of the primary piston, the lip must face away from the centre of the piston. Remember, lubricate the seals with clean brake fluid before fitting them.

9.29 Fit the seal guard over the seal . . .

9.30 . . . then push the spring onto the end of the piston.

9.31 Insert the spring retainer into the spring

9.32 Insert the spring retaining bolt through the retainer and spring and thread it into the piston. Tighten it securely.

9.33 Lubricate the O-ring with clean brake fluid and fit it on the piston. Some primary pistons use a secondary seal instead of an O-ring (some use both) - the seal lip should face the spring end of the piston (the same way the lips of the primary seal face).

Overhaul the proportioning valve and/or the pressure differential warning switch

Note: *This portion of the overhaul procedure only applies to master cylinders with an integral pressure differential warning switch and/or integral proportioning valves.*

Proportioning valve

9.34 Unscrew the proportioning valves from the master cylinder body. Disassemble the valves (one at a time), then lubricate the seals with clean brake fluid and fit the new components, making sure the seal lips are pointing in the right direction. Refit the valves and tighten the caps securely.

9.35 Remove the pressure differential warning switch from the side of the master cylinder, then mount the cylinder in a vice (use wood blocks as shown). Unscrew the switch piston plug.

9.36 Pull out the switch piston assembly. Remove the components from the piston.

9.37 Lubricate the small O-ring with clean brake fluid and fit it on the switch piston

9.38 Fit the metal retainer on the switch piston

9.39 Lubricate the large O-ring with clean brake fluid and fit it on the switch piston

9.40 Fit the plastic retainer on the switch piston

Pressure differential warning switch

9.41 Lubricate the switch piston assembly and fit it into its bore in the master cylinder body. Remove the master cylinder from the vice, then push the piston in until the small-diameter portion of the piston is visible through the pressure differential warning switch hole. Fit the pressure differential warning switch (using a new O-ring) and tighten it securely. Fit a new O-ring on the switch piston plug (be sure to lubricate it with clean brake fluid) and fit the plug, tightening it securely.

Fit the piston assemblies and reservoir

Note 1: *Lubricate all components with lots of clean brake fluid before refitting them into the master cylinder.*
Note 2: *A few manufacturers have named the pistons exactly opposite that of most manufacturers - they call the piston nearest the front of the vehicle the primary piston, and the piston nearest the brake servo (or bulkhead) the secondary piston.*

9.44 On models with detachable reservoirs, lubricate the new reservoir grommets with clean brake fluid and fit them in the openings in the master cylinder. Lay the reservoir face down on a bench and push the master cylinder straight down over the reservoir fittings with a rocking motion. If equipped, fit the retaining screw or roll pins (see illustrations 9.7 and 9.8). If your reservoir is retained by a large bolt (see illustration 9.11), use new sealing washers, if applicable.

9.42 Fit the secondary piston . . .

9.43 . . . followed by the primary piston. Depress the pistons and install the snap-ring or retainer as shown in illustration 9.15, then depress the pistons again and install the piston stop bolt, screw or pin (see illustrations 9.13 and 9.14) Be sure to use a new seaing washer on the stop bolt or screw.

9.45 Fit the reservoir diaphragm in the cover, if applicable.

Bench bleed

Whenever the master cylinder is removed, the entire hydraulic system must be bled. The time required to bleed the system can be reduced if the master cylinder is filled with fluid and bench bled before it's fitted on the vehicle. Since you'll have to apply pressure to the master cylinder piston, the master cylinder should be mounted in a vice, with the jaws of the vice clamping on the mounting flange.

Bleeder tube method

If available, attach a pair of master cylinder bleeder tubes to the outlet ports of the master cylinder **(see illustration)**. These can be made up using scrap brake pipe and unions. Fill the reservoir with fluid, then slowly push the pistons into the master cylinder (a large Phillips screwdriver can be used for this) - air will be expelled from the pressure chambers and into the reservoir. Because the tubes are submerged in fluid, air won't be drawn back into the master cylinder when you release the pistons. Repeat the procedure until no more air bubbles are present.

Remove the bleed tubes, one at a time, and refit plugs in the open ports to prevent fluid leakage and air from entering. Fit the reservoir cover or cap.

Alternative methods

An alternative to the bleed tube method is to insert threaded plugs into the brake line outlet holes and snug them down so that air won't leak past them - but not so tight that they can't be easily loosened. Fill the reservoir with brake fluid of the recommended type.

Remove one plug and push the pistons into the bore to expel the air from the master cylinder. A large Phillips screwdriver can be used to push on the piston assembly.

To prevent air from being drawn back into the master cylinder, the plug must be replaced and lightly tightened down before releasing the pressure on the piston.

Repeat the procedure until only brake fluid is expelled from the brake line outlet hole. When only brake fluid is expelled, repeat the procedure at the other outlet hole and plug. Be sure to keep the master cylinder reservoir filled with brake fluid to prevent the introduction of air into the system.

Since high pressure isn't involved in the bench bleeding procedure, an alternative to the removal and renewal of the plugs with each stroke of the piston assembly is available. Before pushing in on the piston assembly, remove one of the plugs completely. Before releasing the piston, however, instead of replacing the

9.46 One way to bleed air from the master cylinder before refitting it on the vehicle is with a pair of bleed tubes

plug, simply put your finger tightly over the hole to keep air from being drawn back into the master cylinder. Wait several seconds for brake fluid to be drawn from the reservoir into the bore, then depress the piston again, removing your finger as brake fluid is expelled. Be sure to put your finger back over the hole each time before releasing the piston, and when the bleeding procedure is complete for that outlet, refit the plug and tighten it before going on to the other port.

Refitting

Refit the master cylinder by reversing the removal procedure. Don't tighten the mounting nuts until after the fittings on the hydraulic lines have been threaded into the ports by hand. This will allow you to wiggle the master cylinder back and forth, if necessary, to connect

9.47 After the master cylinder is fitted, it can be bled by loosening the fittings (one at a time) and applying the brakes

9.48 Fitting details of a typical vacuum-operated brake servo (not all vehicles have a gasket between the master cylinder and the servo).

the lines without cross-threading the fittings.

If air entered the master cylinder after the bench bleeding procedure (or if you didn't bench bleed it), bleed the cylinder on the vehicle. To do this, have an assistant push the brake pedal to the floor and hold it there. Loosen the fitting nut (start with the one closest to the servo or bulkhead) to allow air and fluid to escape, then tighten the nut. Repeat this procedure on all fittings until the fluid is clear of bubbles **(see illustration)**. **Note:** *Some master cylinders have bleed valves, making it unnecessary to loosen the brake line fittings.*

Bleed the entire brake system as described later in this Chapter.

Brake servos

Vacuum-operated servos

Check

Perform the brake servo checking procedures described in Chapter 4. If a defective servo is not diagnosed from those checks, inspect the check valve. To do this, disconnect the vacuum hose where it connects to the metal pipe or the intake manifold (don't disconnect it at the servo). Apply pressure and suction to the end of the hose, to be sure air only flows away from the servo. If it flows in both directions or if there is no airflow at all, renew the check valve. On some vehicles the check valve is located inside the hose, requiring renewal of the hose.

If the check valve is functioning properly and the hose doesn't have a leak, the engine may be the culprit. If the engine is old and tired, if the ignition timing is way off or

if there's a large vacuum leak, it may not be producing enough vacuum to enable the servo to give satisfactory power assist. A restricted exhaust system could also be the cause of low vacuum.

Connect a vacuum gauge to the servo hose. Place the shifter in park (if the transmission is an automatic), block the wheels and start the engine. Allow the engine to

HINTS & TIPS

- Some engines, including most Diesel engines, are fitted with vacuum pumps which help generate vacuum to power the brake servo and other accessories. A defective vacuum pump will often make a loud rapping sound that rises and falls with engine speed. You can also test the operation of the vacuum pump as outlined in the engine vacuum check in the next paragraph.

9.49 To disconnect the brake servo pushrod from the brake pedal, remove the retaining clip (right arrow) and pull out the clevis pin (left arrow)

9.50 Most vehicles have four servo mounting nuts, accessible from under the dash

Clearance

9.51 Ideally, there should be zero clearance between the servo pushrod and the master cylinder pushrod, but there shouldn't be any interference either - if there is any interference, the brakes may drag; if there's much clearance, brake pedal travel will be excessive.

9.52 Turn the adjusting nut on the end of the brake pushrod to change the clearance - hold the pushrod with pliers to keep it from turning

reach normal operating temperature, then look at the gauge - there should be at least 15 in-Hg indicated at idle. If not, diagnose and repair the cause of low vacuum before condemning the brake servo. **Note:** *Engines with high-performance camshafts will have a lower and somewhat erratic reading at idle. Emission controlled vehicles from the mid 1970s tend to have slightly lower vacuum due to modified valve timing and retarded ignition timing.*

Removal

Note: *Brake servo units should not be disassembled. They require special tools not normally found in most service stations or garages. They are fairly complex and because of their critical relationship to brake performance it is best to renew a defective servo unit with a new or remanufactured one.*

Unbolt the master cylinder from the servo and pull it forward off the mounting studs, being careful not to kink the brake lines. This will usually provide enough room for servo removal. If you can't do this on your vehicle, remove the master cylinder completely.

Disconnect the vacuum hose where it attaches to the brake servo.

Working under the dash, disconnect the brake pedal return spring, then remove the clip (and clevis pin on most vehicles) to disconnect the pushrod from the brake pedal **(see illustrations)**. On some vehicles it may be necessary to remove a panel from under the dash, and maybe even an air conditioning or heater duct, for access to the pedal.

Remove the mounting nuts and withdraw the servo from the engine compartment **(see illustration)**. The mounting nuts on most vehicles are located under the dash. On some vehicles, however, the mounting nuts are removed from the engine compartment, directly behind the servo. Also, it may be necessary on some vehicles to remove one or more support braces.

Refitting

Refitting procedures are basically the reverse of those for removal. Tighten the servo mounting nuts securely. If a split pin was used to secure the clevis pin in the pushrod clevis, be sure to use a new one.

If the brake servo is being replaced, the clearance between the master cylinder and the pushrod in the servo must be measured and, if necessary, adjusted (this applies only to servos with adjustable pushrods) **(see illustration)**. Using a depth micrometer or vernier calipers, measure the distance from the piston seat (recessed area) in the master cylinder to the master cylinder mounting flange. Next, using a hand-held vacuum pump, apply 20 in-Hg of vacuum and measure

1 Nuts
2 Master cylinder
3 Servo unit
4 Nut (4)
5 Gasket

9.53 Mounting details of a hydraulically operated brake servo

the distance from the end of the vacuum servo pushrod to the mounting face of the servo (including the gasket, if any) where the master cylinder mounting flange seats. The measurements should be the same (indicating zero clearance). If not, subtract one measurement from the other - a slight amount of clearance is acceptable (approximately 0.004 to 0.020-inch). An interference fit is not acceptable because this means the servo pushrod would be depressing the master cylinder pistons slightly, even at rest.

If it is necessary to adjust the length of the pushrod, turn the adjusting screw on the end of the pushrod until the clearance is within the desired range **(see illustration)**.

Check the operation of the brakes before returning the vehicle to normal service.

Hydraulically operated servos

Check

Refer to Chapter 4 for the servo checking procedures. Checks that are any more involved than the ones described there require special testing equipment. Take the vehicle to a dealer service department or other garage for further diagnosis, if necessary.

Removal and refitting

Power steering fluid-operated servo

With the engine off, depress and release the brake pedal several times (at least 20) to discharge all pressure from the accumulator. Unbolt the master cylinder from the servo and pull it gently forward without straining the brake lines.

Disconnect the hydraulic lines from the servo unit. Plug all lines and openings to prevent excessive fluid loss and contamination.

Working inside the vehicle, above the brake pedal, disconnect the servo pushrod from the pivot lever, then remove the nuts securing the servo to the bulkhead **(see illustration)**.

Refitting is the reverse of removal. Be sure to tighten the line fittings securely and bleed the power steering system.

To bleed the power steering system, begin by checking the fluid level in the power steering fluid reservoir. Add fluid if necessary, until the level is at the Cold mark on the dipstick.

Start the engine and allow it to run at fast idle. With the wheels in the straight ahead position recheck the fluid level, adding more, if necessary, to reach the Cold mark.

Bleed the system by turning the steering wheel from side-to-side without hitting the stops. This will work the air out of the system. Keep the reservoir full of fluid as this is done. You'll know when the system is fully bled, as the steering wheel action will feel smooth and all strange noises coming from the power steering pump will cease.

Check the operation of the brakes. The brake pedal should not feel "hard" when depressed, and should feel smooth, not jerky.

Electro-mechanical type servo

Warning: Failure to fully depressurise the hydraulic unit before starting this procedure could result in bodily injury and damage to the painted surfaces of the vehicle. Wear eye protection when performing this procedure.

Make sure the ignition key is in the Off position, then disconnect the cable from the negative terminal of the battery. Depressurise the system by firmly pushing the brake pedal down a minimum of 10 times. Cover the wing and the area surrounding the brake master cylinder/brake servo unit.

Disconnect the electrical connectors at the pressure switch and the hydraulic pump. Using a split ring spanner, disconnect the brake lines from the unit **(see illustration)**.

Working under the dash, disconnect the pushrod from the brake pedal. Remove the mounting nuts that secure the unit to the bulkhead.

Carefully remove the servo /master cylinder unit from the engine compartment. **Note:** *The master cylinder portion of the unit should be bench-bled before refitting the unit.*

Refitting is the reverse of removal, but the system must be bled of air. Fill both sides of the reservoir to the Full marks with the recommended brake fluid. Turn the ignition switch to the On position. With the servo pump running, the brake fluid level in the servo side should decrease as the accumulator is pressurised. Watch the level and don't let the reservoir run dry.

Note: *The pump must shut off after 20 seconds. If not, turn the ignition key off after 20 seconds. Perform the following steps if the fluid in the servo side of the reservoir does not drop:*

a) Loosen the servo line fitting at the casting boss, directly below the accumulator.
b) Wait for brake fluid to gravity bleed from the loosened fitting.
c) When fluid starts to flow, tighten the fitting. Check for leaks or flow back to the reservoir.

Refit the reservoir cover. Make sure the ignition is Off, then depress the pedal ten times. Remove the reservoir cover and add fluid, if necessary. Repeat the bleeding procedure again and check the fluid level. Check the operation of the brakes before returning the vehicle to normal service.

Brake caliper

The following procedure depicts the removal, overhaul and refitting procedures for the brake caliper. If an overhaul is indicated (usually because of fluid leaks, a stuck piston or broken bleed screw) explore all options before beginning this procedure. New and factory rebuilt calipers are available on an exchange basis, which makes this job quite easy, and much less time consuming. Before beginning work, check with accessory shops and dealer parts departments for parts availability and prices. In some cases, rebuilt calipers are actually cheaper than rebuild kits.

Removal

Warning: *Dust created by the brake system may contain asbestos, which is harmful to your health. Never blow it out with compressed air and don't inhale any of it. An approved filtering mask should be worn when working on the brakes. Do not, under any circumstances, use petroleum-based solvents to clean brake parts. Use brake system cleaner only.*
Note: *Always rebuild or renew the calipers in pairs - never rebuild just one of them. Loosen the front wheel nuts, raise the vehicle and support it securely on axle stands. Remove the front wheels.*

On models where the brake hose threads directly into the caliper, disconnect the brake line fitting from the brake hose (refer to Hoses and lines in this Chapter, if necessary), then unscrew the hose from the caliper. (If the caliper is only being removed for access to other components, don't disconnect the hose.) On brake hoses with banjo fittings, unscrew the fitting bolt and detach the hose. Discard the two copper sealing washers on each side of the fitting and use new ones during refitting. Wrap a plastic bag around the end of the hose to prevent fluid loss and contamination.

To remove a fixed caliper, remove the bolts that attach the caliper assembly to the steering knuckle. To remove

1	Pushrod	6	Master cylinder
2	Electrical connector	7	Electro-hydraulic
3	Electrical connector		pump
4	Brake lines	8	Accumulator
5	Nut	9	Pressure switch

9.54 Fitting details of an electro-mechanical brake servo

a floating or sliding caliper, refer to the first few steps of the appropriate brake pad renewal sequence in Chapter 5 (caliper removal is the first part of the brake pad renewal procedure for those calipers).

Remove the brake pads from the caliper, also by referring to the appropriate sequence in Chapter 5.

Clean the caliper assembly with brake system cleaner. DO NOT use paraffin, petrol or petroleum-based solvents. And while you've got the caliper off, be sure to check the pads as well and renew them if necessary.

Overhaul

Fixed caliper

On some fixed calipers the pistons are a fairly loose fit in their bores. Try to work the pistons out by hand. If you can't, you'll have to use air pressure to force the pistons out. On most calipers this can be accomplished by removing the bolts holding the caliper halves together, separate the halves, then setting the pistons face-down on the workbench and applying pressurised air to the fluid inlet fitting. However, some manufacturers expressly state NOT to remove the bolts that hold the caliper halves together. These calipers are designed with short pistons which can be removed without separating the halves.

To find out if your caliper is the kind that should not be disassembled, place several rags in the middle of the caliper and apply air pressure to the fluid inlet port. **Warning:** *Wear eye protection, and never place your fingers in front of the pistons in an attempt to catch or protect them when applying pressurised air, as serious injury could occur. Apply only enough air pressure to ease the pistons out. The pressure from a foot pump is usually enough.* One piston may have to be fully depressed in its bore to provide enough space to remove the other piston. If the pistons can be removed without separating the caliper halves, go ahead and remove them (also, ignore any references in this procedure related to disassembling the caliper halves). If they are too long and can't be removed, you have the kind of caliper that is OK to disassemble.

Remove the transfer tube, if equipped. Use a split ring spanner, if available **(see illustrations)**.

Mount the caliper assembly in a bench vice lined with wood or equipped with brass protector jaws. **Caution:** *Clamp on the caliper mounting lugs, NOT the caliper itself!* Remove the bridge bolts that hold the two halves of the caliper together. Separate the two caliper halves.

Peel the dust boot out and away from the caliper

9.55 An exploded view of a fixed brake caliper - this type uses a transfer tube to deliver fluid from one half of the caliper to the other

9.56 This fixed brake caliper doesn't have a transfer tube - instead, internal passages, sealed with O-rings where the caliper halves meet, deliver fluid from one half of the caliper to the other

housing and out of the piston groove **(see illustration)**.

Place each caliper-half face down (pistons facing down) on top of a block of wood and, while holding the caliper-half down against the wood with one hand, plug the hole for the brake hose, apply a brief burst of pressurised air through the hole for the transfer tube and

pop out the pistons. **Warning:** *Keep your fingers away from the pistons while doing this.* The outer caliper-half also has another hole, for the bleed screw, which must be fitted during this procedure, or the air will go in one hole and out the other, instead of pushing out the pistons. If a piston becomes cocked in its bore during removal, don't try to jerk it out with a pair of pliers, or you will damage the piston and the bore. Instead, carefully tap the piston back into its bore until it's square and try again.

Remove the pistons, noting which bore each of them belongs to - they should be returned to the same bores.

9.57 As you peel away the old dust boots, not how they're fitted over both the caliper housing retainer and into the piston groove - that's exactly how the new boots must be fitted during reassembly

9.58 Use a small wooden or plastic tool to peel the old piston seals out of the piston bores - don't use a metal tool or you might damage the bore walls

If there are springs behind the pistons, remove them.

Using a small pointed wooden or plastic tool, remove the piston seals from the groove in the cylinder bore **(see illustration)**. Discard the old seals. And be careful! Don't scratch or gouge the piston bore or the seal groove.

Clean everything with brake system cleaner and allow the parts to dry. Inspect the piston bores in both housings for scratches, scoring and pitting. Black stains in the bore walls are caused by the piston seals and are harmless. Light scratches, scoring and pitting can be cleaned up with crocus cloth. If the damage is deeper, the caliper should be replaced (rebuilt units are

9.59 When you fit the pistons into the caliper halves, coat them with fresh brake fluid, double-check the new seals to make sure they're properly seated into their grooves in the piston bore walls and make sure the pistons are square to the bores

9.60 Exploded view of a floating caliper with an integral torque plate (mount)

available). Light honing is permissible on cast iron calipers, but NEVER attempt to hone an aluminium caliper.

The pistons should be similarly inspected and cleaned up as necessary. If a piston is severely damaged - pitted, scored or the chrome plating worn off - renew the caliper.

Clamp the mounting lugs of the inner half of the caliper in a bench vice with protector jaws. Dip the new piston seals in clean brake fluid and fit them in the caliper grooves. Position each seal into its groove at one spot and gently work it around the piston bore with your finger until it's properly seated. **Warning:** *Do NOT use old seals!*

Coat the outside diameter of the pistons with clean brake fluid and refit them in the cylinder bores with the open end of each piston facing away from the caliper **(see illustration)**. If the caliper is equipped with springs behind the pistons don't forget to refit them first. Position the piston squarely in the bore and apply a slow, steady pressure until the piston is fully seated. If you encounter resistance, remove the piston and make sure the seal is properly fitted.

Fit the new dust boots into their grooves in the caliper and the pistons. Make sure the dust boots are properly seated.

Remove the inner caliper-half from the bench vice and mount the outer caliper-half the same way. Fit the seals, pistons and dust boots using the same method.

If your caliper does not have a transfer tube, fit new O-ring seals in the counterbore(s) around the fluid passage(s) **(see illustration 9.56)**.

Refit the inner caliper-half onto the outer caliper-half that's still clamped into the vice, refit the bridge bolts and tighten. Refit the transfer tube (if applicable) and tighten the fittings securely. Refit the bleed screw, if removed. Refer to page 9-38 for the caliper refitting procedure.

Floating and sliding calipers (except opposed-piston calipers) - front (and rear on models with "drum-in-disc" handbrakes)

If your caliper has an integral torque plate on which the caliper floats, remove the bolts that secure the caliper halves, then separate the halves and remove the inner portion from the torque plate **(see illustrations)**.

If the piston dust boot is held in place by a retaining ring, remove the ring and pull the dust boot out **(see illustrations)**.

Place several rags or a block of wood in the centre of the caliper to act as a cushion (unless you have the kind

9.61 With the caliper held in a vice, remove the bolts that secure the inner and outer halves of the caliper frame together, then separate them (caliper with integral torque plate) . . .

9.62 . . . then slide the inner half of the caliper off the torque plate

of caliper shown in illustration 9.60), then use pressurised air, directed into the fluid inlet, to remove the piston **(see illustration)**. If you separated the caliper halves to remove the torque plate (as shown in illustrations 9.61 and 9.62), place the caliper on the workbench, piston facing down, and direct the pressurised air into the fluid inlet **(see illustration)**.

Use only enough air pressure to ease the piston out of the bore. If the piston is blown out, even with the cushion in place, it may be damaged. **Warning:** *Never place your fingers in front of the piston in an attempt to catch or protect it, as serious injury could occur.*

Remove the dust boot from the caliper bore. Some types of dust boots have to be prised out **(see illustration)**. Now, using a wood or plastic tool,

1	Guide pin (mounting bolt)
2	Sleeve
3	Bush
4	Outer pad
5	Inner pad
6	Wear sensor
7	Pad retainer
8	Dust boot
9	Piston
10	Piston seal
11	Bleed screw
12	Caliper housing

9.63 Exploded view of a floating brake caliper (General Motors/Vauxhall)

9.64 Exploded view of a single-piston floating caliper (Mitsubishi)

1 Guide pin (mounting bolt)
2 Lock pin (mounting bolt)
3 Bush
4 Torque plate (caliper mounting bracket)
5 Guide pin boot
6 Lock pin boot
7 Retaining ring
8 Dust boot
9 Piston
10 Piston seal
11 Brake hose
12 Caliper body
13 Inner brake pad
14 Outer brake pad
15 Shim
16 Anti-rattle clip
17 Shim

9.65 Remove the boot retaining ring with a small screwdriver - be extremely careful not to gouge or scratch the piston or the piston bore

remove the piston seal from the groove in the caliper bore **(see illustration)**. Metal tools may cause bore damage.

Remove the bleed screw, then remove and discard the caliper pin (mounting bolt) bushings, sleeves and boots, if equipped **(see illustration)**.

Clean the remaining parts with brake system cleaner. Allow the parts to air dry. Inspect the surfaces of the piston for nicks and burrs and loss of plating. **Note:** *Some pistons are made of a plastic-like material called phenolic. If your caliper contains this kind of piston, be sure to check it for cracks, chips and other surface irregularities* **(see illustration)**. If surface defects are present, the caliper must be replaced. Check the caliper bore in a similar way. Light polishing with crocus cloth is permissible to remove slight corrosion and stains. Light

9.66 Exploded view of a dual-piston floating brake caliper (Mitsubishi)

1 Guide pin (mounting bolt)
2 Lock pin (mounting bolt)
3 Bush
4 Torque plate (caliper mounting bracket)
5 Dust boot
6 Retaining ring
7 Piston dust boot
8 Piston
9 Piston seal
10 Caliper body
11 Inner brake pad
12 Outer brake pad
13 Shim
14 Shim
15 Anti-rattle clip

9.67 With the caliper padded to catch the piston, use pressurised air to force the piston out of its bore - make sure your fingers aren't between the piston and the caliper

honing is also permissible on cast iron calipers, but NEVER attempt to hone an aluminium caliper. Discard the caliper pins if they're severely corroded or damaged.

Lubricate the new piston seal with clean brake fluid and position the seal in the cylinder groove using your fingers only **(see illustration)**.

If the dust boot on your caliper is held in place by a retaining ring, or if it has a hard casing around its outer diameter which seats in the caliper, fit the new dust boot in the groove in the end of the piston **(see illustration)**. Dip the piston in clean brake fluid and insert it squarely into the cylinder. Depress the piston to the bottom of the cylinder bore **(see illustration)**. Seat the boot in the caliper counterbore using a boot refitting tool (see illustration 9.103) or a blunt punch **(see illustration)**, or refit the retaining ring **(see illustration)**, depending on design.

If the dust boot on your caliper has a lip or flange at the bottom which seats in the upper groove in the caliper bore, refit the boot on the bottom (closed end) of the piston **(see illustration)**. Lower the piston and

9.68 On calipers with integral torque plates, place the caliper piston-side down and direct pressurised air into the brake hose inlet port to eject the piston

9.71 To remove a caliper pin boot, grab it with a pair of needle-nose pliers, twist it and push it through the caliper frame

9.69 If the dust boot has a rigid casing, carefully prise it out of the caliper

PHENOLIC PISTON
INSPECTION

MINOR SURFACE IMPERFECTIONS ARE ALLOWABLE, PROVIDED THEY DO NOT ENTER THE DUST BOOT GROOVE AREA

NO CRACKS, CHIPS, GOUGES, OR ANY OTHER SURFACE DAMAGE ON PISTON OD IS ACCEPTABLE

CRACKS COMPLETELY ACROSS PISTON FACE NOT ACCEPTABLE

BOTTOM OF DUST BOOT GROOVE

9.72 Phenolic pistons must be carefully inspected for signs of damage, as shown

9.70 To remove the seal from the caliper bore, use a plastic or wooden tool - a pencil will do the job

9.73 Position the new seal in the cylinder groove - make sure it isn't twisted

9.74 On calipers with dust boots that have rigid casings (or boots that use a retaining ring), slip the boot over the piston . . .

9.77 On calipers that use retaining rings, seat the boot in its groove, then fit the retaining ring

9.75 . . . then push the piston straight into the cylinder - make sure it doesn't become cocked in the bore

9.78 On calipers where the flange of the boot fits into a groove in the caliper, place the piston boot onto the bottom of the piston . . .

9.76 If you don't have a boot refitting tool, gently seat the boot with a punch

9.79 . . . then tuck the fluted portion of the boot into the upper groove of the caliper bore and bottom the piston in the bore

9.80 If you have trouble refitting the piston and boot as described in illustrations 9.78 and 9.79, fit the big end of the dust boot into the caliper, making sure the fluted portion is completely seated in its groove in the caliper bore . . .

9.81 . . . then place the piston against the open end of the new dust boot. Apply a small burst of filtered, unlubricated pressurised air to the fluid inlet to inflate the boot. Push the piston through the small end of the boot as the boot inflates . .

9.82 . . . as soon as the piston is in the boot, release the pressurised air and push the piston far enough into the bore to seat the ridge on the boot into its groove in the piston. Push the piston the rest of the way into the bore.

9.83 Caliper bush and seal details (General Motors/Vauxhall)

9.84 Be sure to lubricate the caliper bushes

boot assembly into the caliper bore and work the flanged portion (the lip) into its groove in the bore **(see illustration)**. If you have trouble seating the lip of the dust boot in its groove, try this alternative method:

a) Take the boot off the piston and refit the flanged portion of the boot into its groove in the caliper bore **(see illustration)**. Coat the cylinder bore and the walls of the piston with clean brake fluid.

b) Place the caliper in a vice, with the jaws of the vice clamping onto one of the caliper mounting ears. Place the piston against the end of the new dust boot, apply a small burst of pressurised air (make sure it's filtered and unlubricated) to the caliper bore to inflate the boot, then push the piston through the boot opening as the boot inflates **(see illustration)**. **Warning:** Once the piston has been inserted into the boot, stop applying pressurised air. Also, don't place your fingers between the piston and the caliper frame. Although it's possible to push the piston through the boot without applying

9.85 On calipers with integral torque plates, lubricate the torque plate pins with silicone-based grease, then assemble the plate and the inner portion of the caliper - the caliper halves can now be bolted together

9.86 Remove the yoke-to-caliper bolts . . .

9.87 . . . then, using a screwdriver, prise the yoke holder off the yoke

pressurised air, it's extremely difficult and may damage the boot.

c) Continue to push the piston into the bore, then seat the dust boot into its groove near the outer end of the piston **(see illustration)**.

Fit the new mounting pin bushings and sleeves **(see illustrations)**. Be sure to lubricate the sleeves with silicone grease.

If your caliper has an integral torque plate on which the caliper floats, lubricate the torque plate pins with silicone grease and refit the torque plate to the inner half of the caliper **(see illustration)**. Attach the outer half of the caliper to the inner half, refit the bolts and tighten them.

Refit the bleed screw.

On sliding calipers, clean the sliding surfaces of the caliper and the caliper adapter. Refer to page 9-40 for the caliper refitting procedure.

Opposed-piston calipers - front

Remove the two bolts that attach the caliper to the yoke, then prise the yoke holder off the yoke **(see illustrations)**. This disengages the piston from the yoke. The caliper can now be detached from the yoke.

Remove the yoke holder from the inner piston, then remove the dust boot retaining rings from each piston **(see illustrations)**.

Pull the dust boots off the pistons, then push both pistons out of the caliper from the pad side **(see illustration)**. The piston seals can now be removed **(see illustration)**. If you can't remove the seals with

your fingers, use a wood or plastic tool - metal tools can cause bore damage.

Remove the grippers and collars from the yoke.

Clean everything with brake system cleaner and allow the parts to dry. Inspect the piston bore for scratches, scoring and pitting. Black stains in the bore walls are caused by the piston seals and are harmless. Light scratches, scoring and pitting can be cleaned up with crocus cloth. If the damage is deeper, the caliper should be replaced (rebuilt units are available). NEVER attempt to hone an aluminium caliper.

The pistons should be similarly inspected and cleaned up as necessary. If a piston is severely

9.88 Exploded view of a front opposed-piston brake caliper

9.89 Remove the retaining ring from the inner piston dust boot . . .

9.90 . . . then remove the retaining ring from the outer piston dust boot

9.91 Both pistons are removed from the caliper by pushing on the outer piston

9.94 Apply silicone grease to the inside of the dust boots prior to refitting

9.92 Remove the piston seals from the caliper bore

9.95 Fit the outer piston dust boot . . .

9.93 The pistons should be positioned like this when refitting the dust boots

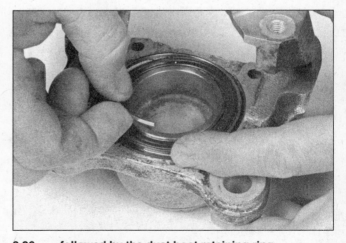

9.96 . . . followed by the dust boot retaining ring

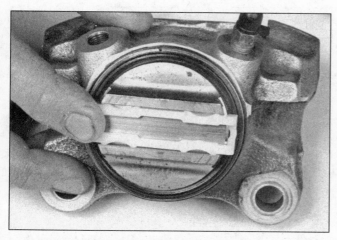

9.97 Fit the yoke holder on the inner piston

9.98 To seat the yoke holder on the yoke, place a crowbar or similar tool across the outer piston, then push down

9.99 Fit the bushes and boots (collars and grippers), lubricating them with silicone grease

damaged - pitted, scored or the chrome plating worn off - renew the caliper.

Check the yoke for cracks, excessive wear or other damage and renew it if necessary.

Lubricate the piston seals with clean brake fluid and fit them into their grooves in the caliper bore, making sure they seat correctly and aren't twisted. Lubricate the walls of the pistons with clean brake fluid (or silicone grease, if it was supplied in the rebuild kit). Refit the pistons into their respective ends of the bore. Don't refit them like you removed them (both pistons through the same side of the caliper).

Press the outer piston into the bore so that the inner edge of the piston seal groove is in line with the inner edge of the caliper seal grooves **(see illustration)**. Apply silicone grease to the inside of the dust boots, then refit the dust boots and retaining rings **(see illustrations)**. Make sure the boots seat properly into the grooves in the pistons and the grooves in the caliper.

Press the yoke holder into its groove on the inner piston face, then position the caliper body in the yoke, making sure the yoke holder is aligned with the yoke **(see illustration)**. Place the entire assembly so the outer piston is facing up, then apply pressure to the outer piston to press the yoke holder onto the yoke **(see illustration)**.

Refit the grippers and collars into their holes in the yoke **(see illustration)**. Be sure to lubricate the collars with silicone grease.

Once the yoke holder is pressed onto the yoke, refit the two mounting bolts that retain the yoke to the caliper housing, tightening them securely.

Refer to page 9-38 for the caliper refitting procedure.

Floating and sliding calipers (except opposed-piston calipers) - rear (calipers with integral handbrake mechanisms)

Note: *If you're not sure what type of rear caliper you have, refer to the component descriptions in Chapter 1. Also, the following procedures are typical for the type of caliper designs they represent. There may be some differences between the calipers shown and the ones on your vehicle. Whenever disassembling a rear brake caliper, make sketches of the relationship of the components and lay the parts out in order as they are removed. As stated in the beginning of this Section, it may actually be more cost effective to purchase factory-rebuilt calipers rather than buy a rebuild kit and overhaul them yourself.*

Chapter 9

1 Nut	10 Pad retainer	20 Balance spring and retainer
2 Handbrake lever	11 Bolt boot	21 Thrust washer
3 Return spring	12 Sleeve	22 Shaft seal
4 Bolt	13 Piston dust boot	23 Cap
5 Bracket	14 Check valve	24 Bleed valve
6 Lever seal	15 Piston	25 Caliper housing
7 Not used	16 Circlip	26 Wear sensor
8 Outer pad	17 Piston locator	27 Mounting bolt
9 Inner pad	18 Piston seal	
	19 Actuator screw	

9.100   Exploded view of a rear brake caliper with an actuator screw-type handbrake mechanism (General Motors/Vauxhall)

9.101   Rotate the actuator screw to remove the piston

Calipers with an actuator screw-type parking brake mechanism

Remove the sleeves and bolt boots from the ends of the caliper, then remove the pad retainer (if equipped) from the end of the piston by rotating the retainer until the inside tabs line up with the notches in the piston **(see illustration)**.

Remove the handbrake lever nut, lever and seal. Place rags between the piston and the caliper frame, then turn the actuator screw with a spanner to work the piston out of the bore **(see illustration)**. Remove the balance spring then push on the handbrake lever end of the actuator screw to remove it. Remove the shaft seal and thrust washer from the actuator screw.

While being careful not to scratch the housing bore, remove the boot **(see illustration)**.

Using circlip pliers, remove the circlip, followed by the piston locator **(see illustration 9.100)**. Using a plastic or wooden tool, remove the piston seal from the caliper bore **(see illustration 9.70)**.

9.102 Carefully prise the dust boot out of the housing, taking care not to scratch the surface of the bore

9.103 Use a seal driver, if available, to seat the boot in the caliper housing

9.104 Sleeve boot refitting procedure
A   Fit the sleeve boot into the groove in the sleeve bore, then push the sleeve into the boot
B   Fit the other boot into the groove in the other side of the bore
C   Push the sleeve back and seat both boots into the grooves in the ends of the sleeve

Remove the bleed valve. Clean all parts not included in the repair kit with brake system cleaner. Allow the parts to dry. Inspect all parts for wear, damage and corrosion. **Note:** *It is okay to remove minor corrosion from the caliper bore using crocus cloth.*

Lubricate all of the internal parts with clean brake fluid. Fit a new piston seal into its groove in the caliper bore (see illustration 9.73).

Fit a new piston locator on the piston. Fit the thrust washer on the actuator screw with the greyish side toward the caliper housing and the copper side toward the piston assembly. Fit the shaft seal on the actuator screw, then refit the actuator screw onto the piston assembly.

Fit the piston assembly with the actuator screw and balance spring into the lubricated bore of the caliper. Push the piston into the caliper bore so the locator is past the retainer groove in the caliper bore. **Note:** *A pair of adjustable pliers might be necessary to press the piston into the caliper. Fit the circlip using circlip pliers.*

With the inside of the boot in the piston groove and

boot fold toward the end of the piston that contacts the brake pad, refit the caliper boot onto the piston. Use a seal driver to seat the caliper boot into the cylinder counterbore **(see illustration)**. If a seal driver isn't available, use a blunt punch and carefully tap around the outer circumference of the seal to seat it **(see illustration 9.76).** Fit the pad retainer on the piston.

Lubricate the outside diameter of the mounting bolt sleeves and the caliper sleeve cavities with silicone grease. Fit one sleeve boot into a groove of the sleeve cavity **(see illustration)**. Fit a sleeve through the opposite side of the sleeve cavity and continue pushing the sleeve until the boot lip seats in the sleeve groove.

Fit the boot in the opposite side of the sleeve cavity groove and push the sleeve through the cavity far enough for that boot to slip into the remaining groove of the sleeve. Repeat the sleeve boot refitting procedure to the remaining sleeve.

Refer to page 9-38 for the caliper refitting procedure.

9.105 Exploded view of a rear caliper with an actuator-spindle handbrake mechanism

9.106 Exploded view of the handbrake lever assembly

Calipers with an actuator spindle-type handbrake mechanism

Remove the caliper guide bush and dust boots **(see illustration)**. Discard all rubber parts. Clean the exterior of the caliper with brake system cleaner.

Prise the retaining ring off the dust boot with a screwdriver. Discard the boot.

Rotate the piston anti-clockwise using a brake piston turning tool (see Chapter 2) or a pair of needle-nose pliers, and remove the piston from the adjuster spindle.

Using a wood or plastic tool, remove the piston seal from the caliper bore groove **(see illustration 9.70)**. Metal tools may cause bore damage.

Remove the caliper bleed screw.

Using a pair of circlip pliers, remove the circlip above the stopper **(see illustration 9.105)**. Remove the adjuster spindle, stopper and connecting link. Separate the adjuster spindle from the stopper. Remove the O-ring from the adjuster spindle. Discard the O-ring.

Remove the return spring from the operating lever of the handbrake mechanism **(see illustration)**. Remove the operating lever nut and lockwasher. Mark the relationship between the operating lever and the shaft. Remove the operating lever from the shaft.

Remove the seal from the caliper housing. Also remove the shaft and the needle bearing.

9.107 Align the opening in the needle bearings with the bore in the caliper housing

9.108 When you fit the operating lever, be sure to align the marks you made before disassembly

9.109 Exploded view of the adjuster spindle and stopper assembly

Carefully examine the piston for nicks and burrs and loss of plating. If surface defects are evident, renew the caliper assembly. Inspect the caliper bore for similar damage and wear. You can lightly polish the bore with crocus cloth to remove light corrosion and stains. If that fails to clean up the damage, renew the caliper. Inspect the mounting bolt - if it's corroded or damaged, discard it. Also inspect the guide pin bushings for wear. If they're worn or corroded, renew them.

Lubricate the needle bearings with multi-purpose grease. Align the opening in the needle bearings with the bore in the caliper housing **(see illustration)**. Fit the needle bearings.

Fit the operating shaft into the caliper housing. Fit the operating lever **(see illustration)**. Align the marks made during removal. Fit the lockwasher nut.

Insert the connecting link into the operating lever shaft. Fit the O-ring onto the adjuster spindle. Position the stopper onto the adjuster spindle so the pins will align with the caliper housing **(see illustration)**. Fit the adjuster spindle and the stopper into the caliper.

Fit the stopper retaining circlip. Be sure the operating lever and adjuster spindle move freely. Fit the handbrake return spring.

Before reassembling the caliper, lubricate the piston bore and O-ring with clean brake fluid. Fit the O-ring into its groove in the caliper bore **(see illustration 9.73)**. Make sure it isn't twisted.

Lubricate the piston with clean brake fluid, then insert it into the caliper bore. Rotate the piston clockwise using a brake piston turning tool or a pair of needle-nose pliers, to refit it onto the adjusting spindle. Screw the piston in fully. Align the notches in the piston with the opening in the caliper.

Fit a new dust boot in the piston groove with the fold toward the open end of the piston. Seat the boot in the caliper bore. Fit the retaining ring.

Fit the dust boots for the guide pin bushings **(see illustration)**. Fit the caliper guide pin bush.

Refer to page 9-38 for the caliper refitting procedure.

9.110 Exploded view of the guide pin (mounting bolt) bushings and dust boots

9.111 Exploded view of a rear opposed-piston brake caliper

Opposed-piston calipers - rear

Unclip the two anti-squeal clamps and detach them from the yoke, then separate the caliper from the yoke and remove the yoke springs **(see illustrations)**.

Remove the caliper retainer clip **(see illustration)**.

Remove the inner and outer dust boot retaining rings, then remove the dust boots and push the pistons from the caliper **(see illustrations)**. Remove the piston seals from the grooves in the caliper bore **(see illustration 9.70)**.

Remove the outer piston from the inner piston by rotating it anti-clockwise **(see illustration)**. Remove the circlip from the outer piston, then lift out the components for inspection **(see illustrations)**.

9.112 Remove the anti-squeal clamps from the yoke

9.113 Separate the caliper from the yoke by pushing outward on the inner piston

9.116 Remove the retaining rings from both piston dust boots . . .

9.114 Prise the yoke springs from the yoke

9.117 . . . and peel the dust boots from the caliper

9.115 Remove the caliper retaining clip

9.118 Push the pistons out of the caliper

9.119 Separate the pistons by turning the outer piston anti-clockwise

9.121 . . . then remove the contents of the piston and lay the components out in order

9.120 Using circlip pliers, remove the circlip from the outer piston . . .

9.122 Remove the dust boot from the inner piston

Remove the dust boot from the inner piston **(see illustration)**. Remove the outer circlip from the inner piston. Lift off the spring cover and spring. Remove the inner circlip from the inner piston. Turn the inner piston upside-down and remove the spring seat and key plate.

Pull the pushrod out of the piston and remove the strut and O-ring. Disengage the return spring from the toggle lever **(see illustration)**. Remove the toggle lever and cam assembly by pulling it out of the inner piston. Remove the toggle lever lip seal from the inner piston.

Use a screwdriver to carefully prise out the seal and bearing retainer from the inner piston.

Check the outer surfaces of the inner and outer pistons for scoring, nicks, rust or other damage. If light rust or scoring is present, it can be removed with crocus cloth. If damage is deep, the piston must be replaced.

Check the threads on the pushrod. Make sure they are in good condition and renew the rod if necessary. Inspect the inner surface of the caliper bore for any nicks, scoring, rust or other damage. Again, if light rust or scoring is present, it can be removed using crocus cloth, but the caliper will have to be replaced if the damage is deeper.

Inspect the needle bearing inside the outer piston for freedom of movement. If any of the rollers are binding, the bearing will have to be replaced by prising it out.

Apply a light coat of silicone-based grease to the needle bearings.

Fit the seal and bearing retainer by gently tapping it into place with a plastic-head hammer. Fit a new lip seal onto the retainer.

Carefully insert the toggle lever and cam assembly

into the outer piston.

Lubricate both ends of the strut with silicone-based grease and refit it into the pushrod. Lightly lubricate the pushrod O-ring with silicone-based grease and refit it into its groove on the pushrod. Insert the strut and pushrod into the piston.

Fit the key plate over the pushrod. Be sure the pushrod is aligned so that the locating pin in the key plate is properly fitted into its hole in the piston. Fit the inner circlip into its groove in the piston.

Fit the spring seat, spring and spring cover then place an appropriately sized socket over the pushrod, so that it sits on the spring cover. Place the assembly in a vice and tighten the vice until the spring is compressed enough for the outer circlip to be fitted in its groove. Be careful that the spring cover is properly centred in the bore so that the tangs don't get damaged.

Fit a new lip seal onto the adjusting screw. Be sure the lip is facing in the proper direction **(see illustration)**. Lubricate the lip seal with silicone-based grease.

Place the adjusting screw into the bore in the outer piston. Place the bearing spacer, wave washer and spacer, in that order, over the adjusting nut. Fit the circlip into the outer piston. Fit the outer piston onto the pushrod.

Apply a light coat of silicone-based grease to the cylinder bore. Fit the new piston seals into their grooves inside the bore **(see illustration 9.73)**. Lightly lubricate the seals with silicone-based grease.

Apply a light coat of silicone-based grease to the seal groove on the inner piston. Wipe off any residual grease that may have got onto the exterior surface of the piston. Fit a new dust boot into position on the inner piston, then refit the retaining ring.

Apply a light coat of silicone-based grease to the outer surfaces of both pistons. Apply a light coat of silicone-based grease into the two dust boot grooves on either side of the caliper housing. Carefully insert the pistons into the caliper bore. Align the inner piston so the inner edge of its boot groove is in line with the inner edge of the caliper boot groove, then pull the boot into position on the caliper.

Align the outer piston in a similar fashion to the inner piston so that the inner edge of the dust boot groove is in line with the inner edge of the caliper seal groove **(see illustration)**. Fit the outer piston dust boot and retaining ring.

Place the caliper retainer into its groove.

Fit the yoke springs into position on the yoke **(see illustration)**.

Apply a light film of high-temperature grease to the indicated surfaces **(see illustration)**.

Fit the caliper into the yoke, then refit the anti-squeak clamps onto the yoke.

9.123 Use a screwdriver to remove the return spring from the toggle lever

9.124 The seal on the outer piston adjusting nut should be fitted like this

9.125 The pistons should be positioned like this when refitting the dust boots. Apply silicone grease to the boots before refitting them

9.126 The yoke springs should be fitted prior to attaching the caliper to the yoke

1 Yoke
2 Caliper body
3 Pad pin

9.127 The frictional surfaces of the yoke and caliper and the pad pin holes should be lubricated with high-temperature grease prior to refitting of the caliper to the yoke

Refitting

If you're servicing a fixed caliper, refit the caliper assembly and the caliper mounting bolts, then tighten the bolts, then refit the brake pads (see Chapter 5). If you're servicing a floating or sliding caliper, caliper refitting is a part of brake pad refitting in Chapter 5. Make sure you tighten the caliper pins/bolts.

On models where the brake hose threads directly into the caliper, connect the brake hose to the caliper and tighten it securely. Position the other end of the hose in its bracket and connect the brake line fitting. Tighten the fitting securely. On models that use banjo fittings, connect the hose to the caliper using new sealing washers. Tighten the banjo bolt securely.

Bleed the brakes as outlined in later in this Chapter.

Fit the wheels and wheel nuts. Lower the vehicle and tighten the wheel nuts securely.

After the job has been completed, firmly depress the brake pedal a few times to bring the pads into contact with the disc. Check the operation of the brakes before driving the vehicle in traffic.

Wheel cylinders

Note: If an overhaul is indicated (usually because of fluid leakage or sticky operation) explore all options before beginning the job. New wheel cylinders are available, which makes this job quite easy. If you decide to rebuild the wheel cylinder, make sure a rebuild kit is available before proceeding. Never overhaul only one wheel cylinder. Always rebuild both of them at the same time.

9.128 Unscrew the brake line fitting from the rear of the wheel cylinder with a split ring spanner, then remove the bolts (arrows) securing the wheel cylinder to the brake backing plate

9.129 On wheel cylinders that aren't retained by bolts, a pair of screwdrivers can be used to remove the wheel cylinder retainer

9.131 Remove the wheel cylinder dust boots

Removal

Remove the brake shoes (see Chapter 6). Unscrew the brake line fitting from the rear of the wheel cylinder **(see illustration)**. If available, use a split ring spanner to avoid rounding off the corners on the fitting. Don't pull the metal line out of the wheel cylinder - it could bend, making refitting difficult.

Remove the bolt(s) or clip securing the wheel cylinder to the brake backing plate **(see illustration)**. Remove the wheel cylinder. Plug the end of the brake line to prevent the loss of brake fluid and the entry of dirt.

Overhaul

To disassemble the wheel cylinder, remove the rubber dust boot from each end of the cylinder, then push out the two pistons, the cups (seals) and the expander/spring assembly **(see illustrations)**. Discard the rubber parts and use new ones from the rebuild kit when reassembling the wheel cylinder.

Inspect the pistons for scoring and scuff marks. If present, the pistons should be replaced with new ones. Examine the inside of the cylinder bore for score marks and corrosion. If these conditions exist, the cylinder can be honed slightly to restore it, but renewal is recommended. If the cylinder is in good condition, clean it with brake system cleaner. **Warning:** *DO NOT, under any circumstances, use petrol or petroleum-based solvents to clean brake parts!*

Remove the bleed screw and make sure the hole is clean.

Lubricate the cylinder bore with clean brake fluid, then insert one of the new rubber cups into the bore **(see illustration)**. Make sure the lip on the rubber cup faces in.

Fit the cup expanders, if equipped, onto the ends of the spring, insert the expander/spring assembly into the

BOOT   CUP   CYLINDER   BOOT

CUP

PISTON   BLEEDER SCREW   RETURN SPRING AND CUP EXPANDER ASSY.   PISTON

9.130 Exploded view of a typical wheel cylinder

9.132 Fit the piston cups with their open ends facing in, toward the cup expanders

9.133 Attach the cup expanders to the spring . . .

9.134 . . . then insert the expander/spring assembly into one end of the wheel cylinder housing (some wheel cylinders don't use expanders - they only have springs)

9.135 Fit a piston into each end of the wheel cylinder housing

9.136 Insert the wheel cylinder pushrods into the new dust boots, then fit the dust boots and pushrods onto both ends of the wheel cylinder (not all wheel cylinders have pushrods)

opposite end of the bore and push it in until it contacts the rear of the rubber cup **(see illustrations)**. Fit the remaining cup in the cylinder bore.

Fit the pistons **(see illustration)**. Insert the pushrods (if equipped) into the boots **(see illustration)**, then refit the boots and pushrods.

Refitting

Refitting is the reverse of removal. Attach the brake line to the wheel cylinder before refitting the mounting bolt(s) or clip and tighten the line fitting after the wheel cylinder mounting bolt(s) have been tightened or the clip has been fitted. If available, use a split ring spanner to tighten the line fitting.

Fit the brake shoes and brake drum, (see Chapter 6).

Bleed the brakes following the procedure described later in this Chapter. Don't drive the vehicle in traffic until the operation of the brakes has been thoroughly tested.

Hydraulic control valves

All vehicles have either a pressure differential warning valve that incorporates a brake warning switch to warn if one half of the hydraulic system fails or a fluid level sensor in the master cylinder reservoir, and most vehicles have a proportioning valve which restricts - at a given ratio - hydraulic pressure to the rear wheels when system hydraulic pressure reaches a certain point. Models with disc brakes in the front and drum brakes in the rear also have a metering valve (or hold-off valve) which limits the front brake pressure until the rear brake shoes have overcome the return springs and contacted the drums. The proportioning valve on some vehicles (notably station estates and pick-up trucks) is load-sensitive - it will allow more pressure to the rear brakes when there is a considerable load in the rear of the vehicle, but reduces the pressure to the rear brakes when the rear of the vehicle is light. The proportioning valves on some vehicles are screwed right into the outlet ports of the master cylinder.

Check

Pressure differential warning valve

The brake warning light normally comes on during the engine start sequence, then goes off again when the

engine starts. It can be checked functionally by opening one bleed screw slightly while an assistant presses down on the brake pedal. The light should come on with the ignition switch On.

Proportioning or metering valve

The testing procedures for these valves require special gauges for checking, as well as individual specifications for each different vehicle. If a problem is suspected with one of these valves, have it diagnosed by a dealer service department or other qualified garage, or simply renew the valve. Refer to Chapter 1 for descriptions of the proportioning and metering valves, and Chapter 3 for problems associated with these components.

Resetting

If the light for the brake warning system comes on, a leak or problem has occurred in the system and must be corrected. Once the leak or problem has been repaired, the pressure differential warning valve must be centred. Once the valve is centred, the brake light on the dash will go out.

Some valves are self-centering. This means that after a brake system failure has taken place and the problem has been fixed, it isn't necessary to reset the valve. Other types of valve must be reset manually. Make sure the master cylinder reservoir is full and the hydraulic system has been bled. Turn the ignition switch to On or Accessory. Slowly press the brake pedal down and the piston will centre itself, causing the warning light to go out. This will work with some valves. If it does not cause

9.137 On many vehicles, the combination valve (A) is located just under the master cylinder, and the pressure differential warning switch (B) is screwed into the centre of the valve

9.138 Typical load sensing proportioning valve mounting details

the light to go out, while an assistant is depressing the brake pedal, loosen the bleed screw in the circuit that did NOT have the problem. Close the bleed screw as soon as the light goes out or you'll have to reset the valve again by opening a bleed screw in the other hydraulic circuit.

Check the brake pedal for firmness and proper operation.

Renewal

Caution: Brake fluid will damage paint. Cover all painted surfaces and avoid spilling fluid during this procedure.

If a hydraulic system control valve is defective or if it is leaking, it must be renewed. Most are non-serviceable units anyway, so there is no point in disassembling one.

Remotely mounted valve (proportioning, metering or combination)

Disconnect the brake warning light connector from the warning light switch **(see illustration)**. Disconnect the brake line fittings from the valve assembly using a flare nut spanner to avoid rounding off the corners of the fittings. Plug the ends of the lines to prevent loss of brake fluid and the entry of dirt.

Remove the bolts and nuts securing the valve assembly to the chassis or bracket. If you're removing a load sensing proportioning valve **(see illustration)**, disconnect the linkage from the rear suspension. Remove the valve assembly. Refitting is the reverse of removal. Bleed the system by following the procedure described later in this Chapter. If necessary, centre the valve as described above (pressure differential valve only).

Master cylinder-mounted valve

If you're replacing a master cylinder-mounted proportioning valve, simply unscrew the line fitting from the valve (using a split ring spanner), then unscrew the valve from the master cylinder. Refitting is the reverse of removal, but be sure to use a new sealing washer if one was present.

Hoses and lines

Note: Refer to Chapter 4 for the brake hose and line inspection procedures.

Flexible hose renewal

Clean all dirt away from the ends of the hose. Disconnect the metal brake line from the hose fitting **(see illustration)**. You'll need a back-up spanner on some fittings. Be careful not to bend the frame bracket

or line. If necessary, soak the connections with penetrating oil. Remove the U-clip (lock) from the female fitting at the bracket and remove the hose from the bracket.

On models that use banjo fittings, unscrew the banjo bolt and disconnect the hose from the caliper, discarding the sealing washers on either side of the fitting. On models where the brake hose threads directly into the caliper, unscrew the hose from the caliper.

Using new sealing washers, attach the new brake hose to the caliper (models that use banjo fittings). Tighten the banjo bolt. On models where the brake hose threads directly into the caliper, tighten the hose fitting securely.

Pass the female fitting through the frame or frame bracket. With the least amount of twist in the hose, secure the fitting in this position. **Note:** *The weight of the vehicle must be on the suspension, so the vehicle should not be raised while positioning the hose. If this is not possible, raise the suspension with a floor jack to simulate normal ride height.*

Fit the U-clip (lock) in the female fitting at the frame bracket. Attach the brake line to the hose fitting using another spanner to counterhold the fitting. Tighten the fitting securely.

Carefully check to make sure the suspension or steering components don't make contact with the hose. Have an assistant push on the vehicle and also turn the steering wheel lock-to-lock during inspection.

Bleed the brake system as described later in this Chapter.

9.139 To disconnect a brake hose from the brake line fitting, place a spanner on the hose fitting (A) and loosen the tube nut (B) with a split ring spanner. Remove the U-clip (C) to detach the hose from the bracket.

Metal brake lines

When replacing brake lines, be sure to use the correct parts. Don't use copper tubing for any brake system components. Purchase steel brake lines from a dealer parts department or accessory shop.

When fitting the new line make sure it's well supported in the brackets and has plenty of clearance between moving or hot components. Make sure you tighten the fittings securely. After refitting, check the master cylinder fluid level and add fluid as necessary. Bleed the brake system and test the brakes carefully before placing the vehicle into normal operation.

> **HINTS & TIPS**
>
> • Prefabricated brake line, with the tube ends already flared and fittings fitted, is available at accessory shops and dealer parts departments. These lines are also sometimes bent to the proper shapes.

Brake system bleeding

Warning: Wear eye protection when bleeding the brake system. If the fluid comes in contact with your eyes, immediately rinse them with water and seek medical attention. Never use old brake fluid. It contains moisture and contaminants which will deteriorate the brake system components and could cause the fluid to boil when braking temperatures rise. This can lead to complete loss of pressure in the hydraulic system.
Note: Bleeding the brake system is necessary to remove any air that's trapped in the system when it's opened during removal and refitting of any hydraulic component.

Models without an Anti-lock Brake System (ABS)

Standard (two-person) bleeding procedure

It will probably be necessary to bleed the system at all four brakes if air has entered the system due to low fluid level, or if the brake lines have been disconnected at the master cylinder. If a brake line was disconnected only at a wheel, then only that caliper or wheel cylinder must be bled. If a brake line is disconnected at a fitting located between the master cylinder and any of the brakes, that part of the system served by the disconnected line must be bled. If you suspect air in the master cylinder, begin by bleeding the master cylinder on the vehicle **(see illustration 9.47)**.

Remove any residual vacuum from the brake servo (if

9.140 When bleeding the brakes, a hose is connected to the bleed screw at the caliper or wheel cylinder and then submerged in brake fluid - air will be seen as bubbles in the tube and container (all air must be expelled before moving to the next wheel)

equipped) by applying the brake several times with the engine off. Remove the master cylinder reservoir cover and fill the reservoir with brake fluid. Reinstall the cover.
Note: *Check the fluid level often during the bleeding operation and add fluid as necessary to prevent the fluid level from falling low enough to allow air bubbles into the master cylinder.*

Have an assistant on hand, as well as a supply of new brake fluid, an empty clear plastic container, a length of 3/16-inch plastic, rubber or vinyl tubing to fit over the bleed valve and a spanner to open and close the bleed valve.

The order of bleeding depends on the design of the brake system. It is worthwhile finding out the vehicle manufacturer's recommended sequence. Generally, the caliper or wheel cylinder farthest away from the master cylinder is bled first, then the other caliper or wheel cylinder, in the same half of the circuit just bled, would be bled of air.

If the hydraulic system in the vehicle being bled is split front-to-rear, as is the case with most rear-wheel drive vehicles, you would bleed the brakes in the following order on a right-hand drive vehicle:
Left rear
Right rear
Left front
Right front

If the hydraulic system is diagonally split, as is the case with most smaller front-wheel drive vehicles, you would bleed the brakes in this order on a right-hand drive vehicle:

Left rear
Right front
Right rear
Left front

Warning: *Regardless of the order used to bleed the brake hydraulic system, the vehicle should NOT be driven unless a satisfactory, firm brake pedal is obtained.*

Beginning at the first wheel cylinder or caliper to be bled, loosen the bleed screw slightly, then tighten it to a point where it's snug but can still be loosened quickly and easily. Place one end of the tubing over the bleed screw fitting and submerge the other end in brake fluid in the container **(see illustration)**.

Have the assistant depress the brake pedal slowly to get pressure in the system, then hold the pedal firmly depressed. While the pedal is held depressed, open the bleed screw just enough to allow a flow of fluid to leave the valve. Watch for air bubbles to exit the submerged end of the tube. When the fluid flow slows after a couple of seconds, tighten the screw and have your assistant release the pedal.

Repeat this procedure until no more air is seen leaving the tube, then tighten the bleed screw and proceed to the next wheel cylinder or caliper in the bleeding sequence, and perform the same procedure. Be sure to check the fluid in the master cylinder reservoir frequently. **Note:** *On the rear brakes of some drum brake systems, only the wheel cylinder on one side of the vehicle is equipped with a bleed screw. Both wheel cylinders are bled through the cylinder that has the bleed screw.*

Refill the master cylinder with fluid at the end of the operation. Check the operation of the brakes. The pedal should feel solid when depressed, with no sponginess. If necessary, repeat the entire process. Bleed the height (or load) sensing proportioning valve, if equipped. **Warning:** *Do not operate the vehicle if you are in doubt about the effectiveness of the brake system.*

Alternative methods

Vacuum bleed method

Several companies manufacture brake bleeder kits that use hand-held vacuum pumps to suck the air out of the hydraulic circuit. The pump is connected to a reservoir, which is connected to the bleed screw. When the bleed screw is opened and the vacuum pump is operated, fluid (and any air bubbles) will collect in the reservoir **(see illustration)**. The pump itself does not

9.141 The vacuum-operated brake bleeding method is a convenient way to bleed the brakes, and you don't need a helper to do it! Just connect the hose from the container to the bleed valve, connect the hand-held vacuum pump to the container, open the bleed valve and apply vacuum. Fluid and air will be sucked out and will collect in the container.

come in contact with the fluid. The normal bleeding sequence can be used.

This is a very convenient method which only requires one person, but it has a couple of potential drawbacks. Since the cups in the wheel cylinder depend on pressure to seal against the walls of the cylinder, negative pressure can cause air to be drawn around the lips of the seal and into the hydraulic circuit. This may not happen in every case, but is more likely if the cups in the wheel cylinder are old or the hydraulic system has not been maintained properly. Air can also be drawn past the bleed screw threads when the screw is loosened.

One-person method

In addition to the vacuum bleed method, which is also a one-person method, another single-handed bleeding method exists. A number of one-person bleeder kits are available, and your local accessory shop will almost certainly stock one of them.

The most common type of one-person bleeder kit is really nothing more than a hose with a check valve in it, and a container to collect the fluid **(see illustration)**. All you have to do is connect the bleed hose to the bleed screw, put the other end of the hose into the container (which must be partially filled with brake fluid) loosen the bleed screw and slowly pump the brake pedal. Fluid and air will be forced out of the circuit, past the check valve and into the container. The check valve prevents old fluid or air from being sucked back into the system.

HINTS & TIPS

- If you just can't seem to bleed all of the air out of a circuit, there are a couple of things you can try. Always keep in mind that air rises to the high points in an enclosed system.
a) Make sure the master cylinder is free of air. Re-bleed it if necessary.
b) Try raising the end of the vehicle being bled. This will help any air trapped in the system to find its way to the bleeder screw, which should be located at the highest point in its caliper or wheel cylinder.
c) Lightly tap the caliper or wheel cylinder with a hammer. This can dislodge air bubbles that cling to the walls of the hydraulic cylinder.
d) Follow the brake lines from the master cylinder, bleeding each line at each connection by loosening the fitting. Work from the closest fitting to the master cylinder to the farthest.
e) Try one of the alternative bleeding methods.

Another type of one-man bleeding kit consists of a hose connected to a bag, which must be suspended above the level of the bleed screw **(see illustration)**. Connect the hose to the bleed screw, open the bleed screw and slowly pump the brake pedal. The old fluid and air will be forced from the caliper or wheel cylinder and into the bag. Since air rises, the bubbles that have been pushed into the bag can't be sucked back into the system.

Gravity bleeding

Gravity bleeding is exactly what it sounds like - the force of gravity pulls the brake fluid through the lines to the bleed screw, and any air trapped in the lines flows out of the bleed screw with it. This procedure can't be used in systems incorporating residual pressure check valves, because the check valves prevent the flow of fluid. When using this procedure you have to be sure to check the fluid level from time-to-time, since the procedure can take an hour or even more. This method might, however, be the answer to a hydraulic system that just can't seem to be purged of air.

To start the gravity bleeding procedure, raise both ends of the vehicle and support it securely on axle stands. Attach a length of clear plastic hose to the bleed screw at each wheel and direct the end of each hose into a container. Open each bleed screw one full turn, making sure fluid flows from each hose. **Note:** *If fluid does not flow, it may be necessary to start a siphon.* **Warning:** *Don't do this by mouth - use a hand-held vacuum pump to start the siphon! Remember, don't let*

9.142 This type of brake bleeding set-up also allows you to bleed the brakes alone. Just attach the hose to the bleed screw and insert the other end into the container partially filled with fluid. Open the bleed valve and slowly pump the brake pedal - fluid and air will be expelled from the caliper, but the check valve in the hose prevents anything from being sucked back in.

the fluid in the master cylinder reservoirs drop too low.

Allow the fluid to drain until the fluid in each hose is free of bubbles. Tighten the bleed screws and check the operation of the brakes. Top up the fluid level in the master cylinder reservoir.

Pressure bleeding

This is the method most garages use to bleed brake systems. It's quick, easy, and probably the most effective way to bleed a hydraulic system.

With this method, an adapter is attached to the top of the master cylinder reservoir. A hose is connected between the adapter and the pressure bleeder unit. Air pressure is connected to the bleeder unit also. (The professional systems use air from a compressor. There is a DIY version which uses air pressure from the spare

9.143 Another type of one-person brake bleeder is this bag-type. In operation it works in a similar manner to the set-up shown in illustration 9.142, but it doesn't have a check valve. Air bubbles rise up into the bag, but they can't flow back into the hose. It is important to pump the pedal slowly in order for this method to be effective.

METERING VALVE BLEEDER

COMPRESS TOOL AND POSITION ONTO VALVE. RELEASE TO ALLOW SPRING ACTION TO FORCE BLEEDER ROD OUT.

9.144 When using a pressure bleeder, you may have to fit a metering valve bypass tool to defeat the metering valve. Otherwise, no fluid will flow to the front brakes.

tyre.) This forces pressurised fluid through the system - all you have to do is open the bleed valve at each wheel until the flow of fluid is free of air bubbles.

When using a pressure bleeder on some vehicles you'll have to use a metering valve override tool, which defeats the hold-off function of the metering valve so pressure can be directed to the front brakes **(see illustration)**. On some metering valves a plunger must be pulled out and held in the extended position - on others a button on the valve must be depressed. Special spring tools are available for this purpose. **Caution:** *Never use a rigid clamp or wedge to depress or pull out the valve plunger, since this can damage the metering valve internally. Either way, the tool must be removed after the bleeding process is complete.* **Note:** *It isn't necessary to defeat the metering valve when bleeding brakes manually, since the pressure created in the system is greater than the hold-off point of the valve (approximately 150 to 165 psi). It also isn't necessary to defeat the valve when using vacuum or gravity bleeding methods, since there basically is no pressure generated in the system.*

There are drawbacks, though. Pressure bleeding outfits are quite expensive and require special adapters to fit different master cylinder reservoirs. Also, great care must be taken to ensure that all pressure in the fluid reservoir is bled off before removing the adapter. If it isn't, brake fluid will "explode" everywhere, possibly causing damage to the vehicle's paint and injury to anyone nearby.

Models with an Anti-lock Brake System (ABS)

Warning: Consult the manufacturer's service information before carrying out any service operations other than brake pad or shoe renewal. Some systems operate at very high pressure (in excess of 2000 psi), and no attempt should be made to work on a high pressure hydraulic system until the system has been depressurised in accordance with the manufacturer's recommendations.

Chapter 10
Anti-lock Braking Systems (ABS)

General information

Note: *The following system and component descriptions offer a general overview of the ABS system, how it works, and the components that comprise a typical ABS system. It is not possible to cover the specifics of all ABS systems nor include in-depth troubleshooting and repair procedures in a manual of this size.*

What is ABS?

When a vehicle is rolling down the road and the driver applies the brakes, the energy of the moving vehicle is converted to heat through the brakes, which slows down the vehicle. The coefficient of friction between the road and the tyres increases too, as the tyres "grab" at the road. If the coefficient of friction exceeds that which the tyre can effectively deal with, the tyre begins to slide along the road surface. This is an example of wheel slip.

Wheel slip can be defined as the difference between the speed of the vehicle and the speed of the wheel against the ground. When a wheel is locked up and sliding, wheel slip of 100-percent is present. If the wheel is rolling along with the vehicle and the brakes are not applied, zero wheel slip is taking place. Normal braking takes place somewhere between these extreme percentages.

Unfortunately, not all instances of slowing down a vehicle fall under the "normal" category. During panic stops or hard braking on slippery surfaces, it's easy to lock up the wheels. When the wheels are locked up, it is impossible to maintain control of the vehicle - the wheels must be rolling in order to have directional control. Besides that, engineers have discovered that a rolling wheel with a slip factor of 8 to 35-percent under braking generates a much greater coefficient of friction between the tyre and the road than a sliding tyre does. When the wheels stop rolling but the vehicle keeps moving, it will follow the path of least resistance. To the dismay of many a motorist, this path of least resistance has lead right into an object of great resistance - like a telegraph pole or the proverbial brick wall!

Anti-lock Brake Systems work to avoid such situations by monitoring the rotational speed of the wheels. When the system senses a wheel turning too slowly in relation to the others, the hydraulic pressure to the brake at that wheel is reduced, preventing it from locking up.

All current anti-lock systems are fail-safe. They all have some form of mechanical override - in the event of a malfunction such as failure of the Electronic Control Unit (ECU), the brakes will function just like a standard (non-ABS) system.

Advantages

Anti-lock Brake Systems have three distinct advantages over a non-ABS brake system:
a) Since brake systems with ABS don't allow the wheels to lock up, tyre wear is improved. It is impossible for the tyres to get flat-spotted with an ABS system.
b) The driver of a vehicle equipped with ABS has a much greater degree of control over the vehicle than the driver of a vehicle not equipped with ABS. Even under hard braking, a vehicle with ABS can be steered.
c) A vehicle with ABS has a reduced tendency to aquaplane when braking in wet road conditions.

Limitations

Although a vehicle equipped with ABS will stop in the shortest possible distance achievable under the design parameters of the system (how much wheel slip the system will allow), there is certainly no guarantee that all accidents will be avoided. Tyres are still a limiting factor, and if the brakes are applied hard during cornering there is a good possibility that the tyres will lose traction. Remember, the system monitors rotational speed of the wheels, not lateral motion against the road (although some systems incorporate a lateral acceleration sensor or switch which, when activated, tells the control unit to reduce braking pressure so the tyres don't get overloaded and break traction).

If the driver applies the brakes too late, the ABS

HINTS & TIPS

- When braking on snowy or icy road surfaces, or in dirt or gravel, an Anti-lock Brake System will not bring the vehicle to a stop in the shortest possible distance. A locked or nearly locked wheel is preferred under these conditions, because a wedge of snow or dirt will build up under the front of the tyres and help stop the vehicle. This can't happen with ABS, so some vehicles equipped with ABS have an override switch on the dash to defeat the ABS system during snowy conditions or when driving on dirt roads.

system will do its job just as it was designed to do, but the vehicle won't come to a complete stop before it hits the object that the driver is trying to avoid.

ABS facts

Here are some important things to know regarding ABS brakes:

a) When the ABS is activated (when a wheel begins to lock up), it is normal for the driver to feel pedal pulsations. This is the result of the modulator valves cycling to reduce pressure in the brake lines. During normal braking no pulsations should be felt.

b) The amount of force on the brake pedal that is required to activate the ABS system depends on the road surface. If the surface of the road is very slippery it won't take much to slide the tyres, in which case the ABS will kick in.

c) If the system experiences a malfunction, it will revert to a normal hydraulic brake system. You won't lose your brakes completely on account of a problem with the ABS portion of the brake system.

d) Some service operations to the ABS system should not be performed by the do-it-yourselfer. Consult the manufacturer's service information before carrying out any service operations other than brake pad or shoe renewal. Some systems operate at very high pressure (in excess of 2000 psi), and no attempt should be made to work on a high pressure hydraulic system until the system has been depressurised in accordance with the manufacturer's recommendations.

e) If you renew a brake disc, brake drum, driveshaft, axleshaft or differential assembly (depending on system design) and the component being renewed is equipped with a toothed signal rotor, make sure the new part is equipped with a signal rotor also. In some cases the signal rotor is pressed onto the component, in which case it will have to be removed from the old part and pressed onto the new one.

f) ABS systems aren't just fitted on vehicles with four-wheel disc brakes. Some vehicles with disc brakes in the front and drum brakes in the rear are equipped with ABS.

g) The presence of an ABS system does not affect normal brake service. Brake pads or shoes must still be checked at the recommended intervals. They don't last any longer, either. Calipers, wheel cylinders, hoses and handbrake mechanisms are also subject to the same amount of wear as in a non-ABS system.

h) Finally, a vehicle equipped with ABS can't out-brake an identical non-ABS vehicle driven by an expert driver on a dry, straight road. This is because a typical ABS system allows the amount of tyre slip to drop as low as 5-percent, which is below the point at which maximum traction is achieved. A skilled driver can use his or her judgement to increase the amount of tyre slip without locking the wheels. An Anti-lock Brake System has no "judgement" whatsoever.

Types of systems

There are two basic types of ABS systems - front-wheel anti-lock systems and four-wheel anti-lock systems. Within these two groupings are two sub-groupings - component systems and integral systems.

1 Brake calipers
2 Master cylinder
3 Wheel speed sensors
4 Hydraulic modulator
5 ECU

10.1 Schematic view of a typical front-wheel anti-lock braking system

Front-wheel anti-lock systems

Front-wheel ABS systems operate on the front wheels only, and have no effect on the rear wheels.

Although the system cannot prevent the rear wheels from locking under extreme braking conditions, the most significant advantage of the system is that it allows the driver to brake as hard as possible and steer the vehicle at the same time.

Most vehicles have a proportioning valve fitted in the rear brake hydraulic circuit (see "Introduction"), which prevents the rear wheels from locking before the front wheels under heavy braking - this valve is not part of the ABS system, and does not sense the rotational speed of the wheels.

Front-wheel ABS systems monitor the rotational speeds of the front wheels. Most systems use electronic wheel speed sensors, which produce a signal in conjunction with toothed rotors mounted on the driveshafts or wheel hubs (these components are described in more detail later in this Chapter). An alternative system was developed by Ford for use on some of their early front-wheel-drive vehicles, using mechanical hydraulic modulators (one for each front brake), driven by toothed belts from the driveshafts.

On some systems, the hydraulic pressure to each front brake is controlled independently, according to the rotational speed of the relevant wheel. On systems where the hydraulic pressure to the front wheels is controlled through a single circuit, the pressure regulation is controlled by the signals from the wheel with the least amount of traction (this is known as the "select-low" principle).

Four-wheel anti-lock systems

Four-wheel anti-lock systems monitor the rotational speeds of all four wheels.

The advantage of this type of system over a front-wheel system is that it reduces the possibility of the vehicle spinning (due to the rear wheels locking) under heavy braking.

On some systems, the hydraulic pressure to all four wheels is controlled independently, according to the rotational speed of the relevant wheel. An alternative type of system controls the pressure to each front brake individually, but the pressure to the rear brakes is controlled through a single circuit (the pressure to the rear brakes is controlled by the signals from the rear wheel with the least amount of grip).

1 Hydraulic unit
2 Wheel speed sensor and toothed signal rotor
3 Main relay
4 ABS control unit

10.2 Typical four-wheel ABS system (Mazda)

BOOSTER PUMP AND MOTOR

MASTER CYLINDER/POWER BOOSTER

BOOST PRESSURE SWITCH (IN MODULATOR)

PRESSURE MODULATOR

PROPORTIONING VALVE/DIFFERENTIAL SWITCH

ECU

ACCUMULATOR AND PRESSURE SWITCH

SENSOR CONNECTORS/WIRES

LEFT FRONT SENSOR

REAR WHEEL SENSORS

RIGHT FRONT SENSOR

10.3 Schematic of a typical four-wheel ABS system (Jeep)

Component systems

The component system is sometimes referred to as an "add-on" system. These types of systems are used on vehicles equipped with a standard master cylinder/brake servo combination. The hydraulic control unit is fitted downstream of the master cylinder.

Although referred to as an add-on system, it is not generally practical to retrofit the relevant components to convert a non-ABS brake system into an ABS system. Considerable work would be involved to achieve this (such as changing wheel hub/driveshaft components, etc).

Integral systems

Integral ABS systems are self-contained units, which combine the master cylinder, brake servo and hydraulic modulator into a single assembly.

FLUID RESERVOIR

FLUID LEVEL INDICATOR 5-PIN PLUG (CANNOT BE SEEN IN THIS VIEW)

ACCUMULATOR

SOLENOID VALVE BLOCK 7-PIN PLUG

PUMP MOTOR 4-PIN PLUG

MAIN VALVE 2-PIN PLUG

ACTUATOR ASSY

PRESSURE WARNING SWITCH 5-PIN PLUG

SOLENOID VALVE BLOCK ASSY

HYDRAULIC PUMP MOTOR

10.4 Details of an integral ABS actuation assembly

Components

Ford belt-driven mechanical ABS system

The system uses two belt-driven mechanical modulators, driven from the driveshafts.

Each modulator contains a shaft which drives a flywheel via a clutch. During normal driving and braking, the modulator shaft and the flywheel rotate at the same speed, and hydraulic pressure is supplied to the front brakes in the normal way. If a front wheel locks, the modulator shaft rotates more slowly than the flywheel, and the flywheel overruns the clutch to operate a hydraulic pressure dump valve, releasing the pressure on the relevant brake. At the same time as the hydraulic pressure is released, the pressure from the master cylinder operates a mechanism to slow down the flywheel. When the speed of the modulator shaft and the flywheel are equal, the dump valve closes, and the cycle is repeated. This cycle takes place many times a second until the vehicle stops, or the brakes are released.

The system incorporates a belt breakage warning light on the instrument panel, which operates if the belt breaks, or if the belt adjustment is too slack. If the ABS system fails, normal braking is still available.

Electronic ABS systems

Most of the ABS systems likely to be encountered are electronic systems, and they comprise the following components.

a) Wheel speed sensors
b) Toothed signal rotors
c) Hydraulic modulator
d) Electric fluid pump
e) Hydraulic accumulator
f) Electronic control unit
g) Lateral acceleration switch (not all systems)

Wheel speed sensors

These sensors are located at all four wheels on vehicles with four-wheel ABS, or at the front wheels of vehicles with front-wheel ABS systems.

The sensors generate small electrical impulses when the toothed signal rotors are turning. The impulses are sent to the electronic control unit, which analyses the signals to determine the rotational speed of the wheels.

All wheel sensors are of a similar design, consisting of a permanent magnet wrapped with wire.

The sensors are positioned very close to the signal rotors, and are usually mounted on the hub carriers, or sometimes in the rear brake backplates.

Toothed signal rotors

The rotors are toothed rings, which turn with the driveshafts or hubs. As the teeth pass the sensor, an electrical signal (alternating current) is produced by the sensor, which is fed to the electronic control unit.

1 Front-wheel speed sensor
2 Steering knuckle
3 Toothed signal rotor (part of 4, 6)
4 Front hub and bearing assembly
5 Rear-wheel speed sensor
6 Rear driveshaft spindle
7 Rear knuckle
8 Rear driveshaft

10.5 Typical wheel speed sensors

Hydraulic modulator

The modulator regulates hydraulic pressure to the brakes, according to signals received from the electronic control unit. The modulator is able to maintain or reduce hydraulic pressure to prevent wheel lock-up.

The unit consists of a set of solenoid valves, which are opened and closed by electrical signals received from the electronic control unit. The valves are capable of cycling at a rate of many times per second, to provide fine control of the hydraulic pressure in each relevant circuit.

Electric fluid pump

The pump is often incorporated in the hydraulic modulator assembly, and operates as a transfer pump. The pump transfers fluid to and from the hydraulic circuits, according to the positions of the valves in the modulator. On some systems, the pump simply acts as a return pump to pump fluid back to the master cylinder when the brakes are released. The pump is controlled by electrical signals received from the electronic control unit.

Hydraulic accumulator

All systems use one or more accumulator to store pressurised fluid. The stored fluid is used to apply the brakes, or (on integral systems) to provide high-pressure power assistance. On some integral systems, the stored fluid is held at a very high pressure (up to 2000 psi).

10.6 The toothed signal rotor is pressed onto the ends of the outer CV joint (lower arrow) - the wheel speed sensor is mounted on the steering knuckle (upper arrow)

Electronic control unit

The electronic control unit analyses the signals from the wheel speed sensors, and any other system sensors, and uses the information to determine whether any of the wheels are about to lock-up. If the control unit detects that a wheel is about to lock-up, it sends signals to the hydraulic accumulator and the electric fluid pump to control the pressure to the relevant brake(s).

On most systems, the control unit is capable of detecting problems within the system, and storing faults codes in an electronic memory. The fault codes can be read by a technician with suitable diagnostic equipment. In the event of a problem, the control unit will illuminate a warning light on the instrument panel.

Lateral acceleration switch

A few systems are fitted with this component

Braking increases the coefficient of friction between the tyre and the road surface, but so does cornering. When heavy braking and hard cornering are combined, it is very easy to lock-up a wheel, which may result in a slide.

The switch operates when a certain lateral G-force is reached, and sends a signal to the electronic control unit, which reduces hydraulic pressure to the relevant brake(s).

Operation

Although the operation of the ABS system has been described in terms of how the individual components work, the components all work together as follows.

When the driver slams on the brakes in a panic stop situation, the system must decide to do one of the following things.
a) Maintain the same pressure that the driver has applied.
b) Reduce the pressure to one or more of the hydraulic circuits.
c) Restore pressure to the original level after the pressure has been reduced.

The electronic control unit constantly monitors the inputs from the wheel speed sensors. If one (or more) of the sensors indicates a higher rate of wheel deceleration than the other sensors, the control unit knows that a wheel lock-up is likely to take place. Initially, nothing happens - the pressure to the wheel in question is maintained. This is called the "pressure holding" phase. The electronic control unit instructs the hydraulic modulator to partially close the solenoid valve, preventing any increase in brake pressure to that wheel. Fluid return is also blocked off by the solenoid, so the pressure stays the same. The electric fluid pump begins to run, but its outlet check valve stays shut unless the pump pressure exceeds the amount of pressure being created by the master cylinder.

If the wheel continues to decelerate at an abnormal rate, the control unit signals the hydraulic modulator to reduce the pressure to the brake at the wheel. The modulator closes the solenoid valve for the wheel, which prevents any more pressure from being applied. In addition, the valve is positioned in such a way as to open a passage back to the fluid reservoir. This bleeds off pressure and allows the wheel to turn.

At this point, the wheel accelerates again because it is not being braked as hard as it was. The control unit will only allow it to gain a certain amount of speed. Once it has been determined that the wheel is no longer in danger of locking up, the solenoid valve stops cycling and normal braking resumes. The hydraulic modulator allows pressure to build up to the level it was at before the pressure reduction took place.

This entire chain of events takes place many times per second, depending on how slippery the surface of the road is.

Precautions

There are several precautions which must be taken when working on or around the components of an anti-lock braking system. If the following points of advice are not heeded, you run the risk of incurring serious injury, either through careless working techniques, or by disabling the system due to incorrect servicing techniques.

a) Some integral ABS systems operate at very high pressures (over 2000 psi). Before working on any part of the vehicle hydraulic system, consult the manufacturer's servicing information to ensure that there is no risk of injury.

b) Before working on any part of the hydraulic system, ensure that, where necessary, the system has been depressurised. Most component systems operate at conventional fluid pressures, and do not need to be depressurised. On many integral systems, the system can be depressurised by pumping the brake pedal a number of times (some systems require as many as 20 pumps) with the ignition switched off - again, consult the manufacturer's servicing information before attempting to depressurise the system. Once the system has been depressurised, always open the bleed screws slowly.

c) When bleeding the complete hydraulic system, always follow the manufacturer's bleeding procedure. Note that most systems have bleed screws on the hydraulic modulator unit. Some integral systems cannot be bled without the use of specialist pressure-bleeding equipment.

d) Do not unplug or connect electrical connectors related to the ABS system while the ignition is switched on. This is necessary to avoid possible damage to the electronic control unit.

e) If it becomes necessary to renew a brake hose or pipe, purchase only genuine parts of original equipment quality and design. DO NOT fabricate your own components.

f) Never strike a wheel speed sensor or a signal rotor with a hammer or any other tool, and don't drop them either.

g) Don't allow grease onto the wheel speed sensors or the toothed signal rotors.

h) If the vehicle is equipped with four-wheel ABS, never refit larger diameter tyres on one end of the vehicle. All four tyres must be of the same diameter, or the electronic control unit will become confused.

i) Do not overtighten the wheel nuts of bolts, as this could damage the brake disc or drum, causing inaccurate speed signals.

j) Whenever a speed sensor is disturbed, where necessary check the gap between the sensor and the signal rotor and adjust (many sensors are not adjustable). Ensure that the sensor is clean.

k) Only use the recommended type of hydraulic fluid in the system. Never use silicone-based hydraulic fluid, unless specifically recommended by the manufacturers.

l) If any ancillary components are fitted to the vehicle, such as a cellular telephone, or a radio transmitter, ensure that the wiring is routed away from the ABS system components and wiring. Certain frequencies can interfere with the system operation.

m) Before carrying out any welding on the vehicle, disconnect the battery negative lead, and the ABS electronic control unit wiring connector.

n) Most manufacturers advise against repairing the ABS system wiring. If one wire becomes damaged, renew the relevant part of the harness. Even slight changes in resistance can lead to inaccurate speed readings from the wheel sensors.

Troubleshooting

All vehicles equipped with ABS have an amber "ANTI-LOCK" warning light on the dash. This light alerts the driver when the ECU has detected a malfunction in the system. The light will also come on whenever the ignition key is turned to the On position, as a bulb check feature. If the light doesn't come on, you should check for a burned-out bulb as soon as possible. Otherwise, you won't know if a problem arises in the ABS system until you need the system to work correctly and find out it doesn't.

In some systems the red BRAKE light also will come

on in the event of a problem. In some cases the light(s) will flash on and off. The flashing of these lights is part of a much more involved diagnostic procedure, and interpreting the flashing sequence must be left to a technician trained in ABS system diagnosis.

If a problem with the ABS system arises, there are a few general checks that can be made. If these checks don't reveal the source of the problem, take the vehicle to a dealer service department or other garage qualified to service ABS systems. Some vehicles will flash fault codes through the warning light on the instrument panel when a diagnostic mode is entered, much like a CHECK ENGINE light for an engine management system. Unfortunately, most ABS systems require expensive electronic test equipment, pressure gauges and adapter fittings to successfully perform diagnostic procedures. Some of this equipment is proprietary to the manufacturers and is not available through motor factors or tool dealers. Furthermore, the ABS diagnosis chapters in a manufacturer's factory service manual frequently exceed one hundred pages or so, making it impossible to provide a comprehensive ABS troubleshooting guide within the covers of this manual. Remember, vehicles equipped with anti-lock braking systems are also susceptible to the same problems as a vehicle that isn't equipped with ABS.

a) Always begin diagnosis to any electrical system with a check of the fuses. If you find a blown fuse, try to figure out why the fuse blew. Never replace a fuse with one of a higher amperage rating or with a piece of foil.

b) Check the battery and make sure it has a full charge. ABS systems depend on an accurate supply of voltage. Batteries should put out 12 or 13 volts without the engine running, and approximately 14.2 volts with the engine running.

c) Make sure all electrical connectors related to the ABS system are securely connected. Remember, however, don't disconnect or connect any of the connectors with the ignition in the On position.

d) Check the gap between the wheel speed sensors and the toothed signal rings. While specifications vary, they should be somewhere in the neighbourhood of 0.5 to 1.0 mm. Also make sure the sensors or rings are not damaged.

Glossary

A

ABS: Anti-lock Brake System.

Accumulator: A vessel that stores hydraulic fluid under pressure.

Adapter: See Caliper mounting bracket.

Air-suspended servo: A type of brake servo that contains atmospheric pressure in both chambers of the servo when the brake pedal is at rest. When the pedal is applied, the front chamber is opened to manifold vacuum, causing the diaphragm of the servo to move toward the master cylinder which assists the driver in the application of the brakes.

Anchor: The stationary portion of a leading/trailing drum brake on which the heels of the brake shoes ride.

Anchor plate: See Caliper mounting bracket.

Anchor pin: The stationary portion of a duo-servo drum brake on which the tops of the brake shoes rest. The secondary shoe bears against the anchor pin when the brakes are applied and the vehicle is moving forward. Conversely, when the vehicle is reversing and the brakes are applied, the primary shoe bears against it.

Anti-lock brake system: A brake control system that monitors the rotational speeds of the wheels and reduces hydraulic pressure to any wheel it senses locking up.

Arcing: A process where the brake shoes are ground to the proper curvature for the drums they are to be used with. Modern brake shoes are pre-arced.

Asbestos: A fibrous mineral used in the composition of brake friction materials. Asbestos is a health hazard and the dust created by brake systems should never be inhaled or ingested.

Asbestosis: An incurable lung disease caused by the inhalation of asbestos fibres.

Automatic adjusters: Brake adjusters that are actuated by the application of the handbrake or by normal brake operation, to compensate for lining wear.

B

Backing plate: The part of a drum brake to which the wheel cylinder(s) and the brake shoes are attached.

Banjo fitting: A type of hydraulic fitting, shaped like a banjo, through which a hollow bolt passes, allowing fluid transfer from a hydraulic line to a hydraulic component.

Bleed screw: The hollow screw that is loosened to open a bleed valve, allowing fluid and air bubbles to pass through during a bleeding procedure.

Bleed valve: A valve on a wheel cylinder, caliper or other hydraulic component that is opened to purge the hydraulic system of air.

Bonded linings: Brake linings that are affixed to the shoe or backing plate with high-temperature adhesive and cured under pressure and heat.

Brake adjuster: A mechanism used to adjust the clearance between the brake linings and the brake drum.

Brake balance: The ratio of front-to-rear braking force.

Brake caliper: The component of a disc brake that converts hydraulic pressure into mechanical energy.

Brake disc: The component of a disc brake that rotates with the wheels and is squeezed by the brake caliper and pads, which creates friction and converts the energy of the moving vehicle into heat.

Brake drum: The component of a drum brake that rotates with the wheel and is acted upon by the expanding brake shoes, which creates friction and converts the energy of the moving vehicle into heat.

Brake dust: The dust created as the brake linings wear down in normal use. Brake dust usually contains dangerous amounts of asbestos.

Brake fade: The partial or complete loss of braking power which results when the brakes are overheated and can no longer generate friction.

Brake lathe: The machine used to resurface the friction surfaces of brake discs or drums.

Brake lines: The rigid steel and flexible rubber hoses composing the portion of the hydraulic system that transfers brake fluid from the master cylinder to the calipers and/or wheel cylinders.

Brake lining: The friction material that is either riveted or bonded to the brake backing plates or brake pads.

Brake pads: The components of a disc brake assembly that are surfaced with brake lining and clamped against the brake disc to generate friction.

Glossary

Brake shoes: The components of a drum brake assembly that are surfaced with brake lining and forced against the brake drum to generate friction.

Brake system cleaner: A type of solvent designed exclusively for cleaning brake system components. It will not destroy plastic, rubber or synthetic rubber components and it dries quickly, without leaving a residue.

Breather port: The small passage between the master cylinder fluid reservoir and the area behind the primary cups of the pistons. This port allows fluid from the reservoir to fill the area behind the primary cups of the pistons, preventing a vacuum from being formed behind the cups when the brakes are applied, which prevents air bubbles from travelling around the lips of the primary cups as the brakes are released.

Bridge bolts: High-strength bolts used to fasten together the halves of a split brake caliper.

Bulkhead: The partition between the passenger compartment and the engine compartment. Sometimes referred to as a firewall!.

Burnish: The process of "running-in" new brake pads or shoes so the linings conform to the disc or drum friction surfaces.

C

Caliper: See Brake caliper.

Caliper mounting bracket: The component that connects a brake caliper to the steering knuckle, hub carrier or rear axle.

Cam: An eccentric shaped device mounted on a shaft that raises and lowers the component in contact with it. Some brake adjuster designs use a cam (or cams) to set the clearance between the brake shoes and the brake drum.

Clevis: A U-shaped device with a pin or bolt passing through it used for attaching the master cylinder or servo pushrod to the brake pedal. Clevises are sometimes used in other parts of the brake system, for instance for attaching the handbrake cable to the handbrake lever at the rear brakes.

Coefficient of friction: A numerical value indicating the amount of work required to slide one surface against another. The coefficient of friction equals the side force acting on the object divided by the weight of the object.

Combination valve: A hydraulic valve usually incorporating a pressure differential warning switch, a metering valve and a proportioning valve. Not all combination valves contain all of these control valves.

Compensating port: The small passage between the master cylinder fluid reservoir and the pressure chamber (the area in front of the primary seals of both pistons) that allows fluid to flow in or out as necessary, depending on requirements.

Component Anti-lock Brake System: A type of Anti-lock Brake System in which the hydraulic control unit is not part of the master cylinder/power servo assembly.

Crocus cloth: A very fine abrasive paper

Cup: A type of lip seal used on hydraulic pistons.

D

Diaphragm: A flexible partition used to separate two chambers or elements.

Discard diameter: The diameter at which a worn brake drum should be renewed.

Discard thickness: The thickness at which a worn brake disc should be renewed.

Disc: See Brake disc.

Disc brake: A brake design incorporating a flat, disc-like rotor onto which brake pads containing lining material are squeezed, generating friction and converting the energy of a moving vehicle into heat.

Dished brake disc: A disc that has worn thinner at the inner part of its friction surface. This is an abnormal form of wear.

Double anchor drum brake: See Leading/trailing drum brake.

Drum brake: A brake design incorporating a drum with brake shoes inside that expand to contact the drum, creating friction and converting the energy of the moving vehicle into heat.

Dual circuit brake system: A brake hydraulic system composed of two separate hydraulic circuits.

Duo-servo drum brake: A type of self-energising drum brake that has servo action in both forward and reverse.

Dust boot: A rubber diaphragm-like seal that fits over the end of a hydraulic component and around a pushrod or end of a piston, not used for sealing fluid in but keeping dust out.

E

Electro-hydraulic pump: An electrically powered hydraulic pump used to create pressure in certain portions of the brake system. Typically found in hydraulically operated power brake servos and in ABS hydraulic control units.

Electronic Control Unit (ECU): The "brain" of an ABS system. The ECU reads impulses from the wheel speed sensors to determine if anti-lock braking needs to take place. If so, the ECU controls the cycling of the solenoid valves in the hydraulic control unit.

Emergency brake: Another term for the handbrake.

Equaliser: A bracket or cable connector which balances tension equally on the cables to the handbrakes.

F

Filler port: See breather port.

Fixed caliper: A caliper containing one or more pistons on each side of the brake disc that is bolted to the steering knuckle, hub carrier or rear axle and is incapable of movement.

Flare-nut spanner: A spanner designed for loosening hydraulic fitting tube nuts (flare-nuts) without damaging them. Flare-nut spanners are like a six-point ring spanner with one of the flats missing, which allows the spanner to pass over the tubing but still maintain a maximum amount of contact with the nut. Also called a split ring spanner.

Floating caliper: A caliper that rides on bushes, has one or more pistons only on one side of the caliper and moves laterally as the piston pushes on the inner brake pad, which pulls the outer pad against the brake disc.

Four-wheel ABS: An anti-lock brake system that operates on all four wheels.

Free play: The amount of travel before any action takes place. In a brake pedal it is the distance the pedal moves before the pistons in the master cylinder are actuated.

Friction: Surface resistance to relative motion.

G

Glazed lining: A brake lining that has been overheated and become smooth and glossy.

Grinding: The process of resurfacing a brake disc or drum on a brake lathe using a power-driven abrasive stone.

Grommet: A round rubber seal which fits into a hole or recess, intended to seal or insulate the component passing through it.

Guide pin: A caliper mounting bolt used for fastening a floating caliper to its mounting plate.

H

Handbrake: The mechanically actuated portion of a drum brake or disc brake caliper, used to prevent the vehicle from rolling when it is parked, usually applied by a lever, or rod. Also called an emergency brake or parking brake.

Hard spots: Shiny bluish/brown glazed areas on a brake drum or disc friction surface, caused by extreme heat. Hard spots can usually be removed by resurfacing.

Hat: The portion of a detachable brake disc that comes in contact with the wheel hub.

Heat checking: Small cracks on a brake disc or drum friction surface caused by heat. Heat checks can usually be removed by resurfacing.

Hold-down pin, spring and retainer: The most common method of retaining a brake shoe to the backing plate. The pin passes through the backing plate and brake shoe. The spring and retainer are fastened to the pin, which holds the shoe against the backing plate.

Hold-off valve: *See Metering valve.*

Hydraulically operated servo: A brake servo that uses hydraulic pressure to assist the driver in the application of the brakes. This hydraulic pressure comes from a belt-driven pump or an electro-hydraulic pump.

Hydraulic control unit: The portion of an anti-lock brake system that houses the solenoid valves and electro-hydraulic pump.

Hydraulic modulator: *See Hydraulic control unit.*

Hydroplane: The action that takes place when an accumulation of water builds up in front of a tyre, causing the tyre to ride on a layer of water instead of on the pavement.

Hygroscopic: The tendency to attract or absorb moisture from the air.

I

Inboard brakes: Disc or drum brakes not mounted out at the wheels, but near the differential. Rarely found on modern vehicles.

Inertia: The tendency of a body at rest to remain at rest, and a body in motion to remain in motion.

Integral Anti-lock Brake System: An anti-lock system that incorporates the master cylinder and servo into the hydraulic control unit.

Glossary

K

Kinetic energy: The energy of a body in motion.

Knockback: The action of a brake disc with excessive runout pushing back the brake pads when the brakes are not applied.

L

Lateral runout: Side-to-side warpage of the brake disc friction surfaces.

Leading shoe: The shoe in a leading/trailing drum brake assembly which is self-energised by the rotation of the brake drum.

Leading/trailing drum brake: A drum brake design in which both brake shoes are attached to an anchor plate, and only one of the shoes is self-energised.

Load Sensing Proportioning Valve (LSPV): A hydraulic system control valve that works like a proportioning valve, but also takes into consideration the amount of weight carried by the rear axle.

M

Manual adjuster: A type of brake adjuster that must be adjusted from time-to-time, with the use of a hand tool.

Master cylinder: The component in the hydraulic system which generates pressure for the calipers and/or wheel cylinders.

Metering valve: A hydraulic control valve placed in the circuit to the front brakes, designed to restrict pressure to the front brake calipers until the rear brake shoes overcome the tension of the retracting springs.

N

Non-servo drum brake: A drum brake design in which the application of one shoe has no effect on the other.

O

Organic linings: Brake lining material using asbestos as its main ingredient.

Out-of-round: The condition of a brake drum when it has become distorted and is no longer perfectly round. In many cases an out-of-round brake drum can be salvaged by resurfacing on a brake lathe.

P

Pad wear indicators: Mechanical or electrical devices which warn the driver when the lining material on the brake pads has worn to the point that they should be renewed.

Parallelism: The relationship between one friction surface of a brake disc and the other.

Parking brake: See Handbrake.

Pascal's Law: The law of physics stating that "pressure, when applied to a confined liquid, is transmitted undiminished." Discovered by Blaise Pascal (1623 - 1662).

Pressure bleeder: A device that forces brake fluid under pressure into the master cylinder, so that by opening the bleeder screws all air will be purged from the hydraulic system.

Pressure differential warning switch: A component of the brake hydraulic system that warns the driver of a failure in one of the circuits.

Primary shoe: The shoe in a duo-servo drum brake that transfers part of its braking force to the secondary shoe.

Proportioning valve: A hydraulic control valve located in the circuit to the rear wheels which limits the amount of pressure to the rear brakes to prevent wheel lock-up during panic stops.

R

Replenishing port: See Breather port.

Reservoir: A container attached to the master cylinder, either directly or by hoses, that stores extra brake fluid for the hydraulic system.

Residual pressure: Pressure remaining in a hydraulic circuit after the brakes have been released.

Residual pressure check valve: A small valve, usually located in the outlet port(s) of the master cylinder, which maintains a certain amount of pressure in the hydraulic circuit(s) when the brakes are released. Used only in drum brake hydraulic circuits to keep the lips of the wheel cylinder cups sealed against the walls of the cylinder.

Resurfacing: The process of machining a brake drum or disc on a brake lathe to remove surface imperfections from the friction surface.

Riveted linings: Brake linings that are riveted to the pad backing plate or brake shoe.

Rotor: *See Brake disc.*

Runout: Side-to-side warpage of the brake disc friction surfaces.

S

Scoring: Grooves or deep scratches on a friction surface caused by metal-to-metal contact (worn-out brake pads or shoes) or debris caught between the friction material and the friction surface.

Secondary shoe: The shoe in a duo-servo drum brake assembly that is acted upon by the primary shoe. It provides more stopping power than the primary shoe (by about 70 percent).

Select-low principle: The method by which the rear brake application of an ABS brake system is monitored and controlled, based on the rear wheel with the least amount of traction.

Self-energising action: The action of a rotating brake drum that increases the application pressure of the brake shoe(s).

Semi-metallic lining: Brake lining incorporating a high-percentage of metal in its composition.

Servo: A device using vacuum or hydraulic power to assist the driver in the application of the brakes.

Servo-action drum brake: See Duo-servo drum brake.

Sliding caliper: Similar to a floating caliper, but instead of riding on guide pins and bushes, the caliper slides on machined "ways" and is retained by keys or spring plates.

Solid brake disc: A brake disc that is solid metal between its friction surfaces.

Split ring spanner: See Flare nut spanner.

Star wheel: The portion of a brake adjuster that turns the adjuster screw.

T

Toothed signal rotor: The component of an ABS system that rotates with the hub, driveshaft, axle or ring gear, used along with the wheel speed sensors for generating impulses to be rear by the ABS Electronic Control Unit (ECU). The ECU counts these impulses and determines if a wheel is decelerating too rapidly.

Torque: A turning or twisting force imposed on a rotating part.

Torque plate: See Caliper mounting bracket.

Traction: The amount of adhesion between the tyre and earth.

Trailing shoe: A shoe in a drum brake assembly that is not self-energised.

Two-wheel ABS: An anti-lock brake system that only operates on two wheels.

Tyre slip: The difference between the speed of the vehicle and the speed between the tyre and the earth, expressed in a percentage.

U

Uni-servo drum brake: A servo-action drum brake that only has servo action when the vehicle is braked in a forward direction.

V

Vacuum: As an automotive term, vacuum is any pressure less than atmospheric pressure.

Vacuum-operated servo: A servo that uses engine manifold vacuum to assist the driver in the application of the brakes.

Vacuum-suspended servo: A type of servo that contains vacuum in both chambers of the servo when the brake pedal is at rest. When the pedal is applied, the rear chamber is vented to the atmosphere, causing the diaphragm of the servo to move toward the master cylinder which assists the driver in the application of the brakes.

Vapour lock: The abnormal condition that occurs when brake fluid contains too much moisture and is overheated, causing the moisture in the fluid to boil. Gas bubbles are formed in the fluid, which causes a spongy brake pedal or a complete loss of hydraulic pressure.

Vented brake disc: A brake disc that has cooling passages cast or drilled between its friction surfaces.

Viscosity: The property of a fluid that resists the force tending to cause the fluid to flow.

W

Ways: Machined abutments on which a sliding brake caliper rides.

Wheel cylinder: The component in a hydraulic system that converts hydraulic pressure into mechanical force to apply the brake shoe(s).

Wheel speed sensor: The component of an anti-lock brake system that picks up the impulses of the toothed signal rotor, sending these impulses to the ABS ECU.

Index

Haynes Manuals – The Complete List

Title	Book No.
ALFA ROMEO	
Alfa Romeo Alfasud/Sprint (74 - 88) up to F	0292
Alfa Romeo Alfetta (73 - 87) up to E	0531
ALFA ROMEO	
Audi 80 (72 - Feb 79) up to T	0207
Audi 80, 90 (79 - Oct 86) up to D & Coupe (81 - Nov 88) up to F	0605
Audi 80, 90 (Oct 86 - 90) D to H & Coupe (Nov 88 - 90) F to H	1491
Audi 100 (Oct 82 - 90) up to H & 200 (Feb 84 - Oct 89) A to G	0907
Audi 100 & A6 Petrol & Diesel (May 91 - May 97) H to P	3504
Audi A4 (95 - Feb 00) M to V	3575
AUSTIN	
Austin/MG/Rover Maestro 1.3 & 1.6 (83 - 95) up to M	0922
Austin/MG Metro (80 - May 90) up to G	0718
Austin/Rover Montego 1.3 & 1.6 (84 - 94) A to L	1066
Austin/MG/Rover Montego 2.0 (84 - 95) A to M	1067
Mini (59 - 69) up to H	0527
Mini (69 - Oct 96) up to P	0646
Austin/Rover 2.0 litre Diesel Engine (86 - 93) C to L	1857
BEDFORD	
Bedford CF (69 - 87) up to E	0163
Bedford/Vauxhall Rascal & Suzuki Supercarry (86 - Oct 94) C to M	3015
BMW	
BMW 316, 320 & 320i (4-cyl) (75 - Feb 83) up to Y	0276
BMW 320, 320i, 323i & 325i (6-cyl) (Oct 77 - Sept 87) up to E	0815
BMW 3-Series (Apr 91 - 96) H to N	3210
BMW 3- & 5-Series (sohc) (81 - 91) up to J	1948
BMW 520i & 525e (Oct 81 - June 88) up to E	1560
BMW 525, 528 & 528i (73 - Sept 81) up to X	0632
CITROEN	
Citroën 2CV, Ami & Dyane (67 - 90) up to H	0196
Citroën AX Petrol & Diesel (87 - 97) D to P	3014
Citroën BX (83 - 94) A to L	0908
Citroën C15 Van Petrol & Diesel (89 - Oct 98) F to S	3509
Citroën CX (75 - 88) up to F	0528
Citroën Saxo Petrol & Diesel (96 - 98) N to S	3506
Citroën Visa (79 - 88) up to F	0620
Citroën Xantia Petrol & Diesel (93 - 98) K to S	3082
Citroën XM Petrol & Diesel (89 - 98) G to R	3451
Citroën ZX Diesel (91 - 93) J to L	1922
Citroën ZX Petrol (91 - 94) H to M	1881
Citroën 1.7 & 1.9 litre Diesel Engine (84 - 96) A to N	1379
COLT	
Colt/Mitsubishi 1200, 1250 & 1400 (79 - May 84) up to A	0600
FIAT	
Fiat 500 (57 - 73) up to M	0090
Fiat Cinquecento (93 - 98) K to R	3501
Fiat Panda (81 - 95) up to M	0793
Fiat Punto Petrol & Diesel (94 - Oct 99) L to V	3251
Fiat Regata (84 - 88) A to F	1167
Fiat Tipo (88 - 91) E to J	1625
Fiat Uno (83 - 95) up to M	0923
Fiat X1/9 (74 - 89) up to G	0273
FORD	
Ford Capri II (& III) 1.6 & 2.0 (74 - 87) up to E	0283
Ford Capri II (& III) 2.8 & 3.0 (74 - 87) up to E	1309
Ford Cortina Mk IV (& V) 1.6 & 2.0 (76 - 83) up to A	0343
Ford Escort (75 - Aug 80) up to V	0280
Ford Escort (Sept 80 - Sept 90) up to H	0686
Ford Escort & Orion (Sept 90 - 97) H to P	1737
Ford Escort Mk II Mexico, RS 1600 & RS 2000 (75 - 80) up to W	0735
Ford Fiesta (76 - Aug 83) up to Y	0334
Ford Fiesta (Aug 83 - Feb 89) A to F	1030
Ford Fiesta (Feb 89 - Oct 95) F to N	1595
Ford Fiesta Petrol & Diesel (Oct 95 - 97) N to R	3397
Ford Granada (Sept 77 - Feb 85) up to B	0481
Ford Granada & Scorpio (Mar 85 - 94) B to M	1245
Ford Ka (96 - 99) P to T	3570
Ford Mondeo Petrol (93 - 99) K to T	1923
Ford Mondeo Diesel (93 - 96) L to N	3465
Ford Orion (83 - Sept 90) up to H	1009
Ford Sierra 4 cyl. (82 - 93) up to K	0903
Ford Sierra V6 (82 - 91) up to J	0904
Ford Transit Petrol (Mk 2) (78 - Jan 86) up to C	0719
Ford Transit Petrol (Mk 3) (Feb 86 - 89) C to G	1468
Ford Transit Diesel (Feb 86 - 99) C to T	3019
Ford 1.6 & 1.8 litre Diesel Engine (84 - 96) A to N	1172
Ford 2.1, 2.3 & 2.5 litre Diesel Engine (77 - 90) up to H	1606
FREIGHT ROVER	
Freight Rover Sherpa (74 - 87) up to E	0463
HILLMAN	
Hillman Avenger (70 - 82) up to Y	0037
HONDA	
Honda Accord (76 - Feb 84) up to A	0351
Honda Civic (Feb 84 - Oct 87) A to E	1226
Honda Civic (Nov 91 - 96) J to N	3199
HYUNDAI	
Hyundai Pony (85 - 94) C to M	3398
JAGUAR	
Jaguar E Type (61 - 72) up to L	0140
Jaguar MkI & II, 240 & 340 (55 - 69) up to H	0098
Jaguar XJ6, XJ & Sovereign; Daimler Sovereign (68 - Oct 86) up to D	0242
Jaguar XJ6 & Sovereign (Oct 86 - Sept 94) D to M	3261
Jaguar XJ12, XJS & Sovereign; Daimler Double Six (72 - 88) up to F	0478
JEEP	
Jeep Cherokee Petrol (93 - 96) K to N	1943
LADA	
Lada 1200, 1300, 1500 & 1600 (74 - 91) up to J	0413
Lada Samara (87 - 91) D to J	1610
LAND ROVER	
Land Rover 90, 110 & Defender Diesel (83 - 95) up to N	3017
Land Rover Discovery Diesel (89 - 95) G to N	3016
Land Rover Series IIA & III Diesel (58 - 85) up to C	0529
Land Rover Series II, IIA & III Petrol (58 - 85) up to C	0314
MAZDA	
Mazda 323 (Mar 81 - Oct 89) up to G	1608
Mazda 323 (Oct 89 - 98) G to R	3455
Mazda 626 (May 83 - Sept 87) up to E	0929
Mazda B-1600, B-1800 & B-2000 Pick-up (72 - 88) up to F	0267
MERCEDES BENZ	
Mercedes-Benz 190, 190E & 190D Petrol & Diesel (83 - 93) A to L	3450
Mercedes-Benz 200, 240, 300 Diesel (Oct 76 - 85) up to C	1114
Mercedes-Benz 250 & 280 (68 - 72) up to L	0346
Mercedes-Benz 250 & 280 (123 Series) (Oct 76 - 84) up to B	0677
Mercedes-Benz 124 Series (85 - Aug 93) C to K	3253
MG	
MGB (62 - 80) up to W	0111
MG Midget & AH Sprite (58 - 80) up to W	0265
MITSUBISHI	
Mitsubishi Shogun & L200 Pick-Ups (83 - 94) up to M	1944
MORRIS	
Morris Ital 1.3 (80 - 84) up to B	0705
Morris Minor 1000 (56 - 71) up to K	0024
NISSAN	
Nissan Bluebird (May 84 - Mar 86) A to C	1223
Nissan Bluebird (Mar 86 - 90) C to H	1473
Nissan Cherry (Sept 82 - 86) up to D	1031
Nissan Micra (83 - Jan 93) up to K	0931
Nissan Micra (93 - 99) K to T	3254
Nissan Primera (90 - Aug 99) H to T	1851
Nissan Stanza (82 - 86) up to D	0824
Nissan Sunny (May 82 - Oct 86) up to D	0895
Nissan Sunny (Oct 86 - Mar 91) D to H	1378
Nissan Sunny (Apr 91 - 95) H to N	3219
OPEL	
Opel Ascona & Manta (B Series) (Sept 75 - 88) up to F	0316
Opel Ascona (81 - 88) *(Not available in UK see Vauxhall Cavalier 0812)*	3215
Opel Astra (Oct 91 - Feb 98) *(Not available in UK see Vauxhall Astra 1832)*	3156
Opel Calibra (90 - 98) *(See Vauxhall/Opel Calibra Book No. 3502)*	
Opel Corsa (83 - Mar 93) *(Not available in UK see Vauxhall Nova 0909)*	3160
Opel Corsa (Mar 93 - 97) *(Not available in UK see Vauxhall Corsa 1985)*	3159
Opel Frontera Petrol & Diesel (91 - 98) *(See Vauxhall/Opel Frontera Book No. 3454)*	
Opel Kadett (Nov 79 - Oct 84)	0634
Opel Kadett (Oct 84 - Oct 91) *(Not available in UK see Vauxhall Astra & Belmont 1136)*	3196
Opel Omega & Senator (86 - 94) *(Not available in UK see Vauxhall Carlton & Senator 1469)*	3157
Opel Omega (94 - 99) *(See Vauxhall/Opel Omega Book No. 3510)*	
Opel Rekord (Feb 78 - Oct 86) up to D	0543

Title	Book No
Opel Vectra (Oct 88 - Oct 95)	
(Not available in UK see Vauxhall Cavalier 1570)	3158
Opel Vectra Petrol & Diesel (95 - 98)	
(Not available in UK see Vauxhall Vectra 3396)	3523

PEUGEOT
Title	Book No
Peugeot 106 Petrol & Diesel (91 - 98) J to S	1882
Peugeot 205 (83 - 95) A to N	0932
Peugeot 305 (78 - 89) up to G	0538
Peugeot 306 Petrol & Diesel (93 - 99) K to T	3073
Peugeot 309 (86 - 93) C to K	1266
Peugeot 405 Petrol (88 - 96) E to N	1559
Peugeot 405 Diesel (88 - 96) E to N	3198
Peugeot 406 Petrol & Diesel (96 - 97) N to R	3394
Peugeot 505 (79 - 89) up to G	0762
Peugeot 1.7/1.8 & 1.9 litre Diesel Engine (82 - 96) up to N	0950
Peugeot 2.0, 2.1, 2.3 & 2.5 litre Diesel Engines (74 - 90) up to H	1607

PORSCHE
Title	Book No
Porsche 911 (65 - 85) up to C	0264
Porsche 924 & 924 Turbo (76 - 85) up to C	0397

PROTON
Title	Book No
Proton (89 - 97) F to P	3255

RANGE ROVER
Title	Book No
Range Rover V8 (70 - Oct 92) up to K	0606

RELIANT
Title	Book No
Reliant Robin & Kitten (73 - 83) up to A	0436

RENAULT
Title	Book No
Renault 5 (Feb 85 - 96) B to N	1219
Renault 9 & 11 (82 - 89) up to F	0822
Renault 18 (79 - 86) up to D	0598
Renault 19 Petrol (89 - 94) F to M	1646
Renault 19 Diesel (89 - 95) F to N	1946
Renault 21 (86 - 94) C to M	1397
Renault 25 (84 - 92) B to K	1228
Renault Clio Petrol (91 - May 98) H to R	1853
Renault Clio Diesel (91 - June 96) H to N	3031
Renault Espace Petrol & Diesel (85 - 96) C to N	3197
Renault Fuego (80 - 86) up to C	0764
Renault Laguna Petrol & Diesel (94 - 96) L to P	3252
Renault Mégane & Scénic Petrol & Diesel (96 - 98) N to R	3395

ROVER
Title	Book No
Rover 213 & 216 (84 - 89) A to G	1116
Rover 214 & 414 (89 - 96) G to N	1689
Rover 216 & 416 (89 - 96) G to N	1830
Rover 211, 214, 216, 218 & 220 Petrol & Diesel (Dec 95 - 98) N to R	3399
Rover 414, 416 & 420 Petrol & Diesel (May 95 - 98) M to R	3453
Rover 618, 620 & 623 (93 - 97) K to P	3257
Rover 820, 825 & 827 (86 - 95) D to N	1380
Rover 3500 (76 - 87) up to E	0365
Rover Metro, 111 & 114 (May 90 - 96) G to N	1711

SAAB
Title	Book No
Saab 90, 99 & 900 (79 - Oct 93) up to L	0765
Saab 900 (Oct 93 - 98) L to R	3512
Saab 9000 (4-cyl) (85 - 95) C to N	1686

SEAT
Title	Book No
Seat Ibiza & Cordoba Petrol & Diesel (Oct 93 - Oct 99) L to V	3571
Seat Ibiza & Malaga (85 - 92) B to K	1609

SKODA
Title	Book No
Skoda Estelle (77 - 89) up to G	0604
Skoda Favorit (89 - 96) F to N	1801
Skoda Felicia Petrol & Diesel (95 - 99) M to T	3505

SUBARU
Title	Book No
Subaru 1600 & 1800 (Nov 79 - 90) up to H	0995

SUZUKI
Title	Book No
Suzuki SJ Series, Samurai & Vitara (4-cyl) (82 - 97) up to P	1942
Suzuki Supercarry (86 - Oct 94) C to M	3015

TALBOT
Title	Book No
Talbot Alpine, Solara, Minx & Rapier (75 - 86) up to D	0337
Talbot Horizon (78 - 86) up to D	0473
Talbot Samba (82 - 86) up to D	0823

TOYOTA
Title	Book No
Toyota Carina E (May 92 - 97) J to P	3256
Toyota Corolla (Sept 83 - Sept 87) A to E	1024
Toyota Corolla (80 - 85) up to C	0683
Toyota Corolla (Sept 87 - Aug 92) E to K	1683
Toyota Corolla (Aug 92 - 97) K to P	3259
Toyota Hi-Ace & Hi-Lux (69 - Oct 83) up to A	0304

TRIUMPH
Title	Book No
Triumph Acclaim (81 - 84) up to B	0792
Triumph GT6 & Vitesse (62 - 74) up to N	0112
Triumph Spitfire (62 - 81) up to X	0113
Triumph Stag (70 - 78) up to T	0441
Triumph TR7 (75 - 82) up to Y	0322

VAUXHALL
Title	Book No
Vauxhall Astra (80 - Oct 84) up to B	0635
Vauxhall Astra & Belmont (Oct 84 - Oct 91) B to J	1136
Vauxhall Astra (Oct 91 - Feb 98) J to R	1832
Vauxhall/Opel Calibra (90 - 98) G to S	3502
Vauxhall Carlton (Oct 78 - Oct 86) up to D	0480
Vauxhall Carlton & Senator (Nov 86 - 94) D to L	1469
Vauxhall Cavalier 1600, 1900 & 2000 (75 - July 81) up to W	0315
Vauxhall Cavalier (81 - Oct 88) up to F	0812
Vauxhall Cavalier (Oct 88 - 95) F to N	1570
Vauxhall Chevette (75 - 84) up to B	0285
Vauxhall Corsa (Mar 93 - 97) K to R	1985
Vauxhall/Opel Frontera Petrol & Diesel (91 - Sept 98) J to S	3454
Vauxhall Nova (83 - 93) up to K	0909
Vauxhall/Opel Omega (94 - 99) L to T	3510
Vauxhall Vectra Petrol & Diesel (95 - 98) N to R	3396
Vauxhall/Opel 1.5, 1.6 & 1.7 litre Diesel Engine (82 - 96) up to N	1222

VOLKSWAGEN
Title	Book No
Volkswagen Beetle 1200 (54 - 77) up to S	0036
Volkswagen Beetle 1300 & 1500 (65 - 75) up to P	0039
Volkswagen Beetle 1302 & 1302S (70 - 72) up to L	0110
Volkswagen Beetle 1303, 1303S & GT (72 - 75) up to P	0159
Volkswagen Golf & Jetta Mk 1 1.1 & 1.3 (74 - 84) up to A	0716
Volkswagen Golf, Jetta & Scirocco Mk 1 1.5,1.6 & 1.8 (74 - 84) up to A	0726
Volkswagen Golf & Jetta Mk 1 Diesel (78 - 84) up to A	0451
Volkswagen Golf & Jetta Mk 2 (Mar 84 - Feb 92) A to J	1081
Volkswagen Golf & Vento Petrol & Diesel (Feb 92 - 96) J to N	3097
Volkswagen LT vans & light trucks (76 - 87) up to E	0637
Volkswagen Passat & Santana (Sept 81 - May 88) up to E	0814
Volkswagen Passat Petrol & Diesel (May 88 - 96) E to P	3498
Volkswagen Polo & Derby (76 - Jan 82) up to X	0335
Volkswagen Polo (82 - Oct 90) up to H	0813
Volkswagen Polo (Nov 90 - Aug 94) H to L	3245
Volkswagen Polo Hatchback Petrol & Diesel (94 - 99) M to S	3500
Volkswagen Scirocco (82 - 90) up to H	1224
Volkswagen Transporter 1600 (68 - 79) up to V	0082
Volkswagen Transporter 1700, 1800 & 2000 (72 - 79) up to V	0226
Volkswagen Transporter (air-cooled) (79 - 82) up to Y	0638
Volkswagen Transporter (water-cooled) (82 - 90) up to H	3452

VOLVO
Title	Book No
Volvo 142, 144 & 145 (66 - 74) up to N	0129
Volvo 240 Series (74 - 93) up to K	0270
Volvo 262, 264 & 260/265 (75 - 85) up to C	0400
Volvo 340, 343, 345 & 360 (76 - 91) up to J	0715
Volvo 440, 460 & 480 (87 - 97) D to P	1691
Volvo 740 & 760 (82 - 91) up to J	1258
Volvo 850 (92 - 96) J to P	3260
Volvo 940 (90 - 96) H to N	3249
Volvo S40 & V40 (96 - 99) N to V	3569
Volvo S70, V70 & C70 (96 - 99) P to V	3573

YUGO/ZASTAVA
Title	Book No
Yugo/Zastava (81 - 90) up to H	1453

AUTOMOTIVE TECHBOOKS
Title	Book No
Automotive Brake Manual	3050
Automotive Carburettor Manual	3288
Automotive Diagnostic Fault Codes Manual	3472
Automotive Diesel Engine Service Guide	3286
Automotive Disc Brake Manual	3542
Automotive Electrical and Electronic Systems Manual	3049
Automotive Engine Management and Fuel Injection Systems Manual	3344
Automotive Gearbox Overhaul Manual	3473
Automotive Service Summaries Manual	3475
Automotive Timing Belts Manual – Austin/Rover	3549
Automotive Timing Belts Manual – Ford	3474
Automotive Timing Belts Manual – Peugeot/Citroën	3568
Automotive Timing Belts Manual – Vauxhall/Opel	3577
Automotive Welding Manual	3053
In-Car Entertainment Manual (3rd Edition)	3363

OTHER TITLES
Title	Book No
Haynes Diesel Engine Systems & Data Book (91 -00)	3548
Haynes Petrol Models Data Book (94 - 00)	3718

CL09.04/00

Preserving Our Motoring Heritage

< The Model J Duesenberg Derham Tourster. Only eight of these magnificent cars were ever built – this is the only example to be found outside the United States of America

Almost every car you've ever loved, loathed or desired is gathered under one roof at the Haynes Motor Museum. Over 300 immaculately presented cars and motorbikes represent every aspect of our motoring heritage, from elegant reminders of bygone days, such as the superb Model J Duesenberg to curiosities like the bug-eyed BMW Isetta. There are also many old friends and flames. Perhaps you remember the 1959 Ford Popular that you did your courting in? The magnificent 'Red Collection' is a spectacle of classic sports cars including AC, Alfa Romeo, Austin Healey, Ferrari, Lamborghini, Maserati, MG, Riley, Porsche and Triumph.

A Perfect Day Out

Each and every vehicle at the Haynes Motor Museum has played its part in the history and culture of Motoring. Today, they make a wonderful spectacle and a great day out for all the family. Bring the kids, bring Mum and Dad, but above all bring your camera to capture those golden memories for ever. You will also find an impressive array of motoring memorabilia, a comfortable 70 seat video cinema and one of the most extensive transport book shops in Britain. The Pit Stop Cafe serves everything from a cup of tea to wholesome, home-made meals or, if you prefer, you can enjoy the large picnic area nestled in the beautiful rural surroundings of Somerset.

> John Haynes O.B.E., Founder and Chairman of the museum at the wheel of a Haynes Light 12.

< Graham Hill's Lola Cosworth Formula 1 car next to a 1934 Riley Sports.

The Museum is situated on the A359 Yeovil to Frome road at Sparkford, just off the A303 in Somerset. It is about 40 miles south of Bristol, and 25 minutes drive from the M5 intersection at Taunton.
Open 9.30am - 5.30pm (10.00am - 4.00pm Winter) 7 days a week, *except Christmas Day, Boxing Day and New Years Day*
Special rates available for schools, coach parties and outings Charitable Trust No. 292048